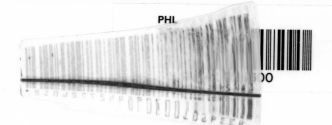

The Department of
PRINTS AND DRAWINGS
in the British Museum

User's Guide

An etching by George Cruikshank of 1828 showing the first Print Room in the Townley Galleries.

The Department of
PRINTS AND DRAWINGS
in the British Museum
User's Guide

Antony Griffiths and Reginald Williams

Published for the Trustees of the British Museum
by British Museum Publications

© 1987 The Trustees of the British Museum
Published by British Museum Publications Limited
46 Bloomsbury Street, London WC1B 3QQ

Designed by Tim Higgins

ISBN 0 7141 1634 3

Set in Linotron Ehrhardt
by Rowland Phototypesetting Limited
Bury St Edmunds, Suffolk
Printed in Great Britain
by St Edmundsbury Press Limited
Bury St Edmunds, Suffolk

CONTENTS

Preface   page vii

PART I

Introduction   1

1 The Print Rooms   1

2 The scope of
  the collection   5

3 The arrangement of
  the collection   6

4 The inventory and
  registers   8

5 The index of artists   10

6 Other indices   12

7 Departmental
  exhibitions   14

8 The curatorial staff   24

**The Collection
of Drawings**   27

**The Collection
of Prints**   33

1 The engraver series   33

2 The master series   39
  Prints after paintings   39
  Prints after sculpture   40
  Prints after drawings   40

3 The subject series   41
  Portraits   41
  History   46
  Topography   47
  Satires   49
  Ornament   51
  Costume   52

4 Illustrated books   53

5 Extra-illustrated
  books and bound
  collections of prints   54

**The Departmental
Library and other
reference material**   60

1 Books   60

2 Periodicals   61

3 Auction and dealer
  catalogues   65

4 Manuscript and
  unpublished material   68

5 Departmental archives   71

6 Microfilms and
  microfiches   73

PART II

The Topic Index   75

Index   185

PREFACE

A department of prints and drawings is like a library in that the display of a small fragment of its collections in changing exhibitions is only a marginal part of its activities. Its service to the public is centred on its Print Room where those who have gone through the necessary formalities to gain a ticket of admission may request to see any part of the collection. The purpose of this handbook is to give them a means of knowing what the collection contains and how it is organised so that they can make the most efficient use of their time.

Since the Department now contains at least two million pieces of paper, and since there is no single catalogue or index which lists the entire collection, it is often a difficult task to locate any individual item. In the same way as the collection itself is divided into many different series and sub-collections organised on quite different principles depending on their nature, so the means of access and retrieval are varied and complicated. They are here described as simply as possible. In general, the drawings and the prints kept under the name of the draughtsman or engraver are the easiest to trace, and thus relatively little space is occupied in this handbook by those parts of the collection that are the concern of the majority of visitors, and which are often well described in published catalogues. By contrast, a great deal of attention is devoted to the documentary collections simply because at present there is no means for the visitor to know that they even exist, much less to get access to them. These collections are of great interest to a wide variety of researchers who are concerned primarily with subject-matter from an historical standpoint.

The only previous handbook which has attempted to cover the entire range of the Department's collections was published by Louis Fagan in 1876 under the title *A Handbook to the Department of Prints and Drawings*. Its one successor, A. E. Popham's *A Handbook to the Drawings and Watercolours in the Department of Prints and Drawings*, published in 1939, was much more limited in its scope. But whereas Fagan's guide is almost completely obsolete, Popham's work is still immensely valuable for the art-historian. It gives an art-historical account of the development of the various schools of drawing, with details of the holdings of the Department by countries. Since post-war acquisitions of drawings have been relatively limited, it is only significantly outdated in a few areas. Two more recent short accounts of the Department and its collections must also be mentioned. The first, by Andrew Wilton, is contained in *Treasures of the British Museum*, edited by Sir Frank Francis in 1971. The second, by J. A. Gere, is in the *British Museum Guide*, first published in 1976.

The present handbook has been compiled by Antony Griffiths, the Deputy Keeper in the Department, and Reginald Williams, former Senior Research Assistant. They have aimed to produce a working tool that is as simple as possible to use, and as exhaustive as the limits of space allow. The first part describes the main series of drawings and prints in which the bulk of the collection is arranged, and the nature of the Departmental library. A few historical sections have been included, but this is only to clarify the background which may help to explain the peculiarities of the present nature or arrangement of the collection. This book is not intended and does not pretend to be a history of the Department; this remains to be written.

The second part of the book is taken up by the 'Topic Index', in which a large quantity of miscellaneous information about special collections, about donors, about the holdings of the works of individual artists and their arrangement, and about types and subjects, have been grouped together in a single alphabetical sequence. The choice of what to include or exclude has not been easy and may appear unduly arbitrary. Decisions have been taken on the basis of experience gained over many years in the Print Room about the questions that most frequently recur. This handbook could be increased in size indefinitely, and still be inadequate to answer many questions. It is offered to the public as an introductory resource in the hope that any help is better than none.

The authors wish me to express their thanks to all the present members of the Department, whose advice and criticism of early drafts has been invaluable. They would also thank two former members of the staff, J. A. Gere and Dudley Snelgrove, for their help. Outside the Department of Prints and Drawings, many colleagues in the museum have given assistance on particular points, but the authors wish to thank in particular Ian Jenkins of the Department of Greek and Roman Antiquities, and Janet Wallace and Christopher Date of the museum's central archives, for their constant help.

JOHN ROWLANDS
Keeper, Department of Prints and Drawings

PART I

INTRODUCTION

1 The Print Rooms

For many years after the opening of the British Museum in Montagu House in January 1759, there was no separate Department of Prints and Drawings. The collections were kept in their original albums and portfolios as part of the Department of Printed Books. A manuscript description of Montagu House of *c.*1805 shows that the prints were then housed in the first apartment of printed books, on the presses numbered V to Y*, sandwiched between the sections on classics and museums. There was no inventory of the collection and no member of staff appointed to look after it. It was the discovery in 1806 of the wholesale thefts committed by Robert Dighton (see p. 108) that brought an end to this situation. In February 1807 the collections were briefly placed in the care of the Department of Manuscripts, before becoming in 1808 a subdivision of the Department of Antiquities under the first Keeper of Prints and Drawings, William Alexander, the artist.

The First Print Room 1808–1828

At this point, the collections were rearranged in part and rehoused in the northernmost room on the top floor of the new Townley Galleries built on to the north-west corner of the original Montagu House between 1804 and 1808. This, the first Print Room, is portrayed in an etching by George Cruikshank of 1828, and is described in an anonymous pamphlet of 1876, *The Print Room of the British Museum. An Enquiry by the Ghost of a Departed Collector.* 'The place appropriated for the reception of Prints and Drawings . . . was a long narrow room . . . above that containing the Towneley marbles, approached by a separate stone staircase, leading to a small vestibule, in the centre of which was the Portland Vase. Passing through a larger apartment, appropriated for the Payne Knight and other bronzes, the Print Room was beyond, shut in with a heavy iron door.' The room was furnished with thirteen wooden presses, of which six can be seen in Cruikshank's etching. These and later presses were transferred to each subsequent location of the Print Room, and must form part of the furnishing of the present Print Room.

The Second Print Room 1828–1842

In 1827 J. T. Smith, the second keeper of the Department, reported to the Trustees that 'the inconveniences of the present Print Room are numerous; it is too narrow, the side lights strike upon the visitor's eye, the floor is stone and ever damp in wet seasons'. The following summer the collections were removed to a newly built room at the southern extremity of the upper floor of the eastern wing – one of the first parts to be finished of the new building designed by Sir Robert Smirke. This room still survives almost unchanged as Room 48, in which the modern collection of the Department of Medieval and Later Antiquities is at present exhibited. Behind the screen built into the room can be found the two offices which housed the Keeper and his single assistant.

   Seven years later the Parliamentary Select Committee investigating the British Museum recommended that the Department of Prints and Drawings should be given its independence, and this was done in 1836. Henry Josi was appointed as the new Keeper the same year, but with almost no staff, very limited storage space and no exhibition galleries.

The Third Print Room 1842–1885

The master plan of Sir Robert Smirke led to almost continuous building works over thirty years from 1823 onwards as old Montagu House was demolished and the new British Museum erected on four sides around a central courtyard. The Department of Prints and Drawings moved into a newly constructed area in the north-west corner of the new building in 1842; this can be clearly seen on contemporary plans. Access was off the first landing on the stairs which now connect the lower and the upper Egyptian galleries. From there a short corridor, which ran alongside two small rooms for staff (all demolished in the 1880s) led to the Print Room. The room still survives, albeit much altered, as the upper half of what is now the Payava Room (number 10); the handsome coffering is still visible round the outside of the ceiling, but a skylight has been pierced through the centre, and the windows blocked up.

   There was, however, still no exhibition space allocated, and what is now the

Nineveh room (the north Assyrian slip room, number 21) was built with the intention of becoming an area for Departmental exhibitions. This scheme was abandoned in 1851 with the arrival of Layard's new discoveries, and as a result from 1858 an area in the King's Library was made available for a display of prints and drawings. A printed catalogue was issued giving a description of each item, this apparently being the first official publication of the Department. The publication by the Trustees of catalogues of the collections began in 1870 with the first volume of F. G. Stephens's catalogue of the collection of satires.

The White Wing 1885–1914

A new wing in the south-east corner of the Museum facing Montague Street was built with a legacy from the estate of William White (1800–23), received in 1879. The Print Room was moved into the mezzanine floor as soon as it was ready for occupation in 1885, where it took up the entire room along the east front. But, as Sidney Colvin pointed out in a memorandum to the Trustees, the room was 'of low proportions and in consequence indifferently lighted, and suffered from being overlooked from the houses in Montague Street'. He therefore proposed, and the Trustees agreed, to transfer the Print Room to one of the two galleries on the upper floor which were intended for the Department's exhibitions. Thus on 23 June 1887 the Print Room reopened in what is now the Later Medieval Room (number 42), and in 1888 the first exhibition opened in the large east gallery (now subdivided into rooms 43, 44 and 45). The exhibition of 1888 was of Chinese and Japanese paintings which, with the prints of those two cultures, formed part of the Department's collections until 1933, although a separate sub-department of Oriental Prints and Drawings was created under Laurence Binyon in 1912. The Department's offices remained on the floor below.

King Edward VII Galleries 1914–present

An extension along the north side of the British Museum on Montague Place was planned in 1904, partly as a result of a bequest from Vincent Stuckey Lean, who died in 1899. The foundation stone was laid by Edward VII in 1907, and the building was completed by May 1914;* it allowed a virtual doubling of the storage area. 150 cases were brought across from the White Wing, and as many

* It had been designed without any decision having been taken as to what collections were to be housed in it, and various possibilities were canvassed, including using the top floor for the Elgin marbles. But in the end it was allocated to Prints and Drawings.

new ones again were constructed to the same pattern as had been first devised in 1808. The galleries and Print Room were adjacent to each other on the top floor, divided by an elaborate wooden screen, with the offices on the mezzanine floor below. Soon after the collection had been transferred war broke out, but the Print Room was not closed until March 1916. The heavier air raids of late 1917 caused the Trustees early in 1918 to evacuate fifteen van loads of printed books, manuscripts, prints and drawings to Aberystwyth from where they returned in the winter of 1918–19. The Print Room had in the meantime been occupied by the Registry of Friendly Societies, and it was not until August 1920 that it reopened, a month after the exhibition galleries.

In August 1939, before the declaration of the Second World War, almost the entire collections of the Department were moved to the basements or evacuated to safer places, the most important part being sent again to the National Library of Wales in Aberystwyth. On the night of 17–18 September 1940 a bomb fell through the roof of the Print Room, penetrating through three floors before ending in the sub-basement. Five nights later a second bomb came through the same hole, but at a slightly different angle. Amazingly, neither exploded, and no part of the collections was damaged except on the mezzanine floor where the bindings of some books were crushed. The Print Room and galleries reopened after repairs in September 1947. A check showed that not a single item had been lost.

It had long been realised that the exhibition gallery with its glass roof did not comply with conservation requirements concerning light levels, and in 1969 it was closed for remodelling. The opportunity was taken to install air-conditioning in the gallery (although not in the Print Room), and internally lit island units were brought in to replace the slope cases and screens. The wall cases were redesigned and rebuilt in the same style. A false ceiling was inserted, and the columns at the far west end of the gallery demolished to make space for a separate Oriental gallery. The new galleries were opened in October 1971. No alterations were made to the Print Room at the time, and it retains substantially the same appearance as in 1914.

2 The Scope of the Collection

The scope of the collection has never been defined by any written or unwritten rule or policy. It has rather been moulded by the accidents of gift and bequest, the changing assumptions of contemporary collecting and the interests of successive members of staff. Above all, it has been affected by the close proximity of what is now the Reference Division of the British Library. Until 1973 this was the Department of Printed Books and the Department of Manuscripts of the British Museum, and until the division there was a constant reshuffling of items back and forth between this Department and the Library.

Physically, the collection is confined to works on paper and excludes oil paintings. It includes prints, drawings, watercolours, works in bodycolour and oil paint if made on paper, and in addition a few pastels, miniatures and drawings on ivory. Chronologically, the collection begins in the XIVc. and continues to the present day. Geographically, it covers Europe and those parts of the world culturally associated with it, such as the United States, Canada and Australia. Works from the Middle and Far East are housed in the Department of Oriental Antiquities (although for a short period Japanese and Chinese prints and drawings used to come under this Department). Those from other cultures may be found in the Department of Ethnography.

The huge range of what is now in the collection is described in this handbook. But some areas are not covered, usually because there are other national collections already active in the field. Thus the British Library contains the national collection of illustrated books, maps and music as well as postage stamps, printed ephemera and excellent topographical collections. Nevertheless, the Department of Prints and Drawings does possess illustrated books, although the collection is greatly inferior to that in the Library, consisting largely of duplicates transferred from it. Many of the bound volumes that are in the Departmental library are strictly books of plates. The distinction, in principle, between the two collections is that if a volume contains letterpress it is a book (and thus for the Library), while if it does not it is a collection of plates (and for this Department).

The Department of Prints and Drawings in the Victoria and Albert Museum has the primary collection of posters, wallpaper, engraved ornament, and drawings for illustration and the applied arts. Both Departments, however, actively collect in areas such as XXc. prints, and British and foreign watercolours. (See the handbook to the collections in the Department of Prints, Drawings and Paintings in the Victoria and Albert Museum, published in 1964 under the editorship of Graham Reynolds, second revised edition 1982.)

Architectural prints and drawings are the province of both the Victoria and Albert Museum and the British Architectural Library (the new name for the library of the Royal Institute of British Architects). The existence of a large collection of prints of the 1960s and later in the Tate Gallery has meant that the British Museum's collection in this field has been restricted, while the Museum of London has a large collection of modern and earlier British printed ephemera. Numerous local museums and art galleries have better collections of prints and drawings of local topography than the Department's, which (with the exception of a few isolated groups) is only rich in views of London.

3 The Arrangement of the Collection

Physical housing

The collection is stored in some 300 cases and a number of metal cabinets. Originally in the XVIIIc. almost everything was kept mounted on to the pages of bound albums. Only a small part of the print collection is still kept in this form. Almost all the drawings and many of the more important prints are now kept on individual sunk mounts stored in solander boxes. These boxes contain, on average, about fifteen mounts. There are five sizes of mount: royal (16″ × 22″), imperial (20″ × 27″), atlas (24″ × 32″), antiquarian (30″ × 45″) and panoramic (20″ × 45″). Most of the print collection is kept unmounted in portfolios. A few special sections (such as the trade cards) have been mounted on to stiff cards and stored in boxes or drawers. A very small number of outsize drawings and prints has long been kept framed, and in recent years this has been extended to a number of modern works which are unsuitable for any other method of storage.

The great part of the collection is stored in the immediate vicinity of the Print Room, and can be produced swiftly upon request. A few sections (which will doubtless change in time) have had to be stored elsewhere on the site at Bloomsbury, and it may be necessary to give advance warning before seeing them.

Although each item in the collection is uniquely identified by its inventory number (see the next section), this number is usually insufficient to allow staff to locate it without difficulty. It is therefore extremely helpful if students can record details of the series in which any item is kept, the number of the case in which it is stored and, if mounted, the size of the mount. These locations are, however, subject to change, and only the inventory number should be quoted in publications.

It should be noted that most cases are divided into upper and lower sections. The lower case is distinguished from the upper in references by the addition of an asterisk. Those books which are kept in cases are given press-marks of the form 176* c.26. This means that it is the twenty-sixth book along the third shelf of the lower half of case 176. The books kept on the open shelves of the Department's working library have references of the form Nn 4 16. This refers to the sixteenth book on the fourth shelf of press Nn.

The principles of organisation

The principles on which the collection is still organised were first drawn up by W. H. Carpenter in the 1840s. It was always regarded as self-evident that all drawings would be kept under the name of the draughtsman. This is still true, and hardly a single drawing is kept according to its subject-matter, unless it forms part of a self-contained collection such as the Crace collection of London topography. This is possible because the collection contains so few ornamental, architectural and suchlike items which tend by their nature to be anonymous.

In the print collection the problem was whether items should be kept under the name of their engraver or designer, or according to their subject-matter. There is of course no satisfactory solution to this question without an elaborate system of cross-referencing from one series to another. This system was never created, although the rudimentary beginnings of one can be seen in the Index of Artists (see section 5). The xixc. solution was, in principle, simply to acquire three impressions of each print and to place one in each of the three possible locations: the finest impression would go in the engraver series, lesser impressions in the designer and subject series. Needless to say, this scheme could not be carried through, and in most cases the Department only possesses one impression of each print. But in general the principle was adhered to that if any impression was particularly fine (such as a proof or early state) it should be placed in the engraver series.

Over and above this, there was a tendency to keep separately as a collection the works of any artist who had an established reputation as an engraver, particularly if his work had been catalogued by an authority such as Bartsch. The portrait series was also regarded as particularly important, and in many cases it tended to be given priority over the master and engraver series. Artists who created prints to their own designs presented no difficulties, and it was only if they were very obscure or if the subjects were unusual that they were placed in the subject series. Anonymous prints tended to be placed in the subject series unless their subject, such as a landscape or a nude, did not lend itself to such classification.

Such are the basic guide-lines for locating items in the collection. But there are certain difficulties, and in the case of many prints (e.g. an engraving of an historical subject) there is no way of telling whether an impression is in the collection without looking in all three of the designer, engraver and history series in order to find it (see later, sections 5, 6).

4 The Inventory and Registers

Every item in the Department's collections has been given a unique number, which has been written or (in most cases) stamped on the verso. These numbers are the primary form of reference to objects, and correspond to entries made in a large number of manuscript volumes. These volumes fall into two categories, the inventory and the register.

When, in 1806, the thefts of Robert Dighton were uncovered, it was a matter of some embarrassment that no inventory existed against which the holdings could be checked. Despite this, the first attempt at a listing of the collections was not made until 1815. This was very rudimentary, and it was left to Henry Josi, between 1836–7, to compile the basic inventory which is still in use. At the time, the prints and drawings in the collections were mounted in a number of large albums which were shelved in 42 cases. These cases were lettered from A to Z and Aa to Qq. Within each case the albums or books were numbered consecutively, and the works within them given sub-numbers. This produced an inventory number of the type C.4–27 or Bb.3–108. In January 1838 the inventory was checked against the collections, and a grand total computed of 9302 drawings and 45,752 prints.

The 1837 inventory produces a number of problems which have not yet been fully resolved. It is documented that between 1808 and 1810 Thomas Philipe was charged with reorganising and pasting into albums the print collection; in February 1810, 83 such albums were finished, 'after being stamped and marked as far as they are known, with the initials of their respective donors'. It follows from this that the provenance of the early prints is often uncertain. On the other hand, the drawings mostly remained in the albums in which they had originally come, and these also bore the press-marks of the Department of Manuscripts in which they had originally been housed. By a strange quirk, it has been Departmental custom to refer to these drawings by the Manuscript press-marks rather than by the 1837 inventory numbers: thus the Sloane Dürers are known by numbers such as Sloane 5218–43 rather than the more proper C.7–43. Before breaking up the original albums in order to integrate their contents, W. H. Carpenter in 1845 compiled more detailed descriptions of the foundation collections of drawings in the Department: those of Sir Hans Sloane (1753), William Fawkener (1769), C. M. Cracherode (1799) and Richard Payne Knight (1824), together with the collection of John Sheepshanks purchased in 1835.

The completion of the inventory entailed the beginning of a new register of supplementary acquisitions. This began on 8 April 1837 and has continued unchanged to the present day. Each item is allocated a number of the type 1837–4–8–1, the first figure being the year, the second the month, the third the day and the last the number. In the case of portfolios and books, a sub-number in brackets is also frequently employed. The item 1837–4–8–1 is in fact a portrait engraving of the former Keeper J. T. Smith by W. Skelton. Until 1913 the Departmental registers included Chinese and Japanese prints and drawings, but in that year the Oriental sub-department was set up and began its own series of registers. In 1985 the total number of volumes of the register of the Department of Prints and Drawings had reached seventy-one.

The intention of the register has never been to record more than the basic details about every item, enough to be able to identify it unambiguously as being the one recorded in the register. It has never been regarded as a catalogue, and so it will only rarely record the publication history of any item or give catalogue references. It has scarcely ever been used as the place to note any later discoveries about the item. In the case of drawings, this information is placed on dossier files which are being compiled for every item. The register does, however, contain details of the source and method of acquisition of everything, and the price paid for purchases. For this reason, the use of the register is restricted and it is only shown with special permission, or in cases where no confidential information is contained in it.

Since the acquisitions are entered in chronological order of receipt, the register can sometimes be used in lieu of a catalogue to provide details of collections. Thus the Ralph Thomas collection of scenes and characters for the Toy Theatre is described in detail under 1886–5–13–17 to 1961. For this reason, the register numbers of collections are sometimes given in this handbook. But this does not always hold good, for at certain periods albums of drawings, sketchbooks, books of prints and even complete collections were entered without giving descriptions of the individual items or pages which make them up.

It was these deficiencies, and the existence of a number of mostly minor prints which had escaped registration altogether, that led the Trustees in 1972 to undertake a project to complete the records of the collection in this and other departments. The entire collection was searched, and any unregistered items found were allocated numbers of the type 1972 U. 123 (the U standing for

Unregistered). These numbers give no clue whatever as to the provenance or the year of acquisition. They also give rise to new problems, since it is clear that in a number of cases the items were indeed listed in the 1837 inventory, but in the intervening years had lost their numbers. These problems cannot be resolved until the entire inventory and register have been transferred to a computer, and items can be matched.

There are, finally, a few anomalies. The Sheepshanks collection of Dutch and Flemish prints and drawings was acquired in 1835 just as the change from inventory to register was taking effect. As a result, it was included in neither, and so has its own unique Sheepshank numbers (such as S.365). In the same way, the Heal collection of trade cards and Franks collection of book-plates were never given register numbers, and have therefore been given their own catalogue numbers. On the other hand, works of reference acquired for the Departmental library were given register numbers until 1960.

5 The Index of Artists

The Index of Artists, which was begun by Sir Sidney Colvin in the mid-1880s, is the fundamental working tool of the Department, and gives access to those parts of the collection (and that is the largest part) which are kept according to the name of the draughtsman, designer or engraver. The indices are large bound volumes with entries mainly in manuscript, arranged alphabetically according to country. They provide the full names and dates of artists, and information about what types of work by each are represented in the Department's collections. They then give the locations where this material is kept. The arrangement of the volumes of indices and their numbers are as follows:

America (including South America, but not Canada)	1
Britain (including Canada, Australia and New Zealand)	10
Eastern Europe (Czechoslovakia, Hungary, Poland, Romania, Russia, in a single sequence)	1
Foreign artists working in Britain (a traditional classification)	1
France	4
Germany (in a single sequence with Austria)	4
Holland and Belgium (in a single sequence)	3
Italy	4
Scandinavia (Denmark, Finland, Norway, Sweden)	1

Spain (including Portugal)   1
Switzerland   1

Despite its importance, the Index of Artists is a most inadequate tool for both staff and students. This can readily be seen by considering a typical (although abbreviated) entry, which reads like this:

DELACROIX, Eugène   b.1798 d.1863
Drawings by: Roy:12, Imp:1
Etchings by: c258*, c271(roy)
Lithographs by: c259*, c278(roy), c67(imp)
Prints after: c291, c76 large   169 a.9, 182 c.10
Repros of drawings by: ERC

To interpret this information, it is necessary to realise that the references in the central column are to single-sheet items, while those in the right-hand column are to bound works. Thus, in order, we have:

DRAWINGS   Individually mounted drawings are listed by mount size, using abbreviations for the five standard sizes (royal, imperial, atlas, antiquarian and panoramic) and giving the number of drawings of each size held. Sketchbooks are usually classified as bound volumes of drawings, and their press-marks entered at the right on the same line as the drawings.
PRINTS   The single sheets are again in the left column. In the case of Delacroix, there are mounted royal etchings and mounted royal and imperial lithographs, as well as unmounted works in both techniques (in cases 258* and 259*). Similarly, prints after his designs are to be found in two wrappers of single prints (case 291, with outsize ones in case 76) and in two bound books (162 a.9 and 182 c.10).
REPRODUCTIONS OF DRAWINGS   This series is described on p. 40. The boxes containing the reproductions used to be kept in cases behind the screens in the exhibition gallery until it was remodelled in 1969; the letters 'ERC' stand for 'exhibition room case'. The boxes are now housed in the print room, but it has not been worth changing the form of reference.

Unfortunately, there is no way of telling how many prints by or after an artist will be found at each location, nor the subject of any of the works. These questions cannot be answered without ordering up the different references and inspecting the works. The only thing that can be done is to consult the blue slip index to find the titles of the books (see p. 13, 60).

The cause of this unhappy state of affairs is the abandoning of Colvin's original scheme. He had intended these indices to serve as the basis for an ultimate complete catalogue of the contents of the Department. The first stage was the publication of the indices themselves, and in 1893 and 1896 his assistant Lionel Cust edited two volumes, the first containing the Dutch and Flemish and German schools, the second the French. Cut-up slips from these form the basis of the present indices; but publication never proceeded to the other schools, and those volumes remain in manuscript. The problems of fleshing-out the indices into catalogues were never solved. A consistent effort was only made in the case of the collection of drawings, and this attempt continues to the present day although the task is nowhere near completion. The publication of the print collection was contracted to a catalogue of a few finite areas of particular interest (early Italian engravings, German woodcuts, British portraits, satirical prints) or of special collections (playing cards, fans).

This history explains a few other curiosities of the Index of Artists. In the three schools for which Cust published indices, references will occasionally be found under an engraver's name of the type: 'see also prints after Rembrandt', or 'see German portraits'. This informs the visitor that one or more engravings by the artist are to be found in those series. But it does not say what they are, and it is scarcely feasible to search through twenty-eight portfolios of German portraits in order to find them. Under the original scheme such prints could have been traced through the index of a published catalogue of German portraits. In the case of the indices of the other schools, no attempt was ever made to trace relevant items in other series, and so no cross-referencing exists. Thus, despite its name, the artist index does not index the locations of all works by artists (whether designers or engravers) in the collection of prints.

6 Other Indices

In the absence of any overall catalogue of the collection, various small sub-indices have been created and other methods devised to make it easier to find out whether a particular print is in the collection. These can be divided into two types: blue slip indices, and marked copies of standard catalogues.

Blue Slip Indices

There are a large number of these, created in the late xIxc. or early xxc., of varying importance and usefulness. Many are of small self-contained collections (such as Banks or Anderdon), and are referred to in the entries on them in the topic index. Others are so outdated and incomplete as not to be worth mentioning. The most useful are the following:

a Index to British topographical prints. This is a topographical index not only to the main topographical collection, but also to topographical prints kept in bound volumes and in the master and engraver series. It is not complete.
b Index to British drawings, according to subject. This index only covers drawings of the British school. It is grouped into sections such as architecture, costume, sculpture and so on. A separate section is devoted to British and foreign topography. This index is not complete.
c Index to the titles of reproductive prints after British painters. This is very incomplete but can be useful for xvIII–xIxc. prints.
d Index, according to subject, of drawings and prints of the Italian school. This is very incomplete but can again be useful.
e There is also a separate but related subject index of prints described by Bartsch in his volumes I to xxII (thus including non-Italian works). The slips are grouped under headings such as saints, mythology, etc.
f There are, finally, several informal subject indices put together by individual staff members of the Department in order to help answer some of the questions that seem to recur frequently.

Other indices, not of the blue slip variety, take the form of duplicate copies of sections of the inventory or register which have been annotated with notes on locations; these are described in the appropriate places.

Marked Catalogues

Many of the standard catalogues of the works of individual or groups of print-makers have been marked with pencil annotations which record the Department's holding of that particular print. It would take too long to list all the catalogues that have been so annotated, but they are always worth checking. The most important of these catalogues is Bartsch's *Le Peintre-Graveur*, which has been completely marked off. (See above for the subject index to this.) So have many of the entries in Passavant, and some of the entries in Le Blanc and Meyer. (For full bibliographical descriptions of these and the following titles, see Antony Griffiths, *Prints and Printmaking*, London 1980, pp. 128–31.) Schreiber, Lehrs and Hind have already recorded the Department's holdings. Chaloner Smith is fully marked, as is Dutuit. But neither of the two Hollstein series on Dutch and Flemish or German prints has been more than occasionally annotated. Of the French school, Robert-Dumesnil, Baudicour, some of Portalis and Beraldi (and of Beraldi's later continuation), and all of Delteil have been marked. Finally standard catalogues contained in periodicals such as *The Print-Collector's Quarterly* (1911–42) have also been annotated.

7 Departmental Exhibitions

The first record of pictures being displayed in the British Museum is found in 1838. The edition of the *Synopsis of the Contents of the British Museum* of that year describes a total of 118 portraits on panel or canvas which were hung above the cases in the Long Gallery above the King's Library (now rooms 49–52). This gallery had just been vacated by the mineral collections, and was then still known as the Mineral Gallery. By 1842 parts of the zoological collection had been moved in, and the gallery was henceforth known as the Eastern Zoological Gallery. The paintings concerned had been acquired from various sources as gifts, beginning with the foundation collections of Sir Hans Sloane and the Old Cottonian library, and then from various donors of which the largest group of eighteen portraits came from Dr Andrew Gifford. The collection consisted of portraits of benefactors, Trustees and staff of the Museum, Kings and Queens, literary figures and others. The paintings remained in situ until the gallery was dismantled for the transfer of the natural history collections, when most of them were transferred to other museums, a large group going to the National Portrait Gallery in 1879. The remainder is now hanging in the Trustees' board room and in other offices of the Museum (see p. 145).

The King's Library 1858–*c*.1883

It was not until 1858 that the first selection of prints and drawings from the Department's collections was exhibited to the public in the King's Library. The first display was of work of the Continental schools, and consisted of 145 drawings and 263 prints hung on screens, and a series of niello plates, casts and prints housed in three table-cases. It was accompanied by a catalogue, *A Guide to the*

Drawings and Prints exhibited to the Public in the King's Library (32 pp.), which was published in three editions in 1858, 1859 and 1860. It was replaced in 1862 with an exhibition of 168 items representing art in England from the xvi–mid-xviiic. A new catalogue of 31 pp. was issued with the same title as the previous one, and published in two editions in 1862 and 1867. In 1869 a third display was put up with a catalogue: *A Guide to that portion of the collection of prints bequeathed to the Nation by the late Felix Slade Esq.* (31 pp.). A second edition followed in 1874. Although no other catalogues seem to have been issued, some part of the collection was continuously on display until at least 1883, and again at times between 1892 and 1914. Even after that, many works from the Department were lent (as they still are) to exhibitions arranged by the Library Departments in the King's Library and elsewhere. Since these were not strictly Departmental exhibitions, they are not mentioned here.

The Northern Galleries 1883–1892

When the natural history collections were transferred to the newly built museum in South Kensington in 1880–3, four rooms (now numbered 55, 56, 64 and 57, and housing Western Asiatic and Egyptian Antiquities) thereby vacated in the northern wing of the Smirke building were allocated to the display of prints and drawings. The catalogue of the first exhibition held there, *A Guide to drawings, prints and illustrative works exhibited in the Second Northern Gallery* (48 pp.), was published in 1883 (new edition 1885). The next exhibition was arranged so that the four rooms were used to illustrate the growth and development of the art of engraving from *c.*1480 to *c.*1850, according to the various processes (woodcuts, line-engravings, etchings and aquatints, mezzotints). The catalogue, *A Guide to the historical collection of prints exhibited in the Second Northern Gallery* (37 pp; first edition 1887, new edition 1890) included 609 prints, ending with twelve plates from the Liber Studiorum by J. M. W. Turner. From 1890, until it was taken down in 1892, this exhibition coincided with the display of drawings in the new gallery in the White Wing. At no later stage has the Department had anything like this number of works again on public view.

The White Wing 1888–1912

For the first time, the Department was allocated its own exhibition space when it moved to its new premises in the White Wing in 1885 (cf p. 3). This room, which was first available in 1888, was referred to as the Print and Drawing Gallery (now divided into rooms 43–5). It was used to display large exhibitions devoted to a single theme, which were changed every two or three years. Most were accompanied by catalogues:

1888 Guide to the exhibition of Chinese and Japanese paintings. 57 pp.

1891 Guide to the exhibition of drawings and sketches by Continental and British masters. 111 pp. (Reprinted 1892 with 18 pp. supplement).

1894 Guide to an exhibition of drawings and sketches by the Old Masters, principally from the Malcolm collection, and of engravings of the early German and Italian schools. 89 pp. (Second edition 1895 of 113 pp.)

1899 Guide to an exhibition of drawings and etchings by Rembrandt and etchings by other masters in the British Museum. 93 pp.

1901 Guide to an exhibition of drawings and sketches by Old Masters and deceased artists of the English School principally acquired between 1895 and 1901. 64 pp. (Revised in 1903 with some new acquisitions. 68 pp.)

1904 Selections from the Reeve collection of works by artists of the Norwich school. (No catalogue.)

1905 Guide to an exhibition of mezzotint engravings chiefly from the Cheylesmore collection. 63 pp.

1909 Drawings, engravings and woodcuts by Albrecht Dürer. (No catalogue.)

1910 Exhibition of drawings bequeathed to the British Museum by the late Mr George Salting. 20 pp.

1910 Guide to an exhibition of Chinese and Japanese paintings iv–xixc. 46 pp.

1912 Guide to an exhibition of drawings and sketches by Old Masters and by artists of the English School principally acquired between 1904 and 1912. vi + 63 pp.

The Edward VII Galleries 1914–present

The last exhibition in the White Wing was taken down in August 1912, and the screens and fittings removed to the newly constructed Edward VII Gallery. In the interim before the opening of the new gallery in 1914, some works were shown in the King's Library. The exhibition policy now changed, and instead of a single show devoted to one theme, the new space was divided into a number of separate areas, each of which held an independent display. Thus while a semi-permanent show of prints was held in the circular stands, the wall cases might be used for an exhibition of watercolours, with three or four groups of exhibits, especially new acquisitions, being shown on screens and in table cases. All works, except those in the table cases, were shown in frames; the wall cases had glass doors until their removal in 1936.

1914–1916

There were five groups of works exhibited in 1914, of which four had catalogues. The most enduring was the first, *A Guide to the processes and schools of engraving represented in the exhibition of select prints, with notes of some of the most important masters* (54 pp., 13 ills in text). Since the exhibition was semi-permanent, this guide remained in print continuously, new editions being issued in 1923, 1933 and 1953 (although the exhibition had been taken down in 1939). The second and third, an exhibition of woodcuts and metalcuts of the xvc., chiefly of the German school, and an exhibition of drawings and sketches by Old Masters and by artists of the British School acquired between 1912 and 1914, were both accompanied by short catalogues each of 36 pp., while the fourth, of Japanese and Chinese paintings, principally from the Arthur Morrison collection, had one of 24 pp. The last was of recent acquisitions, and this was changed in 1915, when selections from the collection of fans presented by Lady Charlotte Schreiber and of the Sale collection of watercolours were put up. None of these had catalogues. The gallery was closed in March 1916 for the duration of the war.

1920–1939

When the gallery was reopened in July 1920, the scheme of constantly changing small exhibitions, only a few of which had any published accompaniment, was intensified. For this reason it is very much more difficult to give a complete listing until after the Second World War. Throughout the period certain areas were reserved for quasi-permanent displays; new acquisitions, for example, were always put out as soon as possible. Thus in 1935 one of the swing-stands and a few screens were occupied by items illustrating the various techniques of printmaking, while other screens held British drawings and selections from the Turner bequest. Two wall-screens held foreign drawings and recent acquisitions, and the second swing-stand sporting prints and drawings. In 1936 the section of foreign drawings was devoted to drawings from Vasari's collection. A summary list is here given of all the more prominent exhibitions that have been traced in the annual reports of these

years, and a note is made whenever a catalogue was published. These were not on
the same scale as before, although all were properly printed by letterpress. The
beginnings of illustration can be found in the occasional frontispiece, the first being in 1923. The Oriental sub-department had an area reserved for its own use at
the end of the gallery, and its displays have not been included in the following list.

1920 Italian, French, Flemish and German drawings, xv–xviiic.
      Drawings by British artists acquired since 1914, including war drawings by
      Muirhead Bone.
      Selection of prints 1780–1820 from the gift of Lady Lucas in 1917.
      Select prints illustrating the processes of engraving.
1921 Three small shows of the work of Meryon, Tiepolo and Frank Short.
1922 Drawings by Crome, Cotman and other artists of the Norwich school.
      Drawings by Girtin; Drawings by J. R. Cozens.
1923 Early Italian engravings (accompanied by *A Guide to the collection of early
      Italian engravings . . . including a catalogue of an exhibition of selected examples*).
      54 pp., 1 pl.
1924 Drawings, engravings and colour prints by William Blake.
      Etchings, colour prints and lithographs by Théodore Roussel.
      Modern prints and drawings presented by the Contemporary Art Society.
1925 Old Master engravings and woodcuts purchased from the Albertina and
      elsewhere.
      Italian drawings of the xviic.
      French line-engravings from Louis xiv–xvi, including the 'Monument du
      Costume'.
1926 The drawings of Claude Lorrain, and artists influenced by him. 54 pp., 1 pl.
      French drawings acquired since 1919 through the H. L. Florence fund.
      Historical prints and portraits illustrating the Napoleonic era.
1927 Flemish drawings; Flemish engravings, etchings and woodcuts.
      Drawings and engravings by William Blake.
1928 The drawings, engravings and woodcuts of Albrecht Dürer. 47 pp., 1 pl.
      Drawings and prints by Francisco Goya.
      Drawings and woodcuts by Thomas Bewick.
1929 Dutch prints; Drawings by Rembrandt.
      British drawings and etchings of the xixc.
      Drawings by William Blake for Young's 'Night Thoughts'.
1930 Italian drawings; Italian woodcuts, engravings and etchings.
      German engravings of the xvc.

1932 French prints and drawings.

1933 The more important prints and drawings acquired during the keepership of Mr Campbell Dodgson 1912–32. 25 pp.
Drawings from the Turner bequest (continuing at least until 1935).
Sporting prints and drawings.

1934 English art (gathered from various departments of the BM). 104 pp. 1 pl.

1934 Drawings by George Du Maurier.

1935 The past hundred years, 1835–1934. 15 pp.
A technical exhibition of the processes of printmaking.

1936 Canaletto to Constable. Drawings and prints of landscape, topography and architecture of the xviii and early xixc.

1937 From Watteau to Wilkie: conversation, portrait and genre in the xviiic. and early xixc. 20 pp. (joint catalogue with the following).
The treatment of water in European and Oriental art.
The work of John Constable (on the centenary of his death).

1938 Drawings and etchings by Rembrandt (summary catalogue of the collection). 32 pp.

1939 Caricature (from Leonardo da Vinci to 1939). 16 pp.

1947–1969

At the beginning of the Second World War the galleries were closed, but a few displays of objects from the Department's collections were mounted in various parts of the Museum. Thus in 1940 groups of fans from the Schreiber collection were to be seen in the Manuscript Saloon, and gifts from the Contemporary Art Society in the Front Hall. The Blitz put an end to these in May 1941, and it was not until September 1947 that the Department's galleries were reopened. The tendency towards larger-scale shows, seen in the later 1930s, was continued, and after about 1953 the whole gallery was taken up by exhibitions with a theme rather than of the miscellaneous character that had marked the inter-war years. Exhibitions, too, were more often accompanied by catalogues, or rather handlists. These were usually cyclostyled and hardly ever properly printed, nor were they illustrated. A few landmarks may be noted. The 1953 Michelangelo exhibition was the first to have a substantial number of loans. The 1963 exhibition of Alpine prints was the first to have a poster designed for it, and that in 1967 of Oskar Kokoschka was the first to be devoted to the work of a living artist. (Its only successor was the 1974 Henry Moore exhibition.)

1947 A selection from the chief treasures of the Print Room.

1948 New acquisitions of British and Italian drawings, 1939–47.

1949 Colonial maps, views and postage stamps (in collaboration with the Map Room).
Drawings by Peter de Wint.
Prints and drawings of French landscape.
The beginnings of English landscape and topographical drawing. 16 pp.

1950 Italian drawings of the XIV and XVc. (to coincide with the publication of the catalogue by A. E. Popham and P. Pouncey).

1951 Watercolours by J. M. W. Turner, his predecessors and contemporaries.
Prints and Drawings acquired from the bequest of Campbell Dodgson.
Emilian drawings of the XVIc. 39 pp.

1952 Dutch prints and drawings from the XVI–XVIIIc.

1953 Canaletto and English draughtsmen. 8 pp.
Drawings by Michelangelo belonging to HM the Queen, the Ashmolean Museum, the British Museum and other English collections. 31 pp.
Drawings from the collection of Sir Hans Sloane.
Prints and drawings acquired by, or with the aid of, the NACF.

1954 Flemish drawings.
Anglo-Flemish art under the Tudors. (in collaboration with the Department of Manuscripts). 16 pp.
Italian drawings and prints acquired during the keepership of Mr A. E. Popham. 2 pp.

1955 Aspects of XVIIIc. art.
Watercolours and colour prints by William Blake.

1956 Rembrandt and his succession. 49 pp.

1957 William Blake and his circle, a bicentenary exhibition. 32 pp.

1958 Eight centuries of landscape and natural history in European watercolour 1180–1920 (in collaboration with the Dept of Manuscripts). 31 pp.

1959 The R. W. Lloyd bequest. 4 pp.
Recent acquisitions 1954–8. 7 pp.
Seven centuries of portrait drawing in Europe.

1960 Recent acquisitions.
Turner drawings from the Lloyd bequest.
Bicentenary of William Beckford (1760–1844). 4 pp.
Drawings from the collection of Sir Hans Sloane. 6 pp.

1961 Forgeries and deceptive copies (a loan exhibition from private owners, other institutions and all departments of the British Museum). 29 pp., 3 pl.

1962 German Gothic and Renaissance prints (joint catalogue with the two following exhibitions). 4 pp.
Sketchbooks and albums of drawings.
Thirteen oil-sketches, c.1820–30, by J. M. W. Turner.
Drawings bequeathed by Iolo Williams (1890–1962). 23 pp.
Raphael and his circle (to coincide with the publication of the catalogue by P. Pouncey and J. A. Gere).

1963 Alpine prints from the R. W. Lloyd collection. 18 pp.
The graphic work of Goya (with loans from the Prado). 18 pp., 11 pl.

1964 The Virginia of Sir Walter Raleigh and John White.
Michelangelo Buonarroti, 1475–1564, to commemorate the 400th anniversary of his death. 23 pp.
Recent acquisitions 1960–4. 8 pp.
William Hogarth 1697–1764: an exhibition in honour of the bicentenary of his death. 49 pp.

1965 Masterpieces of the Print Room. 8 pp, ill. cover.

1966 Turner watercolours from the R. W. Lloyd bequest. 6 pp.
Charles Francis Bell (1871–1966). 14 pp.
Recent acquisitions 1964–6. 9 pp.

1967 Oskar Kokoschka, word and vision 1906–66. 37 pp., 12 pl.
Lithographs by Bonnard, Vuillard and Toulouse-Lautrec.
Artists working in Parma in the XVIc., including Parmigianino and Correggio (to coincide with the publication of the catalogue by A. E. Popham).
Campbell Dodgson (1867–1948), an outstanding benefactor. 4 pp.

1968 Sir Charles John Holmes (1868–1936). 6 pp.
The César Mange de Hauke bequest. 39 pp., 16 pl.
The Eric George Millar bequest (jointly with Dept of Manuscripts. cf. BMQ XXXIII).
Recent acquisitions 1967–8.
Giovanni Battista Piranesi, his predecessors and his heritage. 53 pp.

1969 Turner watercolours from the R. W. Lloyd bequest. 7 pp.
The late etchings of Rembrandt, a study in the development of a print. 32 pp., 25 pl.
Royal Academy draughtsmen 1769–1969. 35 pp.
Recent acquisitions 1969.

1971–present

The exhibition gallery was closed for remodelling in late 1969, and reopened with new artificial lighting and air-conditioning in 1971. From this point onwards it has been usual to hold three exhibitions a year, mostly large shows filling the whole gallery. Occasionally the space has been divided to allow two or three smaller exhibitions to be mounted at the same time. One notable feature of these years has been the increase in the number of exhibitions wholly borrowed from outside the Museum or arranged in collaboration with other institutions. But most remarkable has been the increase in the size and ambition of the accompanying catalogues, and the expansion of the number of illustrations to the point that it is now normal for the majority of items to be illustrated. This development was the direct consequence of the establishment of British Museum Publications Ltd in 1973. The first catalogue that they published for the Department was for the exhibition of portrait drawings in 1974. From 1971 onwards it has been usual to have the labels printed rather than typed, and almost invariably a poster has been designed for each exhibition. The titles given are those of the catalogues rather than the exhibitions in the cases where the two diverged.

1971   The graphic work of Albrecht Dürer. ix + 62 pp., 16 ills.
1972   Modern prints and drawings and other recent acquisitions 1967–72. 27 pp.
        The art of drawing 11,000BC–AD1900 (with loans from other departments).
        79 pp., 22 ills.
1973   Netherlandish prints and drawings: van Eyck to Bruegel.
1974   Auden poems/Moore lithographs. 21 pp., 25 ills.
        Portrait drawings XV–XXc. 112 pp., 54 ills.
1975   Drawings by Michelangelo (with loans from UK collections). 160 pp., 183
        ills.
        Turner in the British Museum. 168 pp., 255 ills.
1976   Recent acquisitions.
        Spanish drawings from the XVII–XIXc. 11 pp. handlist.
1977   Claude Lorrain: Liber Veritatis (leaflet with exhibition; monograph by
        Michael Kitson published 1978). 178 pp., 204 pl.
        Rubens drawings and sketches. 173 pp., 243 ills.
        French landscape drawings and sketches of the XVIIIc. (a loan exhibition
        from France). 112 pp., 68 ills.
1978   From Manet to Toulouse-Lautrec. French lithographs 1860–1900. 104
        pp., 71 ills.
        Gainsborough and Reynolds in the British Museum. xii + 92 pp., 48 ills.

1979 Flowers in art from East and West (jointly with Oriental Antiquities). x + 150 pp., 187 ills. Also a handlist of the labels in the exhibition, 24 pp.

Rubens and Rembrandt in their century. Flemish and Dutch drawings of the XVIIc. from the Pierpont Morgan Library, New York. 320 pp., 136 pl. Also a handlist of the labels in the exhibition, 21 pp.

1980 American prints 1879–1979. 55 pp., 63 ills.

The varieties of Western woodcut.

Watteau drawings in the British Museum. 32 pp., 62 ills.

Dutch landscape prints of the XVIIc. (to coincide with the publication of the book of the same title by David Freedberg; 80 pp., 144 ills.).

British figure drawings.

1981 Recent acquisitions since 1976.

Turner and the Sublime. 192 pp., 133 ills.

Goya's prints: the Tomás Harris collection in the British Museum. 112 pp., 100 ills.

1981 XVIIIc. Venetian drawings.

Francis Towne and John 'Warwick' Smith.

Prints of the School of Fontainebleau.

1982 A century of modern drawing from the Museum of Modern Art, New York. 52 pp., 112 pl.

Masterpieces of printmaking from the XVc. to the French Revolution. 12 pp. handlist.

1983 Italian drawings from the Frits Lugt collection, Institut Néerlandais, Paris (to coincide with the publication of the catalogue of the collection by J. Byam Shaw). 21 pp. handlist.

Wenceslaus Hollar, prints and drawings (a joint exhibition with the National Gallery, Prague). 88 pp., 102 ills.

Sporting life, an anthology of British sporting prints and drawings. 126 pp., 100 ills.

Industry and Idleness: Hogarth and the moral print. 2 pp. leaflet.

Drawings by Raphael from the Royal Library, the Ashmolean Museum, the British Museum, Chatsworth and other English collections. 253 pp., 202 ills.

1984 German drawings from a private collection. 72 pp., 73 ills.

Rembrandt and the Passion. 8 pp., 4 ills.

Landscape in Italy. Drawings of the XVI and XVIIc. 14 pp. handlist.

Master drawings and watercolours in the British Museum. 208 pp., 212 ills.

The print in Germany 1880–1933. The age of Expressionism. 272 pp., 236 ills.

1985 British landscape watercolours 1600–1860. 84 pp., 138 pl.
1986 Five years of collecting, 1981–5. (No catalogue.)
      Florentine drawings of the XVIC. 272 pp., over 200 ills.
      Czechoslovak prints from 1900 to 1970. 96 pp., 67 ills.
      Prints by Jean Morin: the Barnard gift. (No catalogue.)

Since 1982 a few small displays of framed prints and drawings have been mounted outside the public coffee shop at the south-west corner of the Museum. Other small groups of prints have been displayed in cases erected on the north-east staircase from 1984. No catalogue or list has been published of any of these exhibitions, and they are not listed here.

8 The Curatorial Staff

There have so far been fourteen Keepers of Prints and Drawings; engraved portraits or drawings of all of them hang in the Keeper's study. They are as follows:

William Alexander (1767–1816)	Keeper 1808–1816
John Thomas Smith (1766–1833)	1816–1833
William Young Ottley (1771–1836)	1833–1836
Henry Josi (1802–45)	1836–1845
William Holkham Carpenter (1792–1866)	1845–1866
George William Reid (1819–87)	1866–1883
Sidney Colvin (1845–1927) Knighted 1911	1883–1912
Campbell Dodgson (1867–1948)	1912–1932
Laurence Binyon (1869–1943)	1932–1933
Arthur Mayger Hind (1880–1957)	1933–1945
Arthur Ewart Popham (1889–1970)	1945–1954
Edward Croft-Murray (1907–80)	1954–1973
John Arthur Giles Gere (b.1921)	1973–1981
John Kendall Rowlands (b.1931)	1981–

During the years from 1808 until 1865 the Keepers looked after the collections with the help of one (or sometimes two) attendants. The first five Keepers died while still in office. Alexander owed his appointment mainly to his skills as a draughtsman, for in addition to his duties as Keeper, he had to make the drawings for the engraved plates in *Description of the Ancient Marbles and Terracottas in the British Museum*, 1810. Smith seems to have regarded the job as something of a sinecure (see his *Book for a Rainy Day*), while Ottley, although one of the best connoisseurs of his day, was in very poor health. Josi, a printseller in origin, was much more active, but died prematurely at the age of forty-three. Carpenter was also a printseller before he came to the Museum, and was equally successful in expanding the collections and compiling the first manuscript catalogues. Reid's father had been an attendant in the Department, as was Reid himself from 1842, before he became the first assistant (that is Assistant Keeper) in 1865. After his promotion in 1866, his place was taken by Freeman O'Donoghue at the beginning of 1867. A second post as Assistant was created for Panizzi's protégé Louis Fagan in 1869. The first catalogues of the collection were published in the 1870s and 1880s under Reid, and all of these were given to outside scholars to compile.

It was the appointment of Colvin that marked the beginning of the Department's scholarly reputation. In the course of his Keepership he oversaw the introduction of a new breed of university-trained scholars, and managed to persuade the Trustees to add two posts to the complement. The first of these was Lionel Cust in 1884. In 1893 Dodgson took the place of Fagan, who had resigned in 1892, and Binyon succeeded Cust, who went to the National Portrait Gallery in 1895. Hind was appointed in 1904 to the second of the new posts, but on O'Donoghue's retirement in 1909 his post was frozen and not filled until 1913. The first volume of Binyon's catalogue of British drawings in 1898 was the first catalogue to be produced by a staff member of the Department, and it was Binyon who was appointed to fill O'Donoghue's position as Deputy Keeper (then called Assistant Keeper, the new term only being adopted after the First World War).

When Dodgson became Keeper in 1912, Binyon continued as Deputy Keeper and was put in charge of the newly created subsection of Oriental prints and drawings. He still, however, continued his curatorial concern for the British drawings and watercolours. Popham was appointed in 1912 to fill one vacancy, and Arthur Waley in 1913 to help with the Chinese and Japanese collection. Finally, a new post was created in 1915 which was given to Henry Hake. He resigned to go to the National Portrait Gallery in 1928, and was succeeded by Karl Parker. Waley resigned at the end of 1929, and his place was taken by Basil Gray the following year.

In 1933, after Binyon's retirement, the Oriental subsection became the nucleus of a new Department of Oriental Antiquities, to which Gray transferred. Popham became Deputy Keeper to Hind, Croft-Murray took Gray's vacancy and when Parker left at the end of the year for the Ashmolean, the remaining fourth post in the reduced complement of four was given to Elizabeth Senior, the first female member of staff.

She was killed in the Blitz in 1941, and so when Popham became Keeper in 1945, the only Assistant Keepers were Croft-Murray and Philip Pouncey, who had just transferred from the National Gallery. John Gere joined in 1946 and an extra post was made for Paul Hulton in 1951. The vacancy created in 1954 on Popham's retirement was filled by Christopher White, who was replaced in 1965 by John Rowlands. On Philip Pouncey's resignation in 1966, John Gere was appointed Deputy Keeper, and the resulting vacancy filled by Andrew Wilton.

After John Gere became Keeper, Nicholas Turner was appointed to the staff in 1974. In 1975 and 1976 two new posts were created which went to Frances Carey and Antony Griffiths. After the resignation of Andrew Wilton in 1976, his post was filled the following year by Timothy Clifford and, after his departure in 1978, by Lindsay Stainton. With the retirements of Paul Hulton and John Gere in 1981, one vacancy was filled by Martin Royalton-Kisch, who took up his post in 1982. Between 1980 and 1984 Andrew Wilton rejoined the Department as a supernumerary keeper to catalogue the Turner collection; he transferred to the staff of the Tate Gallery in 1985.

The first Research Assistant in the Department was Dudley Snelgrove who was promoted in 1963, having first joined the staff in 1920. He was succeeded in 1964 by Reginald Williams, who was promoted to Senior Research Assistant in 1966 and retired in 1986. Two new posts were created in the early 1970s, Diana Southern joining in 1970 and Paul Goldman in 1974. The former left in 1975, and her place was taken first by Martin Royalton-Kisch, and later in 1979 by Giulia Bartrum.

One other member of staff should be recorded in this short note. This was Alfred Whitman, who wrote a number of valuable works on British prints. He joined the Department in 1885 as an attendant, and was promoted in 1903 to be supervisor of the Print Room, where he gained a considerable reputation for his helpfulness and expertise. His health collapsed in 1908, and he died at the age of fifty in 1910.

Although she was never an established member of staff, Dr M. Dorothy George was employed as a special assistant on the catalogue of personal and political satires for twenty-five years from 1930 to 1954. During this time she worked regularly first in Bloomsbury, and during the war in Aberystwyth. She died in 1971 at the age of ninety-three.

THE COLLECTION
OF DRAWINGS

Reference has already been made to A. E. Popham's *A Handbook to the Drawings and Watercolours in the Department of Prints and Drawings*, published in 1939. This remains the fundamental introduction to the collection of drawings in the Department, and gives an account of its strengths and weaknesses which is only outdated by acquisitions made since the date of publication. The most significant of these are Italian drawings of the xvic. and later, where the collection has been greatly reinforced by the acquisition of the Fenwick collection in 1946. Also of great importance are the collection of British watercolours, including J. M. W. Turner, bequeathed by R. W. Lloyd in 1958, and the sixteen xixc. French drawings bequeathed by César Mange de Hauke in 1965 (see Topic Index). A well-illustrated survey of the collection has been published, *Master Drawings and Watercolours in the British Museum*, edited by John Rowlands, 1984.

The following account is entirely different in nature to Popham's, merely giving a brief description of the way in which the collection is physically divided and of the number of boxes in each division. This may help the student who wishes to gain an overview of a whole section. It also gives a complete list of the official publications that catalogue parts of the collection.

Virtually the entire collection of single drawings has been mounted, and most of the parts which have not should be in forthcoming years. It has been divided by country (as defined by the index of artists), and within each country (in general) by century and then alphabetically. An artist is placed according to the century in which the greater part of his activity falls; in cases of doubt, he appears in the period to which his style more closely approximates. Anonymous drawings are, in general, physically placed at the beginning of each period. Apart from the published catalogues, dossiers of information have been compiled on many of the drawings, and they should be extended to cover the remainder in future years.

In addition to the single-sheet drawings, there is a collection of some 450 sketchbooks, mainly of the British school, housed in nine cases (102a, 196a–202, 204). Included among these volumes are a number of albums in which groups of drawings have been mounted either before their acquisition or by the Department at a later date.

The only drawings which are not kept in sequence by country are some atlas, antiquarian and panoramic works which have been combined together in alphabetical sequences by artist.

American

There are two royal and two imperial solander boxes, containing work by sixteen artists. American artists born before the Declaration of Independence in 1776 have been included in the British school.

See also Topic Index, s.v. Catlin, Whistler.

British

The British drawings are divided into eleven periods, according to the date of birth of the artist. If this is not known, it is taken to be twenty-five years before his first known work, or fifty years before the date of his death. The following table gives the division of the periods, and the number of royal and imperial solanders in each period. Atlas, antiquarian and panoramic size solanders have not been divided into periods, but form a single alphabetical sequence. They total twenty-one, five and five boxes respectively. Unmounted drawings are kept in four royal and one imperial solander. The Lloyd collection, which by the terms of the bequest has to be kept separately, occupies eight royal, two imperial, two atlas and one antiquarian solander.

Period			Royal	Imperial
I	1500–1600	Royal	6	Imperial } 1
II	1600–1664		19	
IIIa	1665–1715		32	5
IIIb	1716–1745		53	18
IV	1746–1774		141	18
V	1775–1790		98	15
VI	1791–1815		110	10
VII	1816–1850		94	13
VIIIa	1851–1885		84	16
VIIIb	1886–1913		29	8
IX	1914–		8	1

CATALOGUES
Laurence Binyon, *Catalogue of drawings by British artists, and artists of foreign origin working in Great Britain*. I, A–C, 1898; II, D–H, 1900; III, I–R, 1902; IV, S–Z, 1907.

Edward Croft-Murray and Paul Hulton, *Catalogue of British Drawings, volume I: XVI–XVIIc.*, 1960 (in two volumes, text and plates).

Lindsay Stainton, *British Landscape Watercolours 1600–1860*, catalogue of an exhibition held in 1985.

See also Topic Index, s.v. Archer, Bewick, Blake, Cotman, Cruikshank, Downman, Hogarth, Lawrence, Reynolds, Stothard, Sutherland, Turner, White.

See also Departmental exhibitions for the years 1934, 1949, 1958, 1962, 1969.

Foreign Artists Working in Britain

This curious classification goes back to the mid-XIXc. and is based on Horace Walpole's *Anecdotes of Painting in England*. Since many if not most of the artists who stand at the beginning of the British tradition of drawing and watercolour were of foreign origins, it seemed sensible to keep these works together for the convenience of students, although the artists concerned do not in any way form a school. They have been divided into three periods, according to date of birth, as follows:

Period I	up to 1660	Royal 22	Imperial 4
II	1661–1774	26	4
III	1775–early XXc.	25	2

CATALOGUES

Binyon's catalogue (see above) also includes the work of foreigners in Britain. Croft-Murray and Hulton's later catalogue (see above) also contains entries on drawings by foreigners in Britain, as well as on pp. 556–78 a handlist of drawings by foreign artists connected with Great Britain, compiled by Christopher White.

See also Topic Index, s.v. Hollar, Le Moyne, Scharf.

See also Departmental exhibitions for the years 1949, 1953, 1954.

Dutch and Flemish

The Dutch and Flemish drawings before the XVIIc. are placed together in a single series, divided into two at the middle of the XVIc. The schools then split for the later centuries. Following the classification followed in the published catalogues, the works of Rembrandt and his school, and of Rubens and van Dyck are separated in independent series. There are two boxes of unmounted drawings.

Dutch and Flemish XV and earlier XVIc.		Royal 16	Imperial 1
Dutch and Flemish later XVIc.		20	2
Flemish XVIIc.	Rubens and van Dyck	18	3
Flemish XVIIc.	Ordinary series	18	1
Dutch XVIIc.	Rembrandt and school	21	0

Dutch XVIIc.	Ordinary series	68	4
Flemish XVIIIc.		1	1
Dutch XVIIIc.		13	1
Flemish XIXc.		2	0
Dutch XIXc.		3	0
Dutch XXc.		1	0

CATALOGUES

Catalogue of Dutch and Flemish Drawings Preserved in the Department of Prints and Drawings. Complete in five volumes.

I   Arthur M. Hind, *Rembrandt and his School.* 1915.
II   Arthur M. Hind, *Rubens, Van Dyck and Other Artists of the Flemish School of the XVIIc.* 1923.
III   Arthur M. Hind, *Dutch Drawings of the XVIIc. (A–M).* 1926.
IV   Arthur M. Hind, *Dutch Drawings of the XVIIc. (N–Z and anonymous),* including a summary list of Dutch and Flemish drawings of the XVIII and XIXc.
V   A. E. Popham, *Dutch and Flemish Drawings of the XV and XVIc.* 1932
       See also Topic Index, s.v. Rembrandt, Rubens, van Dyck.

Eastern European

The royal-size drawings have been separated into the constituent schools as follows: Hungarian (2), Polish (2), Romanian (2), Russian (1). The imperial size of the schools combined fills less than half a box. The number of artists represented is respectively eight, three, seventeen and seven.

French

The French drawings are divided by century, apart from the atlas (5) and antiquarian (6, all by Ducerceau) which are in a single series. The other boxes are divided as follows:

XVIc.	(including some XVc. anonymous)	Royal	5	Imperial	0
XVIIc.	(including 37 boxes of Claude)		55		3
XVIIIc.	(including 5 boxes of Watteau)		13		4
XIXc.			5		4
XXc.			1		2

CATALOGUES

No catalogue of the French drawings has been compiled. There is, however, a handlist of the contents of the boxes, and the drawings by Claude and Watteau (which form the strongest section) have been the subject of independent catalogues by Hind and Kitson, and Parker and Hulton respectively. Paul Hulton has also catalogued the de Hauke bequest (see Topic Index).

See also Topic Index, S. V. Claude, Ducerceau, Watteau.

German

These are divided by century. There are four mounted and one unmounted box of anonymous drawings of the XVI–XIXc. Two atlas boxes cover the entire school. The boxes are divided as follows:

XVc.	(including 2 anonymous boxes)	Royal	3	Imperial	0
XVIc.	(including 14 boxes of Dürer)		29		3
XVIIc.			5		0
XVIIIc.			6		} 2
XIXc.			4		
XXc.			2		2

CATALOGUES

There is no catalogue of the German drawings, although one is being compiled by John Rowlands.

See also Topic Index, s.v. Dürer, Holbein.

Italian

The drawings are divided by century. In the atlas and antiquarian sizes, the centuries are run together in a single series (of five and two boxes respectively).

XVc.	(including a few XIVc.)	Royal	27	Imperial	1
XVIc.			121		10
XVIIc.			52		5
XVIIIc.			20		10
XIXc.			2		} 1
XXc.			1		

Unlike the other schools, the numbers of unmounted drawings are here significant, and the quality, on occasion, good. At present, therefore, both series often need to be consulted. In the unmounted series, there is one box of XVc. works, while the later centuries are run together in one sequence of twenty royal (of which five are anonymous) boxes and one imperial box.

CATALOGUES

There is a projected complete catalogue under the title *Italian Drawings in the Department of Prints and Drawings in the British Museum*. Five parts have at present been published all except the second comprising two volumes of text and plates:

A. E. Popham and Philip Pouncey, *The Fourteenth and Fifteenth Centuries*, 1950.

Johannes Wilde, *Michelangelo and his Studio*, 1953.

Philip Pouncey and J. A. Gere, *Raphael and his Circle*, 1962.

A. E. Popham, *Artists Working in Parma in the Sixteenth Century*, 1967.

J. A. Gere and Philip Pouncey, *Artists Working in Rome c.1550 to c.1640*, 1983.

A number of important drawings have been published by Nicholas Turner in *Italian Baroque Drawings*, 1980, and in *Florentine Drawings of the Sixteenth Century*, 1986.

See also exhibitions 1951 for Emilian drawings of the XVIc.

See also Topic Index, s.v. Bellini, Leonardo, Michelangelo, Raphael.

Scandinavian

The Scandinavian drawings in the collection fill one royal and half an imperial box. There is no catalogue.

Spanish and Portuguese

There are thirteen royal boxes and one imperial box of Spanish drawings. The royal drawings are divided between XVI–XVIIc. (seven boxes) and XVIII–XXc. (six boxes).

A checklist of most of the collection was published on the occasion of the exhibition of Spanish Drawings from the XVII–XIXc., held in 1976.

See also Topic Index, s.v. Goya.

Swiss

The collection fills seven royal boxes (two of XVIc., three of XVIIIc. and two of XIX–XXc.) and one imperial box. There is no catalogue.

THE COLLECTION OF PRINTS

Unlike the collection of drawings, the collection of single-sheet prints is so extensive, and dispersed between so many different portfolios and boxes, that it is impossible to give any list of numbers in a helpful way. This section, therefore, attempts no more than to describe the principal series into which the collection has been divided, and to draw attention to any peculiarities that are to be found among these series.

Any print may be of interest according to its engraver, its designer or its subject-matter. Thus the three main divisions of the arrangement of the print collection are the engraver, designer ('master') and subject series (itself divided into many different classes). Prints bound in book form or illustrating books form a separate shelved sequence apart from the other series, which are all contained in portfolios or solander boxes. It would, in theory, be possible to have other classifications of prints, for example according to their publishers, but this has not been done, and it is impossible at present to trace prints by any particular publisher in the collection except through the index to the catalogue of satires.

1 The Engraver Series

This series contains prints classified according to the name of the printmaker. The artists are arranged according to country (as defined by the Index of Artists), and within each school according to the technique of the print. Only six printmaking techniques are recognised for the purposes of this classification, within which all others are subsumed. These are:

1 Woodcut, including wood-engraving and linocut.
2 Engraving, including stipple.
3 Etching, including drypoint, soft-ground etching, monotype.
4 Aquatint.

5 Mezzotint.

6 Lithography. At present this includes screenprinting, but this would change if the collection of screenprints were to become sufficiently large to warrant a separate classification.

For certain countries and periods, special series of colour prints have been created (see below). For other special techniques (e.g. glass-prints, paste-prints), see the Topic Index.

Within each of these classes, there will often be both a mounted ('select') series and an unmounted ('ordinary') series. The main unmounted sequence is arranged alphabetically in a single sequence, whereas the mounted series is usually divided into centuries. The work of individual printmakers who are particularly important or abundantly represented has been placed in separate boxes or portfolios. For some countries, the series of mounted modern prints has been arranged in a single sequence regardless of the technique of printmaking.

The following notes on the engraver series are not full accounts of each country sequence, since it can be assumed that the basic sexpartite division explained above is valid for all. Rather they draw attention to the existence of special series, or to those of particular interest either because they have published catalogues or some form of index.

American
The select (mounted) xxc. prints are kept in a single series, regardless of technique. See the 1980 exhibition catalogue, *American Prints 1879–1979*, for a listing of some of this part of the collection, and the Topic Index under Whistler.

British
a Engravings   The main series of unmounted engravings is alphabetically arranged in 26 portfolios. Because of the size of the collection, the work of the following engravers has been kept in a separate sequence of 19 individual portfolios: J. Basire i and ii, W. Bromley, G. Cooke, W. B. Cooke, C. and J. Cousen, R. Dodd, R. Earlom, F. Engleheart, E. and W. Finden, J. Fittler, J. Gillray, R. Golding, J. Hall, M. Haughton, C. Heath, T. Higham, F. and W. Holl ii, J. Jones, J. Landseer, C. G. and F. C. Lewis, J. Mason, H. Meyer, J. H. Robinson, C. Rolls, J. Scott, E. Scriven, C. W. Sharpe, J. K. Sherwin, the Smiths, L. Stock, F. Vivares, J. T. Willmore. Besides this sequence, there are special collections of the work of the following engravers: W. Faithorne (6 volumes), J. R. Jackson (1), W. B. Scott (bound in 190* a.20–3, 190* b.26), W. Sharp (4), R. Strange (4), W. Woollett (11).

A separate sequence of unmounted engravings arranged in individual volumes, portfolios or solanders is formed by the work of certain XIXc. engravers of illustrations: E. F. Burney, L. and W. Byrne, R. H. Cromek, J. Emslie, E. Goodall, W. Greatbach, C. and J. Heath, C. H. Jeens, J. Lewis, S. Middiman, J. Neagle, J. Parker, E. J. Portbury, J. Pye II, H. Robinson, R. Smirke, J. Thurston, P. W. Tomkins, W. Walker, C. Warren, R. Westall.

See also Topic Index, s.v. Bartolozzi, Blake, Gribelin, Hogarth, Kirkall.

b Etchings See Topic Index, s.v. Cotman, Cruikshank, Goff, Hills.

c Mezzotints Because of the great interest in mezzotints in the early XXc. when the collection was being arranged, this section was thoroughly sorted and indexed. As a result, it is often possible to find out what is in the collection without having to look in the boxes and portfolios. The system of arrangement and indexing is, however, rather complicated, and needs detailed explanation.

So far as the arrangement is concerned, mezzotints which are classified under the name of their engraver are kept either mounted (the select series) or unmounted. There is a single mounted series that includes works from both the Cheylesmore (see Topic Index) and the ordinary collection. This contains 78 royal, 48 imperial and 45 atlas boxes, There are two unmounted series: the first (the 'O' series) contains only works from the Cheylesmore collection, and is kept in 37 portfolios. The second is kept loose between the pages of 20 large albums, and contains works from the main (non-Cheylesmore) collection. Whereas mezzotints from the main collection may also be kept in the master and subject series, the portrait mezzotints from the Cheylesmore collection are, as far as possible, kept together, and all unmounted works from it are (with a very few exceptions), in a single series according to the engraver.

Since the vast majority of British mezzotints are portraits, the key to cataloguing them is J. Chaloner Smith's *British Mezzotinto Portraits* (4 volumes, 1883). The Department's copy of this has been interleaved and the holdings marked off. The copy has also been annotated with notes of the series in which impressions have been placed. If the impression is to be found in the master or portrait series, there is nothing further to be done than to look in those series and locate the impression; but if the mezzotint has been placed under the engraver's name, references are given either to the Cheylesmore index or to the index to the main collection. These indices take the form of large manuscript volumes and are placed with the Artist Index. By consulting the appropriate volume, it is possible to find the exact solander or unmounted portfolio in which the impression has been placed.

For non-portrait ('subject') mezzotints, it is generally useless to consult

Chaloner Smith, and the first step is to look in the manuscript index of mezzotints under the name of the engraver. If this fails, it is necessary to consult a blue slip index labelled 'Catalogue of mezzotints elsewhere than with engravers'. This should reveal whether the Department owns an impression and, if so, where it is kept. There is also a separate subject index to British mezzotints kept on blue slips (but of doubtful completeness).

Quite apart from the mezzotint series described in the preceding paragraphs, there is another series of 19 volumes labelled 'Early mezzotints'. This contains in a single series the works of von Siegen, Prince Rupert, Vaillant and the other early practitioners of the medium. There is a separate blue slip index of the prints in this series.

There are separate unmounted portfolios of the work of the following mezzo-tinters: S. Cousins (5), R. Earlom (2), V. Green (2), J. Jones (2), S. W. Reynolds (4), W. Say (6), J. R. Smith (2), C. Turner (2).

See also Topic Index, s.v. David Lucas, James Ward.

d XVIIIc. colour prints A series has been created of about 250 select examples of XVIIIc. colour printing in 7 royal and 4 imperial volumes. Almost all these are stipples printed in colour 'à la poupée'; a few are aquatints. There is an index to the prints in the series on white cards.

e XIXc. colour printing Various separate boxes and portfolios have been created. See also Topic Index, s.v. Baxter, Colour printing, Oleographs.

f XIXc. woodcuts (containing mostly wood-engravings). The main unmounted series is divided into two, one by name of the designer, the other by the name of the engraver. This division is maintained in the mounted select series of 9 and 3 boxes respectively. See also Topic Index, s.v. Bewick, Dalziel, Landells, Swain.

g XXc. woodcuts The select mounted series has been divided into two. The first sequence of 20 boxes contains woodcuts and wood-engravings (undifferentiated) printed in monochrome. The second (15 boxes) is of those printed in colour. This includes colour linocuts.

Dutch and Flemish
a For XVc. works see below, s.v. German.

b The main part of the collection of XVIIc. etchings is kept mounted into a number of albums known as the Sheepshanks albums. When the Sheepshanks collection, comprising almost entirely XVIIc. Dutch works (see Topic Index), was acquired in

1835, it was mounted into these volumes which thereby acquired their name. But even at that stage the opportunity was taken of incorporating related prints from the rest of the collection, so that many of the prints in the albums are not from the Sheepshanks collection. Conversely, a number of prints that were from the Sheepshanks collection never found their way into them, and were placed loose in the parallel series of unmounted etchings in portfolios. The albums have been rearranged several times since the 1830s, and a number of prints extracted for mounting (e.g. those by Segers). At present it comprises two sequences, the first of 45 albums of prolific printmakers whose work occupies a good part of an album or more, and the second of 7 albums of other artists' work, arranged ten or more to an album, in alphabetical sequence. See also Topic Index, s.v. Rembrandt, and exhibitions 1980.

French

a There is a mounted select series of XVIIIc. colour prints, arranged alphabetically in 11 royal and 2 imperial solanders. It has been indexed on white cards.

b The two portfolios of unmounted XIXc. woodcuts (wood-engravings) have, like the British, been divided, one by designer, the other by engraver.

c The catalogue of the 1978 exhibition entitled *From Manet to Toulouse-Lautrec, French Lithographs 1860–1900*, contains at the end a complete listing of all the lithographs in the Department's collection by the artists included in the exhibition (principally Bresdin, Manet, Redon, Pissarro, Degas, Toulouse-Lautrec, Bonnard and Vuillard).

See also Topic Index, s.v. Gavarni.

German

a XVc. woodcuts The collection has been arranged according to the catalogue by W. L. Schreiber, *Handbuch der Holz- und Metalschnitte des XV Jahrhunderts* (Leipzig, 1926–30). It follows Schreiber in including the few Netherlandish and French works of this period in the collection, and occupies 12 solander boxes. There are also 6 supplementary boxes of prints cut from XVc. books.

b XVc. engravings The collection has been arranged according to the catalogue by Max Lehrs, *Geschichte und kritischer Katalog des deutschen, niederlandischen und französischen Kupferstichs im XV Jahrhundert* (Vienna 1908–34). It occupies 35 boxes. The early work by W. H. Willshire, *Catalogue of Early Prints in the British Museum: German and Flemish Schools* (I 1879, II 1883), is now entirely superseded apart from various sections in which he describes impressions from plates which were never intended for printing, and which have not been redescribed in any subsequent catalogue.

c XVIc. woodcuts The collection has been arranged according to the two published volumes of Campbell Dodgson's *Catalogue of Early German and Flemish Woodcuts in the British Museum* (1903 and 1911). Unfortunately, Dodgson's scheme was not completed, and did not reach the Flemish school. With the German School it never extended beyond the middle of the XVIc. and did not touch the artists of the lower, middle and upper Rhine and Switzerland, such as Holbein and Hans Baldung. Thus works of these areas and of the later XVIc. were left loose in portfolios, awaiting Dodgson's attention. Since his death, the work of a number of these artists has been mounted according to more recent published catalogues, notably those in the Hollstein series. It should, incidentally, be noted that although Dodgson included xvc. woodcuts in his catalogue, these have been arranged by Schreiber's order (see above), as have the other relief prints which Dodgson published in 1937 in his *Prints in the Dotted Manner and Other Metal Cuts of the XVc. in the Department of Prints and Drawings.*

d The mounted XXc. prints are kept in a single series, regardless of technique. The catalogue of the 1985 exhibition *The Print in Germany 1880–1933, The Age of Expressionism*, contains the greater part of the Department's collection of German prints by artists of the avant-garde of those years.

Italian

a XVc. engravings A. M. Hind published in 1910 an official *Catalogue of Early Italian Engravings preserved in the Department of Prints and Drawings in the British Museum* (two volumes, text and plates). His findings were later revised and incorporated in his magnum opus, the seven-volume corpus *Early Italian Engraving* (1938–48). The Department's collection is arranged according to this later catalogue.

b Nielli The collection is arranged according to A. M. Hind's catalogue of 1936: *Nielli, chiefly Italian of the XV century, plates, sulphur casts and prints, preserved in the British Museum.*

c XVI–XVIIc. etchings The work of most Italian 'peintres-graveurs' of this period was included in volumes XIV–XXI of Bartsch's *Le Peintre Graveur*. Most of the collection of their works is kept according to Bartsch's order and numbering.

Works by artists who never found a place in Bartsch's work are kept in the separate unmounted series of Italian etchings or engravings.

d Chiaroscuro woodcuts These are kept according to the order of Bartsch XII. The corresponding volume of *Le Peintre Graveur Illustré* published by Caroline Karpinski in 1971 has been marked with a complete record of the Department's holdings. There is also a complete finding list.

e The work of a number of the leading Italian reproductive engravers of the late XVIII–early XIXc. is kept in seven volumes labelled 'Italian School'.
   See also Topic Index, s.v. Morghen.

2 The Master Series

This series contains prints classified according to the designer of the composition. Thus it pays no heed to the method of reproduction, and contains a large medley of works of many different media and periods. There are probably as many photo-mechanical reproductions included as prints made by the traditional methods of printmaking. The series has been divided into three classes, depending on whether the original reproduced was a painting, a sculpture or a drawing.

Prints after paintings

This is the major series, and contains a very large number of portfolios. There is no mounted series in parallel with the unmounted works in the portfolios. A separate sequence for each country is arranged alphabetically without any subdivision by century. A number of artists, whose work was frequently reproduced, have been pulled out of the main series and given separate portfolios. In general, it will be found that the contents of the portfolios have been built up from the following sources:

1 Single-sheet engraved reproductions.
2 Sheets from broken-up albums of reproductions of works in particular collections (the so-called 'Gallery' works). There are hardly any of these albums still intact in the Department; the remaining sheets containing letterpress text have been rebound and are shelved on presses Oo and Pp. The theory (which does not always work in practice) which justified this was that the main library (now the British Library) would always have a second complete copy, and that the

convenience to students of finding all prints after a single master together in one place would more than outweigh any disadvantages.

3 Photographs or photogravures, usually made in the XIXc., of paintings and frescoes.

4 Cuttings taken from auction and other sale catalogues, reproducing paintings on the market. The work involved in making and filing these cuttings was always time-consuming, and after the opening of the Witt Library to the public, the practice was abandoned. The series, therefore, contains mainly cuttings from catalogues of the period between the two World Wars.

Prints after sculpture

This is a very much smaller series than with paintings. It contains only six portfolios in all, two each of British and Italian masters, one of French, and one for all the other schools. All are arranged alphabetically. There is no mounted series. The contents are a miscellany of engravings, photographs and cuttings from catalogues.

Prints after drawings

This is a very extensive series. All the prints are housed loose in solander boxes, arranged alphabetically by school. Most schools have been subdivided by century. There is no mounted series. The core of the series is formed by the plates from a number of broken-up copies of XVIII and XIXc. volumes of reproductions of Old Master drawings. On this subject see appendix III of Popham's *Handbook to the Drawings and Watercolours in the Department of Prints and Drawings*, especially the last paragraph. It is also worth noting that Popham has annotated the Department's copy of Weigel's *Die Werke der Maler in ihren Handzeichnungen* (Leipzig 1865) with notes of the press-marks of all the volumes to be found both in the Departmental library and in the main (British) library.

Nevertheless, it will be found that the large majority of works contained in this series are photographs of drawings taken in the great collections of Europe and the United States, as well as many private collections. The great period of their accumulation was the second half of the XIXc. and the early years of this century, and they were collected in the first place as an aid to Departmental staff in cataloguing the collection. Since the Second World War this function has been largely taken over by the Gernsheim Corpus Photographicum of drawings (see the Topic Index). For this reason, growth of the series in more recent years has been limited.

3 The Subject Series

There is a large number of portfolios containing prints classified according to their subject-matter. For many of these subject series (e.g. Architecture, Heraldry, or Shipping) there is no more than a single portfolio, and these small groups are described in the Topic Index. This section only describes the six main subject series, all of which occupy a number of boxes or portfolios.

Portraits

The main series of engraved portraits is kept unmounted in portfolios, arranged by countries according to the nationality of the sitter. This section gives a brief description of this series alone. In addition to the series described here, there are numerous portraits which will be found elsewhere in the collection. Some of the finest impressions of engraved portraits will have been placed under the name of the engraver, and of those more interesting to the art-historian under the name of the master. Moreover, many others will be in special collections, especially Grangerised volumes. For some references to these and other locations, see the entry for portraits in the Topic Index which complements this entry.

As a general remark, it is worth pointing out that the collection of portraits is primarily a collection of engravings, although it includes a number of photographs and photomechanical reproductions. Its strength is therefore in portraits of the XVI–XIXc.; it is very much weaker for the late XIXc., and almost useless for the XXc. In these areas recourse must be had to the National Portrait Gallery.

Blue slip indices exist for all the following countries. The indices will, however, only reveal whether the Department possesses any portrait of the sitter. They will not state what portraits are in the collection, which can only be ascertained by looking in the relevant wrapper. In the case of Continental royal portraits, however, in addition to a blue slip index, there are entries for each print contained on white cards made in the XIXc. as the skeleton for an unpublished catalogue.

America
All the nationalities of the American continent are combined in a single alphabetical series, which occupies three portfolios. Portraits of Franklin, Washington, and Webster have been placed in a separate portfolio.

Belgium and Holland (Netherlands)

There is a single alphabetical series which occupies ten portfolios. There are also two separate portfolios of Dutch royal portraits, arranged chronologically.

Britain

This is by far the largest of the series, and is the most complicated in its arrangement, which is based on that in Bromley's *Catalogue of Engraved British Portraits* of 1793. All sitters have been classified into one of a number of groups depending on their status or occupation. Within each group, they have been further subdivided into periods according to the date of their death. The following table gives details, and the number of portfolios in each class:

Class 1 Royalty (the Kings and Queens of England and Scotland from Egbert to George IV – including the Cromwells – mounted in 42 royal and 3 imperial solanders, to which must be added 2 containing the Stuart Pretenders; the rest from William IV in 9 portfolios, of which one is outsize. There is a separate series of royal offspring arranged in 5 portfolios according to the parent, from the Normans and Plantagenets to George V.)

Class II	Nobility	20 portfolios, plus one outsize
III	Gentry	27 plus one outsize
IV	Clergy	
	subclass 1 Bishops	7 (there is one outsize portfolio for IV–X)
	2 Others	17
V	Lawyers	
	subclass 1 Judges	3
	2 Others	2
VI	Military, Naval	8
VII	Literary	30
(VIII	Artists, tradesmen, etc. has been incorporated into class VII)	
IX	Female	
	subclass 1 Nobility	13
	2 Others	8
X	Convicts, etc.	6 (including freaks and the like)
No class	Theatrical	7
No class	Foreigners	3 (resident in Britain)
No class	Groups	one outsize portfolio

The periods are as follows, depending on the date of death:

Period 1   827–1625   Egbert to James I
        2   1626–1684   Charles I to Charles II
        3   1685–1760   James II to George II
        4   1761–1837   George III to William IV
        5   1838–1901   Victoria
        6   1902–present Edward VII onwards

The portraits of foreigners in England and the groups are in a single series, which has not been divided into periods.

There are separate portfolios for Garrick, the Kemble family (including Sarah Siddons), Nelson, Shakespeare, and Wellington.

See also Topic Index, s.v. Burney, Irving, Mary Queen of Scots.

The British portrait series is the only one to have been catalogued: *Catalogue of Engraved British Portraits preserved in the Department of Prints and Drawings in the British Museum.*

by Freeman O'Donoghue I   A–C   1908
                        II   D–K   1910
                        III L–R   1912
                        IV   S–Z   1914
and Henry M. Hake   V   Groups (with index to names in groups) 1922
by Henry M. Hake   VI   Supplement and Indices   1925

(the supplement is alphabetical; the indices are to artist and engraver. It also contains a useful appendix listing the books and periodicals with portraits which have been included in the catalogue)

There is a blue slip index which gives (as the catalogue does not) the class and period of any sitter. It also gives references (as the catalogue does not) to the locations of any portraits kept elsewhere than with the main portrait series, but without stating which they are (although all are included in the catalogue unless they are more recent acquisitions).

Finally, it must be noted that a series of reproductions of British portraits (but not of any other nation) was compiled between 1928 and the Second World War in seven boxes. It has now been discontinued, but references to it will be found on the blue slip index. There is also a portfolio of anonymous unidentified portraits.

Bulgaria
Part of a single portfolio.

Czechoslovakia (Bohemia)
Part of a single portfolio; royalty are kept in a separate portfolio.

Denmark
A single portfolio; royalty are kept separately.

France
French portraits are arranged in a single alphabetical series in 5 portfolios. There are separate portfolios for Victor Hugo, Marat and Molière. Kings of France from Pharamond to Louis-Philippe are arranged chronologically in 5 portfolios. Napoleon and members of his family take up 3 portfolios, while another 3 are devoted to the royal houses and domaines: Alençon, Anjou, Angoulême, Berry, Bourbon, Brittany, Burgundy; Condé, Conti, Guise, Lorraine, Navarre, Valois; the house of Orléans occupies the third portfolio by itself.

Germany and Austria
The main alphabetical series occupies 28 portfolios, with separate ones for Erasmus, Goethe and Luther. The German ruling houses are arranged as follows in 15 numbered portfolios:

1–4   German ruling houses, alphabetically:
1   Anhalt, Baden, Brandenburg (Electors), Brandenburg-Ansbach, Brandenburg-Bayreuth.
2   Carolath, Cleves, Dietrichstein, Fürstenberg, Hanau, Hesse-Cassel, Hesse-Darmstadt, Hesse-Homburg.
3   Hohenlohe, Hohenzollern, Isenburg, Leiningen, Leuchtenberg, Liechtenstein, Limburg, Lippe, Luxemburg, Lobkowitz, Löwenstein-Wertheim, Mecklenburg, Schwerin and Mecklenburg-Strelitz, Metternich.
4   Oettingen, Oldenburg, Pomerania (Stettin), Reuss, Salm, Schaumburg, Holstein-Schauenburg with Holstein-Gottorp and Schleswig-Holstein, Schwartzenberg, Schwarzburg, Solms, Stolberg, Thurn und Taxis, Waldeck.
5–11   German royal houses, thus:
5   Bishops.
6,7   Bavaria and the Palatinate.
8   Brunswick, Hanover, Württemberg.
9   Prussia, German Emperors.

10, 11 Saxony.

12–14 Holy Roman Emperors, from Charlemagne to Franz Joseph.

15   Archdukes of Austria, alphabetically.

Greece
One portfolio for ancient Greeks; modern Greeks occupy part of a portfolio.

Hungary
Part of a portfolio; royalty are kept separately.

Italy
The main alphabetical series occupies 15 portfolios. There are also the following separate portfolios:

1 Popes (2 portfolios).
2 Ancient Rome.
3 Royal portraits (Savoy and Naples).
4 Ruling Houses (Ferrara, Mantua, Milan, Modena; Parma, Tuscany, Urbino; arranged in 2 portfolios).

Norway
Half of a portfolio; royalty are kept separately.

Poland
A single portfolio; royalty are kept separately.

Romania
Part of a portfolio.

Russia
A single portfolio, with a separate one for royalty.

Portugal
A single portfolio; royalty are kept separately.

Serbia
Part of a portfolio.

Spain
A single portfolio, with 2 separate ones for royalty.

Sweden
Half of a portfolio; royalty are kept separately.

Switzerland
A single portfolio.

Turkey
A single portfolio.

Others
African and Asian portraits, as well as those of members of primitive societies, are kept in a single portfolio.

History

Prints showing historical events have been classified in two separate series, depending on whether the event relates to British or Foreign history. Although there is no catalogue of either series, a complete microfiche has been made of both of them, following the order in which they are arranged. This fiche is ideal for quick consultation, and will show whether a print is in the collection.

British History 55BC–AD1936
The prints are arranged chronologically according to the date of the event shown, not according to the date of publication of the print. They are kept unmounted in folders kept in 12 drawers; outsize prints are in a separate large portfolio. The series begins with events connected with Julius Caesar's invasion, continues through the Roman and medieval period, but of course only begins to include contemporary prints from the XVIIc. onwards. From the mid-XIXc. the role of the historical print was increasingly taken over by photography, which in principle falls outside the scope of the collection. There are, nevertheless, a few photographs included in the series. The last print in the series is dated 1936.

There is no published catalogue or index, and nothing has been entered in the Index of Artists. In the XIXc., a catalogue was prepared, and printed as far as page-proof. The projected title (recorded in manuscript on the title-page of the Department copy) was: *A Catalogue of Prints and Drawings illustrating English*

History, and it is dated 1882. The period covered is 55BC–AD1685. It was never published because it was thought to be too badly compiled. There is a single bound set of the proofs in the Department library, which is sometimes useful. In particular it includes many prints that are kept elsewhere in the Department (especially the Grangerised books), as well as in the British Library, and gives references to their locations. It also sometimes gives the source of a single detached book-illustration.

Foreign History AD31–1968

The prints are arranged chronologically in a single sequence, regardless of the country to which they relate. They are kept loose in folders in 14 drawers, while outsize prints are kept separately in a large portfolio. They are mostly German, Dutch or French in origin, with a few Italian, Spanish and others. Some are rare, particularly the xviic. German broadsheets. References to the German, Dutch and French prints (only) are in general included in the Index of Artists. The subjects include political and ceremonial events, religious allegories, military and naval history, scientific or natural phenomena and many others. This very miscellaneous character distinguishes the series from that of British History. Some prints in it have very little to do with historical events, and seem to have been placed here mainly because they were dateable.

There is no catalogue or index. The collection has, however, been marked off against Drugulin's Historical Atlas of 1867. See also Topic Index, s.v. Broadsheets.

See also Topic Index, s.v. History, for references to other historical prints kept in different places or series.

Topography

There are two series of single-sheet topographical prints, one of British topography, the other of foreign topography. There is no catalogue of either series. In general, the collections contained in this series are not good. The Department has never attempted to collect topographical prints in any systematic way, and has always regarded local museums and archives as the appropriate repositories. For these see M. W. Barley, *A Guide to British Topographical Collections*, 1974. The only important exception to this rule is the collection of London prints (see below). The prints in the topographical series are frequently anonymous; high-quality prints of this class have often been placed in the Master or Engraver series. There is no published catalogue. See the Topic Index, s.v. Topography for references to topographical drawings and prints kept elsewhere in the collection.

The British Library possesses an extremely fine collection of topographical views and maps covering the whole world, which is, in general, of much greater importance than the collection in Prints and Drawings. It is also much better indexed and therefore more accessible. The most important part is formed by the King's Topographical Collection, which comes from the library of George III. It has been mounted into 120 albums, and is at present housed in the Map Room. There is a published catalogue: *Catalogue of Maps, Prints, Drawings etc. forming the Geographical and Topographical Collection attached to the library of his late Majesty King George the Third*, 1829. This is arranged alphabetically and includes an index. The other topographical drawings acquired before the mid-XIXc. were catalogued in the *Catalogue of the Manuscript Maps, Charts and Plans, and of the Topographical Drawings in the British Museum*, two vols 1844 (Britain and France), one vol 1861 (the remainder). Most of these drawings are now in the Department of Manuscripts, but a few of the albums are still kept in this Department. See further the Topic Index, s.v. Buckler and Kaye (for drawings by S. H. Grimm). There are also many topographical prints illustrating books in the Department of Printed Books. A useful reference book for these is J. P. Anderson: *The Book of British Topography: a classified catalogue of the topographical works in the library of the British Museum relating to Great Britain and Ireland*, 1881.

British Topography
The prints are arranged in the first place by country (England, Wales, Scotland, Northern Ireland), and within each country by county. For the purposes of this classification the county names are those that existed before the county reorganisation of 1974. The prints occupy 16 drawers.

Prints and drawings of London topography consist of a group of collections. The foundation is the Crace collection (see Topic Index), which is organised in 38 portfolios. Other London views from other sources have been arranged in the same sequence as the Crace collection in 8 drawers labelled the 'Crace supplement'. See also Topic Index, s.v. London, Archer, Scharf and pp. 55, 58 for the Crowle and Marx extra-illustrated copies of Pennant's *Some Account of London*.

There is an incomplete alphabetical blue slip index to British topographical prints which covers not only this series, but also some of those kept in bound volumes and elsewhere. There is a separate blue slip index to British drawings of topographical subjects, which is helpful, although incomplete.

Foreign Topography

The prints are arranged in the first place by country and then alphabetically by town or place within that country. The organisation is as follows in 18 drawers: Belgium and Holland (1 drawer), France (4) with Paris separately (1), Germany (1), Italy (2) with Rome separately (2), Russia (1), Spain (1), Portugal (1), Rest of Europe (2), America and Australia (1), and Asia (1).

There is no blue slip index to foreign topographical prints. A few references to foreign locations will be found in the blue slip index to British drawings of topographical subjects.

Satires

The Department possesses a very large and important collection of satirical prints. Its importance is increased by the existence of a catalogue published in eleven volumes, and of a microfilm which reproduces most of the items. The catalogue falls into two parts, the first published in the XIXc., the second in the XXc.

The first four volumes were published under the following title: *Catalogue of Prints and Drawings in the British Museum, Division I: Political and Personal Subjects.* (In the first volume only this read *Satirical and Personal Subjects*.) The title reflects the intention formulated by G. W. Reid to catalogue the entire collection in different divisions. The author commissioned to compile the volumes was Frederic George Stephens, and he based his work on the notes of Edward Hawkins (although this fact was only stated on the title-pages of volumes 3 and 4). Hawkins had been the Keeper of Antiquities in the British Museum, and his extensive collection was purchased in 1868, the year after his death. Stephens (the former member of the Pre-Raphaelite Brotherhood) was initially expected merely to edit Hawkins's notes, but the intention was soon expanded to include the many other satirical prints and the few drawings already in the Department's collection and in the main library.

Volume I	1870 Covering the years	1320–April 1689 Satires nos	1–1235
II	1873	June 1689–1733	1236–2015
III	1877 Part I	March 1734–*c.*1750	2016–3116
	Part II	1751–*c.*1760	3117–3804
IV	1883	1761–1770	3805–4838

These first four volumes have no index to titles, engravers or publishers. One is at present being compiled, but in the meantime the only aid is four volumes of manuscript index of titles (often defective) kept in the Department. Another peculiarity is the arrangement of the entries by the date of the earliest event directly illustrated by each print. After Colvin became Keeper in 1884 Stephens's publication was discontinued, and the project was not resumed until 1930 when Mary Dorothy George was commissioned to complete the sequence up to the end of the great age of British caricature in 1832. Her seven volumes were published under a slightly altered title-page: *Catalogue of Personal and Political Satires preserved in the Department of Prints and Drawings in the British Museum.*

Volume V	1935	Covering the years	1771–1783	Satires nos	4839–6360
VI	1938		1784–1792		6361–8283
VII	1942		1793–1800		8284–9692
VIII	1947		1801–1810		9693–11703
IX	1949		1811–1819		11704–13500
X	1952		1820–1827		13501–15496
XI	1954		1828–1832		15497–17391

Mrs George's volumes, unlike Stephens's, have excellent indices which cover persons, titles, selected subjects, artists, and printsellers and publishers. Moreover, her volumes are arranged according to the date of publication of the print, not the date of the event referred to. She also avoids Stephens's practice of giving separate catalogue numbers to different scenes on a single print.

As has been mentioned above, all eleven volumes of the catalogue contain entries for prints that are in the collection of the British Library, and are therefore not in the Department; it has been calculated that ten per cent of the total is to be found there. In this respect, Stephens's volumes differ in emphasis from Mrs George's. Whereas he made a deliberate attempt to find all such works in the Library, she only included those which had come to her notice, or were an important addition. When, in the late 1970s, a microfilm was prepared of all the prints in the catalogue and of the catalogue volumes, the attempt was made to include all the items from the British Library by splicing them into the film at the appropriate points. Nevertheless, a large number had to be omitted because they were contained in collections such as the Thomason Tracts, which could not be filmed. The microfilm also omits all acquisitions – a significant number in total – made by this Department since the publication of the catalogue.

The collection is arranged in the following manner. Numbers 1 to 4838, being the prints in Stephens's catalogue, were mounted on large boards which are housed in 24 imperial solanders. The remainder, from 4839 to 17391, is in 27 portfolios. There are, however, important exceptions. Many of the prints are in books, and some are kept under the name of the designer or engraver. In most cases, the catalogue will give the locations or press-marks. The work of the three great English caricaturists is also kept separately. Gillray's etchings are in 6 portfolios, with his non-satirical work being placed in a separate one. Rowland-son's are in 3 portfolios, also chronologically arranged. Cruikshank's etchings are arranged in 15 portfolios according to the numbers of Reid's catalogue raisonné.

Supplementary prints have been placed in a separate folder within the appropriate year. This could not usually be done for the years before 1771, as the series had been mounted; those additions which could not be fitted on to the boards of the mounted series have therefore been placed unmounted in a separate portfolio. Works later than 1832 are in two portfolios, while undated prints occupy a third. Finally, there is a small collection of foreign satires kept in one portfolio. Other foreign satires, apparently if they are of British interest, have been catalogued and placed in the main series. But the main series of German, Dutch and French satirical prints before the xviiic. will be found in the Foreign History series. Many of these come from the Banks collection, the H. W. Martin gift, and the collection of the Earl of Crawford, of which a large part was purchased in 1925.

Three separate items also require notice. There is a portfolio of caricatures, both French and German, relating to the Franco-Prussian War of 1870–1 and the subsequent Commune. Many of these prints were purchased in 1871 (1871–7–8–214 to 292); another group was presented by Sir C. W. Dilke in 1874 (1874–7–11–39 to 110). There are also five volumes containing some 1200 caricatures and cartoons, mainly cuttings from the Irish Nationalist Press (such as Weekly News, Weekly Freeman, Pat, United Ireland, St Stephens Review) of 1880–92 (298*; 1894–5–16–106 to 110, no list). Finally, among the Italian drawings, is a group of 106 anonymous political cartoons dealing with events in Rome and Italy, many of which were published in *Don Pirlone*, Rome 1848–9 (1948–10–9–20 to 125, list).

Ornament

There is a series of 15 solander boxes of ornament prints. The works are arranged in a single alphabetical series according to the designer, disregarding country or century or origin. Although they are all included in the Index of Artists, and there is a finding list that gives the names of artists and engravers represented, there is no separate catalogue. In general, ornament prints have been kept in this separate series, and will not be found in the main series of masters or engravers. The exceptions to this rule come with various important engravers, such as Dürer or Delaune, of whose work the Department has assembled special groups.

There are also numerous ornament prints kept in sets in bound volumes, mostly shelved in cases 168–168*. Most of these volumes can be traced through the book index under the subject-heading Ornament. Other books of engraved ornament are in the British Library. See also the Topic Index, s.v. Ornament for further references.

The collection of ornament prints, although of high quality, has nothing of the range and size of the collection in the Victoria and Albert Museum, which has been built up as an adjunct to its function as a museum of applied art. The Department has therefore ceased to collect on any scale in this area, but instead attempts to round out the collection by obtaining examples of styles that are lacking, or techniques of engraving that are unrepresented.

Costume (Authorities for Artists)

There is a series of unmounted prints, mostly of costume, known under the title 'Authorities for Artists' after the function originally intended when it was put together. It occupies 15 large boxes, and is arranged as follows:

1 Britain   55BC–AD1603
2   1603–1760
3   1760–1901
4 France   752–1589
5   1589–1804
6   1804–c.1900
7 Germany and the Netherlands
8 Italy
9 Other European countries (Denmark, Sweden, Lapland, Spain, Canary Islands, Russia, Finland, Poland, Austria, Hungary, Bohemia, Yugoslavia, Switzerland, modern Greece, Malta, Romania, Portugal, Bulgaria)
10 Greenland, the Levant, Armenia, Persia, Japan, China, Tartars, Syria, Bokhara, Siam, Sumatra, Java, North and South America, Egypt, Africa, Madagascar, Tripoli, Abyssinia, Morocco, Algeria, India, Ceylon, Australia, Pacific Islands
11 Turkey (both European and Asiatic)
12 Military uniforms (foreign)
13 Military uniforms (British)
14 Ecclesiastical, Theatrical, Fancy
15 Instruments, Armour, Military appliances, Furniture

Within each country, the prints are often subdivided by class of person or by type of dress.

The series contains, in general, documentary prints of little quality as works of art, and has not been actively increased for many years. There is no catalogue, and no references to it have been recorded in the Index of Artists. Many costume prints, such as those by Hollar, have been placed in other series under the name of the engraver or designer if this was thought to be of more importance. There are also many costume prints bound in book form, and references to these will be found in the book index under the heading Costume. These books are, as a rule, shelved in cases 169–171. Other costume prints will be found in Grangerised books, or kept in special collections. Thus the Lloyd collection (see Topic Index) contains a fine collection of the costumes of Swiss cantons. Many parodies of costume are kept in the series of satires, and may be found through the index to its catalogue. For further references, see the entry on Costume in the Topic Index.

4 Illustrated Books

A very large number of prints (mostly original, but also some high-quality modern reproductions) is kept in the original books or albums in which they were published. These are shelved in various cases reserved for this purpose; the system of press-marks is explained on p. 7. There is a card index to all these volumes, in which works can be found both under the name of the author or artist and by subject. The same card index also contains the index to the books in the Departmental working library which are kept on open shelves (see p. 60). References will also be found to these case books in the Index of Artists (see p. 10), which goes further than the book index by indexing every print by designer and engraver.

A rough classification system (not invariably adhered to through lack of space) has been adopted when shelving case books. A key to this is given below:

Cases 1–1*	Hogarth, Blake, Bewick	72–72*	Rembrandt
		156–157*	Dutch and Flemish
3	Blake	158–158*	German 1470–1550
36–37*, 39*	Dürer, Holbein and related early German books	159	German 1550–1600
		159*	German 1600–1700
		160–160*	German 1700–present
49	Goya	161–162*	French

163–164*	Italian	183–183*	Gallery works
165	British	184–184*	Cruikshank
165*	British (small), American, Spanish	185	Heitz: series of Einblattdrucke
166–167	British	186	Leonardo facsimiles
167*	Drawing books		
168–168*	Ornament, Fans, Toy theatre, Playing cards	188*–193*	XIX–XXc. books and albums of prints (mostly)
169–170*	Costume	196a–201	Sketchbooks (see p. 27)
171	Queen's costume books (on loan)	201*	Pornographic material
171*	Denkmaler des Theaters (Vienna): 12 portfolios	206*–210*	Portraits
		230*	Portraits
172–173	British topography	242–245*	Miscellaneous (mostly antiquities)
173*–175*	Foreign topography	246–246*	Outsize volumes (including modern portfolios)
176–178*	Reproductions of drawings		
179–180*	Reproductions of prints	248–249	Wood-engravings
181–182	Gallery works (i.e. plates reproducing collections)	266*–268*	Swiss Alpine views (Lloyd collection)
		270	Leonardo facsimiles
182*	Exhibition catalogues	274a	Modern portfolios
		298–298*	Satires

5 Extra-illustrated Books and Bound Collections of Prints

The custom of extra-illustrating appropriate texts with prints has been named after J. Granger's *Biographical History of England . . . adapted to a Methodical Catalogue of engraved British Heads*, 1769–74, which established the fashion. The Department possesses a number of works of this type, which contain a very considerable quantity of prints and a few drawings of mainly documentary interest. Many of these volumes are equipped with their own indices to the illustrations (rather than the texts), but in most cases the prints concerned are not included in the main Departmental catalogues, or the Index of Artists. (Most of the drawings are, however, in the Index of Artists.) It is therefore worth listing all these volumes, since they are an important supplement to the main series of loose prints. They are described in order of acquisition.

1 The Crowle Pennant

Thomas Pennant (1726–98): *Some Account of London*, 1793 (third edition; first edition 1790). Extra-illustrated and bound in 14 folio volumes by John Charles Crowle. Bequeathed by him in 1811, and inventoried as G 1 to 14. There is a manuscript index to topography, persons, artists and engravers compiled by Edward Carpenter in 1853 placed with the Index of Artists. The volumes contain a superb collection of 3347 drawings and prints of London topography, and of portrayals of historical events and persons connected with the history of London. The British portraits and watercolours are included in the respective published catalogues, but otherwise nothing is included in the Index of Artists. A number of the most important drawings and watercolours have been taken out and mounted, and the large panoramic prints that were formerly folded in volume 13 have been placed in a separate portfolio. On this and the Marx Pennant, number 14 below, see Bernard Adams in *The London Journal*, VIII 1982, pp. 123–39.

2 Clarendon's History of the Rebellion

Edward Hyde, first Earl of Clarendon (1609–74): *The History of the Rebellion and Civil Wars in England, begun in the year 1641*, 1702–4. Extra-illustrated and bound in eight folio volumes in 1796. Bequeathed by HRH William Frederick, Duke of Gloucester in 1834. Inventory Kk 5–1 to 8. The illustrations are consecutively numbered within each volume. There is a manuscript index to topography, persons, artists and engravers compiled by Edward Carpenter placed with the Index of Artists. The text is illustrated with a remarkable collection of 1700 portraits, historical prints, maps, plans, views, and engravings of seals, medals and coats of arms relating to the English Civil War.

3 Whitelocke's Historical Memorials

Bulstrode Whitelocke (1605–75): *Memorials of the English Affairs . . . from the beginning of the Reign of King Charles the First, to King Charles the Second his happy Restauration*, 1732 (first edition 1682). Extra-illustrated with 579 prints and bound in two folio volumes in 1796. Companion to the above, also bequeathed by HRH William Frederick, Duke of Gloucester in 1834. Inventory Ll 7–1 to 2. The prints are consecutively numbered within each volume. There is a manuscript index by E. Carpenter compiled on the same lines as the one above.

4 Mme de Sévigné's Letters

Marie de Rabutin-Chantal, Marquise de Sévigné (1626–96): *Lettres*, Paris 1823 (edited by M. Gault de Saint-Germain; first edition published 1725). The twelve volumes of the 1823 edition have been extra-illustrated with 9316 prints by Ellis Ellis, Esq. of Bath and rebound in thirty-eight quarto volumes in 1847. Bequeathed in 1859. Register 1859–5–14–306 to 343; within each volume the prints have been consecutively numbered. There is a manuscript index (shelved at Ss 7 8–10) in three volumes, two being devoted to portraits, the third to history and topography. There is no index to artists and engravers, or to the many other sorts of print (book-illustration, costume plates etc.) in which the volumes are very rich. The quality is high, with many proofs; larger prints, however, have had to be cut or folded.

5 Walton's Complete Angler

Izaak Walton (1593–1683): *Compleat Angler*, with the second part by Charles Cotton (1630–87), edited by John Major, fourth octavo edition 1844. Extra-illustrated with 98 prints (above the original 12 illustrations) in 1850, and given by H. W. Martin in 1861 (1861–10–12–874 to 981, and 1863–4–18–195,6). Placed at 166* a.32.

6 Anderdon Royal Academy Catalogues

A complete set of the catalogues of the annual Royal Academy exhibitions from the first exhibition in 1769 to 1849. Bound together in thirteen quarto volumes, and extra-illustrated with numerous manuscript notes, prints, drawings and documents collected by J. H. Anderdon, Esq. Presented by him in 1867. Register 1867–11–9–1(1 to 6985). Each sheet, whether of text or illustration, is stamped with one of these sub-numbers; the prints and drawings included have been numbered in a separate sequence for each volume. It is these latter numbers (which add up to 1696) which are referred to on the index on blue slips. This index has headings for engravers, topography, artists, masters and portraits. The portraits are included in O'Donoghue's catalogue and on the portrait-slip index, and the few drawings are in Binyon's catalogue and the Index of Artists. (Another set of extra-illustrated RA catalogues was presented by Anderdon to the Royal Academy.) On Anderdon himself see Lugt 50.

7 Anderdon Society of Artists Catalogues

A complete set of the catalogues of the annual exhibitions of the Society of Artists of Great Britain from the first exhibition in 1760 to the last in 1791. Bound together in nine quarto volumes, and extra-illustrated with a large number of prints and drawings, and enriched with copious notes by the donor. Presented by J. H. Anderdon, Esq. in 1869. Register 1869–12–24–603(1 to 2105). These volumes are exactly similar to the previous set, except that there is a manuscript index (shelved on Desk C), and only one numbering sequence which refers to every sheet in the albums.

8 Edwards Anecdotes of Painters

Edward Edwards (1738–1806): *Anecdotes of Painters who have resided or been born in England*, 1808. Extra-illustrated with 591 illustrations and numerous notes by J. H. Anderdon, Esq. and presented by him in 1869. Register 1869–12–24–604(1 to 591). Bound in two quarto volumes, in which the extra illustrations are individually numbered up to 591. There is an index on blue slips, and in a bound volume shelved on Desk C, to portraits, masters, artists and engravers. This and the two previous items form a set together.

9 Anderdon Collectanea Biographica

Collectanea Biographica, being an historical and pictorial biography of illustrious, celebrated and remarkable persons of all ages, nations and professions . . . founded on a work by Mons. Jacob . . . bound by Henry Massey . . . 1853. This is not strictly a Granger, since there is no single text that is illustrated. The foundation of the collection is one compiled by Jacob and bound together in 1823. This consisted of portions of the Biographie Universelle and other biographical works used to elucidate a mass of engraved portraits, autograph letters and autographs. Anderdon bought these thirty-eight volumes in 1833, and used them as the basis for his own expansions of both text and illustration. In 1853 he had the results bound together in 105 volumes, large octavo, 'interleaved to admit of further illustration'. After his death in 1879, the volumes, with a total of over 11,000 prints, were purchased at a nominal price in 1881 (register 1881–7–9–631 to 735). The form of reference used, however, is not the register number, but the volume and sub-numbers stamped on each print (e.g. Anderdon Collectanea 24–78). The illustrations include letters, topographical and historical prints, title pages and plates from books, engravings after paintings and theatrical scenes. Unfortunately, because of the small size of the volumes, all the larger prints have been folded. There is no separate index. The arrangement of the text is alphabetical by person, but the illustrations are not always bound in predictable places: thus Garrick between Tragedy and Comedy is placed under Angerstein, the owner of the painting. All the British (but not the foreign) portraits are noted on the blue slip portrait index, but nothing is entered in the Index of Artists. It is usually worth looking under any name that is the subject of research: thus under Ackermann will be found a view of the Repository of Arts, his trade card, an advertisement in engraved verse, and an illuminated letter B printed by Ackermann's lithographic establishment.

10 Tartt Byron English Bards and Scotch Reviewers

George Gordon, sixth Lord Byron (1788–1824): *English Bards and Scotch Reviewers, a satire*, 1810 (third edition; first edition 1809). Extra-illustrated with 145 prints, mostly portraits but with some topography collected by W. M. Tartt, and presented in 1882 (see the register 1882–5–13–390 to 533 for a complete listing of the contents). There is an index on blue slips.

11 Knowles Life of Fuseli

John Knowles (1781–1841): *The life and writings of Henry Fuseli, Esq.*, 1831, volumes two and three only, octavo. Bound in four volumes and extra-illustrated with 394 prints, mostly of the artists and paintings mentioned in the text, by Miss Julia Moore by whom it was presented in 1885 (register 1885–3–14–297 to 300; the prints in each volume are sub-numbered) together with Fuseli's Roman album (1885–3–14–201 to 296, now broken up and mounted). There is no index, but manuscript lists of illustrations have been bound in.

12 Evans Byron English Bards and Scotch Reviewers

George Gordon, sixth Lord Byron (1788–1824): *English Bards and Scotch Reviewers, a satire*, 1811 (fourth edition). Extra-illustrated with 173 mostly portrait prints compiled and presented by William Evans, Esq. (Register 1886–11–22–5(1 to 173)). There is an index on blue slips.

13 Simes House of Medici

J. T. Simes, *House of Medici*, unpublished manuscript, dated 1836. Being a collection of 160 portrait engravings of members of the Medici family c.1250–1790 with genealogical tables extracted from Noble's *Memoirs of the House of Medici* and accompanying biographical notes by J. T. Simes. Purchased, 1914–12–15–6 to 164. There is an index of persons included.

14 Marx Pennant

Thomas Pennant (1726–98): *Some Account of London, Westminster and Southwark*, printed for the illustrator, n.d. (c.1942). Extra-illustrated with 1607 illustrations by

Hermann Marx between 1935–42, and bequeathed by him in 1948 (1948–3–15–1 to 13). The text and illustrations are bound in twelve volumes, while the index (written by Marian Marsh) forms a thirteenth volume; each volume, moreover, has its own sub-index. The content is described on the subtitle: 'illustrated with numerous views of houses, monuments, statues, and other curious remains of antiquities; historical prints, and portraits of kings, queens, princes, nobility, statesmen, and remarkable characters'. Although similar in type to the Crowle Pennant (number 1 above), these volumes for magnificence of presentation form the finest Grangerised book in the Department. The content, however, lacks any drawings or the other extreme rarities that distinguish the Crowle volumes. For Marx himself, see Adams's paper (quoted above item 1); his own account of the formation of the collection is to be found at the beginning of the index. It is worth noting that a complete set of the Wheatley *Cries of London*, printed in colour, form the frontispieces to the volumes.

15 Second Folio Shakespeare

William Shakespeare (1564–1616): *The workes of William Shakespeare*, 1632 (the second folio edition). Extra-illustrated with thirty-eight drawings and water-colours: six by William Blake, the others by Robert Ker Porter, William Hamilton, John Thurston, G. H. Harlow, William Mulready, possibly John Flaxman and other unidentified artists. Purchased 1954–11–13–1(1 to 38). The illustrations were commissioned between about 1801–9 by the Rev. Joseph Thomas. See T. S. R. Boase in BMQ XX (1955) pp. 4–8. The watercolours by Blake have been extracted, but are placed with the album at 200 b.12.

See also Topic Index, s.v. Landseer.

THE DEPARTMENTAL LIBRARY
AND OTHER
REFERENCE MATERIAL

1 Books

The Departmental library contains all those books and pamphlets which are on open shelves rather than in locked cases. These shelves have press-marks beginning with a letter rather than a number. Thus E 5 23 will refer to the twenty-third book on the fifth shelf of press E. If a number of offprints or pamphlets have been bound together, the individual item is further distinguished by a sub-number: e.g. E 5 23(3).

In principle, reference books in the library are distinguished from case books in that the latter form part of the collections, while the former do not. But this distinction is blurred in practice. Until 1960 all reference books were allocated register numbers in exactly the same way as books containing original prints. A number of books which were originally regarded as reference material have since been redefined as part of the collection: an example of this is Senefelder's treatise on lithography. Finally, a number of books which are only of importance for reference have now become so rare and valuable that they have had to be locked in cases.

All books in the Departmental library are freely available to visitors, and anything in it may be read in the Print Room. Those books shelved on the presses near the student tables may be taken directly by visitors: these will have press-marks beginning with the word Desk. All other works will be brought to the tables on request by the Print Room staff. Every work in the library is catalogued in a card index, which also contains the cards that index the case books. There is also a blue slip index arranged by shelf order, which is useful to identify a book which is noted in the Index of Artists by its press-mark. No catalogue of the Departmental library has ever been published.

Books are indexed by author and by subject. Monographs on artists are indexed under the artist as well as the author. Exhibition catalogues are indexed in the first place under Exhibitions, followed by the town in which it was held and then the institution. (For example: Exhibitions, London, British Museum, Department of Prints and Drawings.) They will also be indexed under artist or subject, and under author if this is considered of significance. Catalogues of collections are entered under the town and then the gallery; there will also be entries under the name of the author or subject. The subject indexing is not systematic, and it is always worth looking under a variety of possible headings. Three headings under which there are many entries are Painting, Drawing and Topography. The entries for Print-making are, in general, divided between the different techniques. References to some other important headings will be given at appropriate points in this hand-book.

The Departmental library contains over 15,000 volumes to which over 600 new volumes, catalogues, parts of periodicals, offprints and articles are added every year. It has been put together as an aid to staff and students, and therefore concentrates on works connected with prints and drawings. Monographs on painters and sculptors are included if they relate to works in the collection. Specialised works on iconography and other subjects have only been acquired in limited numbers. The strengths of the library lie in its comprehensive groups of oeuvre catalogues of printmakers' work, and in its many scarce publications of the XIXc. It is more complete in areas in which members of staff of the Department have specialised than in those in which the collection is weak.

2 Periodicals

The Department library contains a number of periodicals, often in extensive runs. Most of these are listed below; the listing also includes notes on a few other important journals that are available elsewhere in the British Museum.

A card index has been compiled of the articles contained in the volumes of periodicals in the library. This index is primarily by artists and subject, but there are also cross-references to authors. It is complete until the late 1950s, but has been abandoned after this date as more recent bibliographies have taken over its function.

A complete list of the periodicals available in the library (even if only in a single part) is contained on cards placed at the beginning of this index; these cards also give the press-marks.

L'Amateur d'Estampes. 1921–34 (all published)

Amstelodamum. Jaarboek. 1956–present
Maanblad 1964–present

Amsterdam. *Bulletin Rijksmuseum.* 1953–present

Amsterdam. *De Kroniek van het Rembrandthuis.* 1970–present (incomplete)

Annals of the Fine Arts. 1817–20 (all published)

Antichità Viva. 1963–present

Antologia di Belle Arti. 1981–present

Apollo. March 1962–present only. (From 1939 to present in Dept. Medieval & Later Antiquities)

Archief voor Nederlandsche Kunstgeschiedenis. 1877–90

Archiv für die Zeichnenden Künste, ed. R. Naumann. 1855–70 (all published)

Archives de l'Art Français. 1851–62 only

Archivio Storico dell'Arte. 1888–97 (continued as *L'Arte*)

Arnold's Library (later *Magazine*) *of the Fine Arts,* 1831–4 (all published)

L'Art, ed. E. Veron. 1875–84 only

Art Bulletin. 1948–present only

Art History. 1978–83 only

Art in America. 1913–40

Art Journal. 1844–89

Art Journal (College Art Association). 1947–present

The Art Quarterly. 1938–present

L'Arte. 1898–1963 (all published)

Arte Antica e Moderna. 1958–66 only

L'Arte in Italia. 1869–73

Arte Lombarda. 1955–present

Arte Veneta. 1947–present

Baden-Württemberg. *Jahrbuch der Staatlichen Kunstsammlungen in Baden-Württemberg.* 1964–present

Berlin. *Berliner Museen,* (Amtliche) *Berichte.* 1907–43, 1951–73

Berlin. *Jahrbuch der Preussischen Kunstsammlungen.* 1880–1943

Berlin. *Jahrbuch der Berliner Museen.* 1959–77 (incomplete)

Blake Newsletter. 1967–present

Bollettino d'Arte (including *Cronaca delle Belle Arti*). 1907–38, 1938–43 (as *Le Arti*), 1948–67, 1972–4, 1979–present

Bollettino dei Musei Civici Veneziani. 1957–present (incomplete)

The Bookplate Journal. 1983–present

The Bookplate Society. Newsletters. 1972–present

Boston Museum of Fine Arts Bulletin. 1903–70

The British Museum Quarterly. 1926–73 (all published)

British Museum Society Bulletin. 1969–present

Brussels. *Bulletin des Musées Royaux des Beaux-Arts.* 1959–62, 1968–80

Budapest. *Jahrbuch.* 1918–41 only

Budapest. *Acta Historiae Artium.* 1953–71 (incomplete)

Budapest. *Bulletin du Musée Hongrois des Beaux-Arts.* 1954–73 (incomplete), 1974–present (complete)

Bulletins of museums. See under town of publication

Bulletin de la Société de l'Art Français. 1956–7 only

Bulletin (later *Jaarboek*) *van den Nederlandschen Oudheidkundigen Bond.* 1908–38

Burlington Magazine. 1903–present

'Byblis.' 1922–31 (all published)

Le Cabinet de l'Amateur, ed. E. Piot.
  1861–3 only
Chronik für Vervielfältigende Kunst
  (Vienna). 1888–91
Chronique des Arts et de la Curiosité.
  1861–1922 (later part of *Gazette des
  Beaux-Arts*)
Der Cicerone. 1909–23, 1929 (then
  merged with *Pantheon*)
Cleveland, *Bulletin of the Museum of
  Art.* 1953,5,7 only
Cologne. *Wallraf-Richartz-Jahrbuch.*
  1952–present
Connoisseur. Not in Dept. Prints and
  Drawings; complete in Dept.
  Medieval & Later Antiquities
Commentari. 1950–76 only
Critica d'Arte. 1935–40, 1949–50,
  1954–present

Dedalo. 1920–32 (incomplete)
Deutsches Kunstblatt. 1850–4
Drawing (Published by the Drawing
  Society of New York). 1979–present

Emporium. 1915–18, 1946–65 only

Fine Arts Quarterly Review. 1863–7
Frankfurt. *Städel-Jahrbuch.*
  1967–present

Gazette des Beaux-Arts. 1859–present
  (complete)
Gordon's Print Price Annual.
  1978–present
Die Graphischen Künste (Vienna).
  1905–43 (incomplete) (see also
  Mitteilungen)

Hamburg. *Jahrbuch der Hamburger
  Kunstsammlungen.* 1948–9, 1978
  only

Harvard. *Bulletin of the Fogg Art
  Museum.* 1931–50 only (incomplete)

Jahrbuch. For Museum Jahrbücher,
  see under town of publication
Jahrbuch der Bildenden Kunst. 1902–7
  only
Jahrbuch für Kunstwissenschaft. See
  Monatshefte
Jahrbücher für Kunstwissenschaft, ed.
  A. von Zahn. 1868–73
Journal of the Ex-Libris Society.
  1892–1908
Journal of the Playing-Card Society.
  1972–present (incomplete)
*Journal of the Warburg and Courtauld
  Institutes.* 1937–present

Kunstchronik. 1961–present only. See
  also *Zeitschrift für Bildende Kunst*
Kunstmarkt. See *Zeitschrift für
  Bildende Kunst*

Leeds Art Calendar. 1953–present
  (incomplete)
Liverpool Bulletin. 1951–64
  (discontinued)
Le Livre et l'Estampe. 1923 only

Madonna Verona. 1907–13 only
Madrid. *Bulletin del Museo del Prado.*
  1980–present
Magazine of Art. 1878–89
  (incomplete)
Maso Finiguerra. 1936–40
Master Drawings. 1963–present
*Mitteilungen der Gesellschaft für
  Vervielfältigende Kunst.* 1901–33
*Mitteilungen des Kunsthistorischen
  Institutes in Florenz.* 1908–present
Monatshefte (later *Jahrbuch*) *für
  Kunstwissenschaft.* 1908–32 (merged
  with *Zeitschrift für Kunstgeschichte*)

Münchner Jahrbuch der Bildenden Kunst.
1906–present
Das Museum. 1896–1912

Netherlands Institute for Art History,
Bibliography of the. 1943–present
New York. *Bulletin of the Metropolitan*
Museum of Art. 1923–present
Nouvelles de l'Estampe. 1963–present

Old Master Drawings. 1926–40
(complete)
Old Watercolour Society's Club Annual.
1923–present
Oud-Holland. 1883–present

Pantheon. 1928–39, 1960–present
Paragone. 1950–present (*Arte* numbers
only)
Parma per l'Arte. 1951–64 (incomplete)
Portfolio. 1870–98
Print Collector (Il Conoscitore di
Stampe). 1972–83
Print Collectors' Newsletter.
1971(volume 2)–present
Print Collector's Quarterly. 1911–42
Print Quarterly. 1984–present
Prints, ed. W. Salisbury. 1930–8
Proporzioni. 1943–63 only
Prospettiva. 1975–present (incomplete)

Rassegna d'Arte. 1901–22
Repertorium für Kunstwissenschaft.
1876–1932 (merged with *Zeitschrift*
für Kunstgeschichte)
Revue de l'Art. 1968–present
Revue de l'Art Ancien et Moderne.
1897–1929

La Revue des Arts (later *La Revue du*
Louvre et des Musées de France).
1951–present
Rivista d'Arte. 1903–62 only
Rotterdam. *Bulletin Museum Boymans.*
1937–67 (incomplete)

Simiolus. 1966–present
Stockholm. *Nationalmusei Årsbok.*
1941–50 only

Turner Studies. 1981–present

Il Vasari. 1927–43
Venice. See *Bollettino*
Vienna. *Jahrbuch der Kunsthistorischen*
Sammlungen des Allerhöchsten
Kaiserhauses. 1891–3 only

Walpole Society. 1911–present

Zeitschrift für Bildende Kunst.
1869–1932 (then retitled *Zeitschrift*
für Kunstgeschichte). It was published
with several supplements, of which
the following have been bound
separately:
Kunstchronik. 1887–1918
Der Kunstmarkt. 1904–18
Kunstchronik und Kunstmarkt.
1918–26
Zeitschrift des Deutschen Vereins für
Kunstwissenschaft. 1934–40, 1943,
1963–present
Zeitschrift für Kunst. 1947–50 only
Zeitschrift für Kunstgeschichte.
1932–present
Zeitschrift für Kunstwissenschaft.
1947–62 (incomplete)

3 Auction and Dealer Catalogues

Catalogues of auction sales

The Departmental library contains an important collection of British and foreign auction catalogues, ranging in date from c.1716 to the present day. It includes many rare catalogues from the XVIII and early XIXc., most of which were presented by William Smith in 1850. There are almost complete runs of Sotheby and Christie catalogues from the 1870s, and strong groups of the major Continental sales of the early decades of this century, notably those of Boerner and Amsler & Ruthardt. Most of the catalogues include lists of the prices fetched and the names of the purchasers. Whereas the collection of early catalogues is almost exclusively confined to sales of prints and drawings, during the XXc. sales of paintings have also been covered.

All the auction catalogues in the Department library are recorded on blue slips mounted in chronological order in a number of large ledgers. Three are devoted to sales taking place in Britain, and two to those abroad. Besides these, there is a card index of names of vendors divided into two series, according to whether the sale was in Britain or abroad. Both the blue slips and cards give the press-marks of the catalogues, which are shelved on a number of separate presses which can be distinguished by their SC prefixes (e.g. SC A 2 3, with a sub-number whenever a number of catalogues have been bound together in a single volume).

Most of the auction catalogues in the Department have been recorded in the three volumes so far published by Frits Lugt under the title *Répertoire des Catalogues de Ventes Publiques*, covering the years 1600 to 1900. Since the publication of his volumes, a number of further catalogues have been acquired, as well as a large number of photocopies, including sixteen bound volumes of the Northwick Park collection which is now in the British Art Center at Yale. All of these have been entered in the indices.

Apart from these, the Department library contains a photocopy of a two-volume manuscript in the Victoria and Albert Museum Library (L 867/8–1938) which transcribes the catalogues of 176 principal collections of pictures sold at auction in England 1711–59. It was probably compiled by Richard Houlditch, father and son, and is bound in three volumes; each part contains an index of owners. None of these catalogues has been entered in the blue slip index, and 120 are not recorded by Lugt. See the article by Frank Simpson in the *Burlington Magazine*, 1953 pp. 39–42.

Dealers' catalogues

The collection of dealers' catalogues is uneven. There is an important group of the rare priced catalogues issued by London firms in the late xviiic., which will be found entered as though they were auction catalogues. The occasional catalogues of xixc. dealers, such as Evans or Woodburn, are usually entered under the author's name. It is only in the xxc. that dealers have tended to publish catalogues at regular intervals, and these were kept as far as possible as bound series in the library.

During the 1950s this system broke down, and catalogues were generally bound up as they arrived in randomly grouped volumes on the S press. These can be retrieved by consulting the book index. From the late 1970s a new system has been devised by which they have been separated into a separate series, arranged alphabetically according to the name of the firm. This series has not been given conventional press-marks, but is referred to on the index cards as DC (for dealers' catalogues) followed by the name of the dealer.

This untidy history has given rise to inconsistencies in the indexing of dealers' catalogues. The present system is that they are recorded on the cards of the main book index under, firstly, the name of the town in which the dealer operates, and then under the name (e.g. Düsseldorf, C. G. Boerner). In previous years they have been indexed simply under the name of the dealer, or occasionally under the heading Exhibition Catalogue, when linked with a public exhibition. They have not been indexed by subject.

4 Manuscript and Unpublished Material

Although no efforts have ever been made to collect work of this type, a number of manuscripts or typescripts containing unpublished material, as well as albums of cuttings, have been acquired, usually as gifts or bequests, over the course of years by the Departmental library. In this section, a list is given of the more important of such items, arranged in alphabetical order.

1 Breun

Twenty-three bound and thirty-nine unbound albums containing records of British and Foreign portraits, compiled by H. A. J. Breun. The notes are either in manuscript or are cuttings from sale catalogues, and are arranged in alphabetical order by sitter. When they came to the Department the notes were in fifty-nine unbound folders. Twenty of these were mounted into twenty-three bound albums by Department staff; these contain the sequence of British portraits from A–SY. Those from T to Z, as well as all the notes on foreign portraits, remain in the unbound volumes. Breun (d.22 January 1933) was a printseller in Greek Street, Soho, in which trade he had succeeded his father and grandfather. The albums are his own record of every portrait that passed through his hands during some forty years. 1937–6–12–322.

2 British Library
Two bound volumes of photocopies of the Art section of the old class catalogue of the Department of Manuscripts in the British Library. Volume I contains the entries of the subjects of drawings in their collection in alphabetical order from Agriculture to Trophies. Volume II contains a similar subject index for the prints, calligraphy and bindings in the collection. Z 6.11–12

3 Buckley
One manuscript volume of 102 pp. in which Francis Buckley collected notices of engravers and advertisements extracted from periodicals and newspapers for prints published in England between the 1680s and 1790s. The preface gives a complete list of journals consulted. Certain notes are in the hand of A. W. Aspital, former higher executive officer in the Department, who transcribed them from Buckley's notes. Dd 8.7; 1939–11–27–1. A complementary volume of notes on painters is in the Victoria and Albert Museum Library.

4 Cuttings
There are various albums of cuttings compiled by former members of staff, containing reviews of books and exhibitions and obituaries.
a 1884–1912 Four albums containing obituary notices of British and foreign artists. Dd 7.10–13
b 1893–1943 Campbell Dodgson's album of offprints and reviews written by himself. 133 pp. with index. Ee 6.16
c 1932–1945 Press-cuttings collected by A. M. Hind. Two volumes, 70 + 72 pp. Cc 6.19,20
d Other albums contain press notices of Departmental exhibitions, and occasionally labels or typescripts of labels from exhibitions which had no catalogues. Many are on Desk B. Complete files of press notices concerning the British Museum are maintained by the Museum's Press Office.

5 Farington

Typescript of the diaries of Joseph Farington (1788–1821) from the original manuscript in the Royal Library at Windsor Castle. In twenty-eight volumes including index, and two boxes. Desk B, C. A microfilm of both the original diary and the transcript is commercially available (although no copy is in the Department); and a full edition of the diary is being published at the time of writing.

6 Finberg

a Fifteen loose-leaf folders compiled by A. J. Finberg, containing sheets with notices of books and prints listed under the name of their author in alphabetical order. Most are cuttings from catalogues; some are in manuscript. Af 6.

b The Department also possesses microfilms of three sets of albums compiled by Finberg of records of the work of J. M. W. Turner, Edward Dayes and Thomas Girtin. The originals were for many years kept here, but were transferred to the Tate Gallery in 1986 with the Turner Bequest.

7 Gold

Four typescript volumes compiled by Sidney M. Gold in 1957, containing transcripts and indices to the records of masters and apprentices of the Painter-Stainers and other companies. B 2.19–22

a Alphabetical list of masters with the names of all apprentices registered under them, in two volumes. The information is predominantly derived from Ms 5669 of the Guildhall Library (the binding book of the Painter-Stainers Company 1666–1715 with others to 1720), the Chester Painters Manuscripts (1571–1691), and the Edinburgh Apprentice Registers.

b A general transcript of the apprentices entered at the Painter-Stainers Company 1666–1715 (from the above manuscript), in chronological order. The transcript also records the name of the master and the county of the apprentice's origins.

c One volume with various contents. Important names from the records of the Chester Painters Company; Scottish apprentices and painters from various sources; American, Irish, Female, and Welsh painters from the BM catalogue of painters born before 1699. Concluding with transcripts of the wills of John Rowell, Leonard Fryer, Edward Polehampton, Richard Neve, Robert Walker, Rowland Lockey and Nicholas Hilliard.

8 Heathcote

A volume of letters from various amateur artists of the 1870s addressed to John Heathcote. 167 c.24; 1955–5–2–3(1 to 115).

9 Lance

Miscellaneous letters by George Lance (1802–64) to his wife, daughter and others; also a manuscript list of his works, and letters addressed to him. 167 c.23; 1954–4–7–5(1 to 23).

10 Landseer

Catalogue of the works of Sir Edwin Landseer. This volume was compiled and given by Algernon Graves. It contains an almost complete photographic record of Landseer's output, based on Graves's own 1875 catalogue of his paintings, drawings and etchings; it also includes a few drawings and letters. The catalogue indexes every item by title. Case 35; 1919–8–7–1.

11 Lawrence

Seven manuscript letters written by Sir Thomas Lawrence to Mrs Emma Forster (later Mrs Ambrose Poynter) 1827–9. Presented by C. F. Bell. 165 a.26; 1948–5–4–12(1 to 7).

12 Monro

A small miscellaneous collection of correspondence of the Monro family and circle, including Sir George Beaumont, Thomas Hearne (with an abstract of his will), Henry Edridge and John Henderson was presented by P. D. O. Coryton. 167 b.26, 27; 1973–12–18–17.

13 Morland

A manuscript catalogue on 146 pp. of the drawing-books published between 1792–1807 with soft-ground etchings after drawings by George Morland. Compiled by Francis Buckley. Nn 5 2; 1931–8–17–9.

14 Percy

The catalogue of his own collection of British watercolours compiled by Dr John Percy (1817–89). It takes the form of an annotated and enlarged copy of the catalogue of the 1871 Burlington Fine Arts Club exhibition of drawings in watercolour. In addition to Percy's text, autograph letters from many artists, signatures cut from mounts, and numerous press cuttings are included. M 6 7; 1890–5–12–154. The Department also purchased part of his collection which has been registered as 1890–5–12–1 to 153.

15 Resta

A bound photocopy of Lansdowne mss. 802 and 803 in the British Library, containing a copy by Jonathan Richardson (father and son) of the voluminous 'Remarks' written by Sebastiano Resta (1635–1714) in the volumes of drawings, which formed one of his collections, and which were imported into England *c.*1710. Ms 802 contains 'Father Resta's remarks on the drawings' (Books A to O), while 803 has an alphabetical index of artists' names, a chronological list of artists and an index of unnamed drawings. Case 202; see A. E. Popham in *Old Master Drawings*, XI (June 1936), pp. 1–15.

16 Rossetti

An album of material relating to Dante Gabriel Rossetti (1828–82) collected by A. J. and E. J. Hipkins. Included are letters, portraits, cuttings and a drawing attributed to W. B. Scott. 165 a.21; 1936–11–19–1(1–34).

17 Sharpe

Typescript of letters from Sutton Sharpe (1756–1806) to his wife Marion (née Rogers), written in 1802 in France. P 5.17.

18 Steer

A collection of biographical material, including manuscript records, exhibition catalogues, articles, correspondence, etc. together with a card index, assembled with a view to compiling a catalogue of the paintings of Philip Wilson Steer (1860–1942). Presented by Mrs B. Kay, G. L. Behrend and Miss D. E. Hamilton. Press Ae; 1946–2–27–1 to 4.

19 Thomas

A scrapbook of printed cartoons and other designs by Bert Thomas (1883–1966) cut from published sources, notably *Punch*. Included are a few newspaper cuttings and one drawing. Case 282; 1966–12–10–1.

20 Turnbull

An album containing photographs, letters, drawings, notices of exhibitions and other records relating to A. W. Turnbull. 25.7; 1957–10–12–182.

21 Walker

A collection of prints, drawings, photographs, reproductions and letters assembled by E. E. Leggatt, to form a complete record of the work of Frederick Walker (1840–75), case 20*; 1915–7–10–1 to 128. See Topic Index.

22 Whitley papers

Volumes of newspaper cuttings and typewritten slips collected by William Thomas Whitley (1858–1942) for his books on the history of English art in the XVIII and early XIXc. These provide the references which he deliberately omitted from the books themselves. The collection passed in separate parts to Miss L. M. Redfern (his executrix) and Mrs H. Finberg, who jointly presented them to the Department in October 1943. Most of the collection was arranged by artist and mounted into fourteen large albums by Mrs B. Croft-Murray. (These volumes only have been microfilmed; this film is commercially available.) The remainder, which is stored in two wooden cases, consists of material concerning Reynolds (two guard books), Gainsborough (four guard books and six notebooks), Lawrence (one guard book), together with various other records. There is a bound manuscript index of some 2500 entries to the entire collection compiled by Mrs H. Finberg. Jjj 5.3; 1945–7–14–2.

23 Wright manuscripts

The three manuscripts relating to the prints of Fyfe, Meryon and Sickert bequeathed by Harold Wright are described in the entry on him in the Topic Index.

5 Departmental Archives

The greater part of the British Museum's records are kept in the central archives, under the charge of the Museum archivist. The minutes of the Trustees' subcommittee on Prints and Drawings, the resolutions of the full board of Trustees and the Museum accounts will all be found there. The following list is of most of the records stored in the Department. Since many papers deal with confidential matters, they can only be seen by permission.

1 Reports to the Trustees by the Keeper of Prints and Drawings. 1811–present. This is the single most important source of information about the activities of the Department, and duplicates a series in the Central Archives. There is an index covering the years 1811–77.

2 Resolutions of the Trustees relating to the Department. 1831–present. These are the formal records of the Trustees' decisions on matters raised in the Keepers' reports. They also duplicate a series in the Central Archives.

3 Copies of papers in the Principal Librarian's Office relating to the Department. 1766–1877. There is also an index to these papers which were extracted from the main series because of their importance to the history of the Department.

4 Letter books 1802–present (including one volume of undated papers, many of which predate 1802). From 1960 the letters have not been bound. The letter books contain that part of the incoming correspondence from the public which was thought worth keeping. Since replies were made in manuscript, copies were not kept until after the Second World War. Copies of some official correspondence of the years 1884–1911 have been bound in a single volume titled 'Letters Sent'.

5 Visitors' books 1867–present. From 21 May 1867 the names of all visitors to the Department were recorded by staff on entry; from 3 February 1900 visitors themselves wrote their names and address on entering the Print Room. These volumes will provide precise information about the period of artists' study in the Department. Between 1901 and 1916 they also record the name of the Duty Officer on each day.

6 Deposit books 1878–present. These record every item left on deposit in the Department.

7 Records of work sent into the mounters' shop (later Department of Conservation). 1885–present.

8 Bill books 1878–present. These contain records of payments made, with some original invoices.

9 Loan files These only begin in 1963 when the new British Museum Act permitted the Trustees to lend items from the collections to exhibitions abroad. A separate file is created for each transaction. The files of the period 1963–73 have been retained in the Department. Following the reorganisation of the Central Registry in 1974, they have become part of a centralised system, and have been returned to the Central Registry after the Department has finished with them.

10 There are also various separate files on **individual purchases or bequests**, dating in the main to the 1950s and 1960s. Since the establishment of the central registry such files have been part of the central filing system, and are therefore no longer kept in the Department.

11 The Department archives also contain an **album of letters** addressed to G. W. Reid, the Keeper of the Department between 1866–83. This contains 400 pages with letters usually relating to Department business. It remained in his possession, and was purchased in 1969 (register 1969–6–14–47).

6 Microfilms and Microfiches

In order to save damage in handling the originals, parts of the collection have been filmed on microfilm or microfiche, and it is intended in forthcoming years to continue this policy. A complete list is given here of the films of works in the collection available at the time of writing for consultation in the Print Room. In addition to these, a number of films have been acquired of works in other collections. They will be found useful in answering questions more quickly than is possible by consulting the collection itself. In a number of cases, for conservation reasons, visitors are asked to consult films rather than the original works. Access is only given to the originals by special request.

All the works described below (with the exception of 8) have been made commercially available by several outside publishers; they are not obtainable from the Department. Details can be given on request.

Films of Works in the Department's Collection

1 Personal and Political Satires 1320–1832 This 35mm microfilm reproduces on 21 reels the entire series of satirical prints catalogued by Stephens and George; the catalogue volumes themselves are reproduced on 12 extra reels. See pp. 49–51.

2 The Crace collection, and the supplement to it. Available on 8 reels of 35mm microfilm, which include the two volumes of catalogue. See p. 103.

3 Historical Prints This microfiche contains on 204 sheets of fiche the complete series of British and Foreign History, as described on pp. 46–7 above.

4 The Banks and Heal collections of Trade Cards Available on 36 reels of 35 mm microfilm. See pp. 84, 174–6.

5 The Franks collection of Bookplates Only the mounted series of British bookplates from the Franks collection has been filmed on 10 reels of 35mm microfilm. See p. 86.

6 French Lithographs 1860–1900 This is a set of 7 colour microfiche, based on the catalogue of the 1978 exhibition entitled *From Manet to Toulouse-Lautrec*. This includes as an appendix a complete list of lithographs in the Department by artists included in the exhibition. The fiche contains all 395 of these prints.

7 The Windsor Raphael collection The collection of prints and photographs of the work of Raphael put together by Ruland for Prince Albert (see p. 156) does not belong to the Department but is on indefinite loan from HM the Queen. It has been filmed on 61 microfiche, which are vastly easier to handle than the bulky volumes of the original collection.

8 Many sketchbooks in the collection have been filmed for security and conservation reasons. A complete list of these is available for consultation. They include almost all works with press-marks between case 196a and case 198 a.15. None of these films has been published.

Films of Works in Other Collections

9 **The Royal Collection of drawings and watercolours** This is a 35mm microfilm which contains on 23 reels the entire sequence of drawings in the Royal Library at Windsor in the order of the 17 published volumes of catalogue.

10 **Hollar etchings in the Royal Library, Windsor** The collection of Hollar's etchings at Windsor is even finer than that in the British Museum, and so this set of 71 microfiche is very useful as a visual index to the Department's own collection.

11 **The collection of watercolours in the Victoria and Albert Museum** This set of 80 colour microfiche (plus 2 fiche of index) accompanies the catalogue *British Watercolours in the Victoria and Albert Museum*, edited by L. Lambourne and J. Hamilton (1980), and reproduces every work described in it as well as some 235 foreign watercolours.

12 **Drawings and watercolours by J. M. W. Turner** This records the entire Turner Bequest, formerly housed in the Department, but now in the Tate Gallery, on 43 reels of microfilm. The works have been filmed in the order of Finberg's Inventory.

13 **French Popular Lithographic Imagery 1815–70** A set of microfiche of lithographs selected from the collections of the Bibliothèque Nationale in Paris. They are arranged according to various topics, and accompanied by a text by Beatrice Farwell.

PART II
The Topic Index

Introduction

The Topic Index contains in a single alphabetical sequence entries of the following types:

1 Artists Artists are only included if the collection of their work is particularly famous and much consulted; or if the existence of an important collection might not be well known; or if there is some special complication in nature or arrangement; or if there is a separate published catalogue produced by the Department.

2 Donors An attempt has been made to give notes on all the most important donors to the Department, but many more have had to be left out through lack of space.

3 Types Entries have been given for particular types of material such as pastels, paste prints and polygraphs, in order that some idea of the Department's holdings can be given, although not always a complete list.

4 Subjects Every subject portfolio in the collection has been listed and described. Beyond that, the choice of entries may appear arbitrary, but is based on our experience of the questions that frequently arise. As is mentioned elsewhere, the Department maintains an informal card index of other subjects (e.g. smuggling, bathing machines, rhinoceroses) which may be of interest to researchers.

Notes

1 The content of the entries is restricted to information which is specific to the Department's collection. Information of a more general nature is only rarely and sparingly given, as this handbook is not a general guide to research. Its aim is to make the Department's collections better known and more accessible to researchers.

2 In the entries, references are normally given to inventory or register numbers; if

the item is shelved, the press-mark is given first. This is to help in identification and the ordering of photographs. The terms '(list)', or '(no list)' occasionally occur after references to series of individual objects. This means that a complete description of the items concerned is, or is not, to be found in the volumes of the inventory or register.

3 Abbreviated references are frequently given to the following Departmental catalogues:

O'Donoghue and Hake: *Catalogue of Engraved British Portraits preserved in the Department of Prints and Drawings . . .*, 1908–25. See p. 43.

Stevens and George: *Catalogue of Personal and Political Satires preserved in the Department of Prints and Drawings . . .*, 1870–1954. See pp. 49–50

Other Departmental catalogues referred to in abbreviated form should be easily traceable from the first half of this handbook, by looking in the appropriate context. References to other standard print reference works can be traced from pp. 128–31 of Antony Griffiths, *Prints and Printmaking*, 1980. Lugt refers to Frits Lugt, *Les Marques de Collections*, Amsterdam 1921 (*Supplément*, The Hague 1956).

4 All relevant officially published works dealing with the collection have been mentioned in the appropriate places, but references have only been given very sparingly to other publications in order to keep this handbook within a reasonable length. Departmental exhibitions are only mentioned if a handlist or catalogue of the exhibits is available.

Altered Plates

The Department possesses a remarkable collection of some 200 engraved British portraits printed from plates which were altered by the engraver so as to change the sitter: for example, a plate of Queen Victoria riding out from Windsor Castle with Lord Melbourne was altered in the third state so that her companion became Prince Albert. This was frequently done by publishers in the XVIIc. and XVIIIc. to avoid the expense of making a new plate. The collection was formed for the 6th Marquess of Sligo by G. S. Layard, and was the basis for his two books, *A Catalogue Raisonné of Engraved British Portraits from Altered Plates*, 1927, and *The Headless Horseman*, 1922. The collection was presented by the 7th Marquess in 1935, and is mounted in six royal and one imperial solanders. 1935–4–13–12 to 219 (list).

Amateurs (Draughtsmen and Engravers)

There is a large collection of prints by amateur artists formed by Richard Bull (d.1805) under the title 'Etchings and Engravings done by the Nobility and Gentry of England'. It is in two volumes lettered on the spines 'Honorary Engravers', one containing works by male artists, the other by female artists. There is a manuscript index to each volume compiled by A. W. Aspital; these have been consolidated and amplified in a typescript index by David Alexander. 189* b.22, 23; 1931–4–13–1 to 517 (list).

Other prints by amateur artists have been distributed under the names of the individual artists. Apart from the work of numerous British watercolourists, there is a complete set of etchings and some lithographs by Queen Victoria and Prince Albert, 1926–1–9–1 to 91 (list). A group of drawings and etchings by Princess Augustus Sophia, George IV when Prince of Wales, Princess Charlotte and others is now distributed, 1857–5–20–65 to 337 (list).

Other works, by figures more famous in other walks of life, worth noting are:

1 John Evelyn, an album containing a drawing, Ezekiel receiving the word of God, together with six etchings by him and other prints relating to him. 190* a.1; 1838–5–30–1 to 18 (list); also a drawing of Naples from Vesuvius, 1911–10–18–2.
2 Sir Christopher Wren, Head of a Moor and a bust of a negro child, mezzotints; as well as three drawings (Croft-Murray 1–3).
3 Prince Rupert, three drawings (Croft-Murray 1–3) and mezzotints (marked off in Chaloner Smith, pp. 1772–5).
4 Louis XIV, a landscape etching of 1650. 1927–10–8–143.
5 Dirk Bogarde (placed as Dierek van den Bogaerde), View from my tent, 3 July 1944, pen and wash. 1945–12–8–60.
6 Enrico Caruso, Self-portrait caricature, 1906, pen and ink. 1915–3–15–1.

Anastatic Drawings

The collection contains the publications of the Anastatic Drawing Society from 1854–63 only. The volumes contain antiquities, seals, coats of arms, churches, abbeys, tombs, etc. There are no references in the Index of Artists. 189* a.14–21; 1882–8–12–616 to 1156 (list).

Anatomy

There is no separate collection of anatomical prints and drawings. Titles of books of engravings on the subject will be found under the heading Anatomy in the index of the Departmental library. A few other interesting items are:

1 Baccio Bandinelli (1488–1559/60): An album of anatomical studies with an engraved portrait of the artist as the frontispiece. 197 c.3; 1866–12–8–640 to 669.
2 John Singleton Copley (1737–1815): An album of anatomical studies with descriptions of various muscles. 200 a.2; 1864–5–14–136 to 143 (Binyon I, pp. 247–8).
3 Coloured woodcut of a seated man and woman with movable pieces of paper to show their anatomy, a plate from Thomas Geminus, *Compendiosa totius Anatomiae Delineatio*, 1559. 1860–4–14–264; Hind I pp. 48–52. See also s.v. Pornography (for Eric Gill).

Animals

There is no separate collection. An anthology of some of the material held in all departments of the British Museum (including this one) on the subject will be found in the catalogue of the exhibition *Animals in Art* held in 1977–8. Individual types of animal can often be traced through the subject cards on the Duty Desk. A general collection is the Bestiary by Graham Sutherland (q.v.).

Anonymous Works

Prints and drawings by anonymous artists are in general placed at the beginning of the relevant section of the collection. Thus anonymous British drawings are at the beginning of that period to which they are thought to belong, while Italian aquatints will be found at the beginning of the series of unmounted Italian aquatints (or, if mounted, at the beginning of the mounted series of Italian select prints). The main exceptions are as follows:

Early prints These are kept in the order of the catalogues by Schreiber, Lehrs and Hind.

British prints There are separate portfolios of etchings (1) and engravings (2), and a solander box in which the unmounted woodcuts are kept. Anonymous mezzotints are mostly to be found in a volume labelled 'Specimens of early mezzotints'. Otherwise anonymous British prints are kept at the beginning of the relevant classification.

Netherlandish and German prints These are kept together in one portfolio regardless of technique.

French prints These are kept together in one portfolio regardless of technique.

Italian drawings See above p. 31.

Italian prints There is a separate portfolio each for anonymous etchings and engravings.

Other There is a portfolio of portraits of unidentified sitters; there is also a portfolio of anonymous foreign mezzotints which contains only portraits from the Cheylesmore collection.

Works by identifiable monogrammists can be traced through the Index of Artists, where they have been entered usually under the letter M. Many of the prints have also been marked off in the Department's copy of G. K. Nagler, *Die Monogrammisten*, Munich 1858–79.

Antiquities

The Department contains four portfolios of prints of classical antiquities. These are labelled *Antiquities*, *Greek and Roman Statues*, and *British Museum Antiquities*. The fourth contains loose engraved plates from *Ancient Marbles in the British Museum*. Many books of prints on the subject are shelved in cases 242–3. Kept elsewhere is a bound set of the 26 plates in colour by various engravers of the Roman paintings discovered at the Villa Negroni in 1777 (1917–12–8–23(1–26)); there is also a second incomplete copy in c.242*.

The Department possesses many drawings of classical antiquities by Francis Towne (1740–1816), William Pars (1742–82), John 'Warwick' Smith (1749–1831), William Alexander (1767–1816), Benjamin Robert Haydon (1786–1846), John Foster (1787–1846), Henry Corbould (1787–1844), Charles Robert Cockerell (1788–1863), James Stephanoff (1788–1874) and Samuel James Ainsley (1806–74). Many more are in the collection of the Department of Greek and Roman Antiquities. An exhibition *Classical Sites and Monuments* was held jointly with that Department on the mezzanine gallery above the Payava Room in 1971. The catalogue of 16 pp. contains entries for 79 drawings.

See also s.v. Elgin Marbles and British Museum.

Archer, John Wykeham (1808–1864)

There are 17 portfolios containing 479 watercolours by Archer of buildings and antiquities in London. They are described in Binyon's catalogue, volume I, pp. 34–61. They include the Roman remains in the City of London, and views and interiors of many places including St Paul's, Southwark, the Strand, Covent Garden, Bloomsbury, the British Museum and Whitehall. One portfolio contains street names, street signs, badges, monuments and inscriptions. 1874–3–14–1* to 479 (list). Cf. Scharf, London.

Architecture

There is a single portfolio containing a small collection of prints mostly of the XVIIc. and XVIIIc. arranged by country: Austria, France, Germany, Italy, Netherlands, Scandinavia and Spain. Others will be found among the topographical collections, particularly those of London (q.v.). The collection of ornament prints will contain some items of interest to the architectural historian. In general, however, the Department contains very little work of this type. Architectural prints were usually published in book form, and have therefore been considered part of the British Library's collection. Architectural drawings have never been consciously acquired; the national collections are those in the Victoria and Albert Museum and the Royal Institute of British Architects (now the British Architectural Library). The Department of Manuscripts of the British Library also contains a good number of architectural drawings, often indexed under place as well as by architect.

Some of the most notable items in this Department are:

1 Two albums of drawings by Ducerceau (q.v.).
2 A copy of Antoine Lafréry, *Speculum Romanae Magnificentiae* (see s.v. Rome).
3 Attributed to Inigo Jones, Elevations and plans for Whitehall Palace

(Croft-Murray 11–15), and elevation and plans for a large palace (Croft-Murray 16–18).
4 Sir Christopher Wren, Designs for the finial of the Monument, the cupola of St Paul's, and a reredos at Hampton Court (Croft-Murray 1–3).
5 François Cuvilliès, senior and junior. The works in architecture, published in the 1770s. 179 b.16; 1962–12–31–1(1–352). A typescript index is placed as 179 b.16*.
6 Sir Jeffrey Wyattville, Album of watercolours and architectural designs. 198 c.15; 1912–4–16–65 to 206.
7 Augustus Welby Pugin, two sketchbooks. The first of topography, architectural details and objects seen in France 1836–7 (199 a.19; 1984–6–9–13(1–71)), the second of similar contents, drawn mostly in 1847 (199 b.17; 1985–7–13–48(1–214)). Both have been published by A. Wedgwood in the volume devoted to the Pugin family in the catalogue of the RIBA drawing collection, 1977, pp. 90ff, nos 105, 106.
8 Charles Rennie Mackintosh, Three designs for the Studios, Cheyne House, Chelsea. 1981–12–12–22 to 24.
9 See s.v. British Museum, for plans and drawings of the buildings.

Arts and Sciences

Under this title there is a portfolio containing a curious mixture. The core is formed of plates, taken mostly from the *Universal Magazine*, of Trades (glass makers, printers, hat makers, papermakers, printmakers, etc.), Agriculture (farm scenes, a brewhouse 1747), and Chemistry and Physics (including means of measuring air, air pumps, machines for taking likenesses, water works at London Bridge, etc.). To this have been added curiosities as follows: 6 lithographs of the highest towers, mountains, waterfalls and other wonders of nature, 1931–10–8–25 to 30; 3 programmes of Royal Entertainments performed by Her Majesty's servants at Windsor Castle, 1852, 1853 and 1861; and 20 samplers containing manuscript inside engraved borders, c.1785–7. In addition there will be found a puzzle picture (The Magic Egg or Birth of Harlequin, 1770), a sand print (A view of the Needles by E. Dove, 1848), an example of paper splitting by W. Baldwin, and a visiting card of 1927 for Lewis W. Douglas, printed on a thin sheet of Arizona copper.

Aviation

There is a portfolio of Aviation prints, 35 of which related to ballooning (q.v.), as well as 4 lithographs of the 'Ariel' steam carriage designed by William Samuel Henson in 1843.

Bagford, John (1650–1716)

The materials assembled by John Bagford for his projected history of printing came to the British Museum via the Harley and Sloane collections in 1753. Most of the collection remains divided between the Departments of Manuscripts and Printed Books in the British Library. See *Catalogue and Indexes to the title-pages of English printed books preserved in the British Library's Bagford Collection*, compiled by Melvin H. Wolf, 1974. Over 1000 prints of varying importance were transferred at various times to this Department, where they have been distributed between different series. This makes it impossible to study them as the Bagford collection, although the items may be retrieved individually. The main section was transferred in 1814 and listed

in the 1837 inventory under the numbers Gg 4. A–W, each part of which had separate sub-numbers. In 1900 256 further prints were transferred; a complete list is at 1900–10–19–1 to 251. See also s.v. Ballads and Title-pages.

Ballads

There are two great collections of ballads in the British Library:

1 The Bagford Ballads. C.40 m.9–11. Edited in three volumes by J. W. Ebsworth, 1876–80.
2 The Roxburghe Ballads. C.20 f.7–10. Edited by J. W. Ebsworth or William Chappell, nine volumes, 1869–99.

References to other ballad collections in the British Library are given in Alison Gould, *Named Special Collections in the Department of Printed Books* (British Library, Reader Guide 9, 1981).

There are only a few ballads in this Department; most are scattered in the series of satires with a few more in the Banks collection. There is also a watercolour by Richard Dadd, The Ballad Monger, of 1853 (1953–5–9–2).

Ballooning

There are 35 ballooning prints included in the Aviation portfolio. Among them are views of Lunardi's ascent from the Artillery Ground in 1784 and Major Mony in the sea off Yarmouth after a failed attempt in 1785. There are also impressions of two satirical prints: 'Prime Bang up at Hackney' (1811, George 11775), and 'A King bestowing favors' (1824, George 14667). For six other portrayals of balloons, see *Sporting Life* nos.36–41 (see s.v. Sporting Prints). Other interesting items kept elsewhere are:

1 A drawing of Lunardi's ascent by George M. Woodward (Binyon 3; 1890–1–18–8).
2 Two watercolours by Robert Schnebbelie of Mr Graham's ascent at Lords Cricket Ground in 1837 (Binyon 2, 3; 1879–8–9–652, 3).
3 A lithograph by Édouard Manet, 'Le Ballon' of 1862 (1949–4–11–3334).

Bank Notes

The main collection in the British Museum is contained in the Department of Coins and Medals. An album of specimens of bank note engraving was presented by the American Bank Note Company to the Department of Prints and Drawings in 1869, where it was described by Fagan (p. 203). This has now been transferred to the Department of Coins and Medals. The following are the most notable items that remain in the Department:

1 A specimen of a one pound note (engraved by Finden after R. Smirke); a design for a bank note 1818; and specimens of bank note engraving. 1849–5–12–849 to 863 (complete list).
2 Satirical bank notes. See George 10123, etc. 1857–12–12–19 to 44 (complete list). Other examples are George 7839, 8564, 11780, 13109.
3 George Cruikshank's 'Bank Restriction Note' of 1819 is Reid 965 (= George 13198; a rejoinder is George 13200).
4 A group of items relating to the forgery of bank notes is in the Crace Supplement XXII nos.25–33.
5 Some bank notes engraved by Bewick (q.v.) are in the unmounted supplementary box.
6 See also Banks collection D 3.185–233 and Franks collection for other security printing.

Banks, Sir Joseph (1743–1820)

A group of 811 bound and unbound prints and drawings of natural history subjects from the collection of Sir Joseph Banks was transferred from the Library to the Department in 1914. It was registered fully under 1914–5–20–1 to 811. In the group are six albums of Banksian drawings:

1 Sydney Parkinson (1745–71), Birds, animals, fish, etc. 199* b.1; 1914–5–20–1 to 67 (the first 44 items are bodycolour on vellum, the rest are grey wash on paper).
2 idem. Insects and marine flora. 199 a.8; 1914–5–20–68 to 134 (bodycolour on vellum).
3 Various artists, including John Cleveley, J. F. Miller, Capt. P. D'Auvergne, Sawrey Gilpin, Peter Paillou. Birds, insects, animals, fish. 199* b.4; 1914–5–20–135 to 267 (watercolour and bodycolour).
4 Various artists, including N. Dance, Wilhelmina King, J. W. Lewin, Francis Masson, Frederick Nodder, F. Reichel, A. Schouman, J. E. de Sève, J. Stuart, Thomas Davies, R. Wright, W. Watson, George Edwards, George Garrard, George Stubbs. Natural history drawings. 197* d.4; 1914–5–20–268 to 330 (various media; the three drawings by Stubbs of lemurs have been mounted separately).
5 John Greenwood (1727–92), Insects of Surinam. 199* a.6; 1914–5–20–331 to 357 (bodycolour).
6 John Webber (1753–93), Fish and birds drawn on Captain Cook's third voyage 1776–80. 199* b.2; 1914–5–20–358 to 403 (watercolours). Cf s.v. Cook.

Most of the rest of the loose Banksian drawings and prints are kept in the portfolio of Natural History (q.v.); a few have been distributed in the series of engravers and topography as given in the register, 1914–5–20–404 to 811.

Banks, Miss Sarah Sophia (1744–1818)

Sarah Banks was the only sister of Sir Joseph Banks. During her life she assembled, in addition to coins, medals and books, a remarkable and pioneering collection of printed and engraved ephemera; this she bequeathed to her sister-in-law, Lady Dorothea Banks, who at once in 1818 presented it to the British Museum. The Department of Prints and Drawings now houses about 19,000 items from her collection. In addition there are nine volumes of broadsides, newspaper cuttings and other prints in the British Library (LR 301 h.3–11). The collection is only summarily mentioned in the main inventory volumes; a fuller listing is to be found in a separate Banks inventory, although even this only gives block entries for the visiting cards, trade cards and admission tickets. The easiest way to describe the character of the collection is to list the contents of its various sections as recorded by the inventory:

C 1 1 to 5346 Visiting cards, newspaper paragraphs, views, admission tickets, envelopes, ms notes, etc.
C 2 1 to 2011 Visiting cards, admission tickets, newspaper paragraphs, maps, tradesmen's cards.
C 3 1 to 197 Admission tickets engraved by Bartolozzi.
C 4 1 to 468 Ladies' fashions, newspaper paragraphs, being mostly leaves from almanacs, magazines and pocket books.
D 1 1 to 1482 Foreign visiting cards.
D 2 1 to 4392 Trade cards, bill heads, bills, prospectuses, plans.

D 3 1 to 702 Election cards, bankers' cards, lottery tickets, passports, coats of arms, tea certificates, receipts for the delivery of coal, leaves from magazines, paragraphs from newspapers, frontispieces, Handel's commemoration prints, King's Bench rules, Montem tickets.
J 1 1 to 170 Political caricatures.
J 2 1 to 147 Political caricatures.
J 3 1 to 147 Political caricatures by Gillray.
J 4 1 to 368 Political caricatures, ms notes, music, etc.
J 5 1 to 168 Various caricatures.
J 6 1 to 112 Caricatures after Bunbury.
J 7 1 to 53 Political caricatures.
J 8 1 to 388 Anniversary tickets, admission tickets, letters of thanks, invitations, prospectuses, play bills, etc.
J 9 1 to 655 Anniversary tickets, advertisements, admission tickets, newspaper paragraphs, invitations.
J 10 1 to 425 Prints and newspaper paragraphs relating to the Jubilee, visiting cards.
J 11 1 to 193 Maps, views, portraits.
Y 5 1 to 329 Various, mostly portraits, engravings on wood, labels.
Y 7 1 to 125 Funerals.
Y 8 1 to 191 Public ceremonies.
Y 9 1 to 157 Funeral of Charles, Duke of Lorrain, 1608.
Y 10 1 to 247 Political caricatures by Sayer.
Mm 1 1 to 190 Portraits, costume prints by Hollar.
Mm 2 1 to 245 Public festivals, Danish costume.
Mm 3 1 to 116 Miscellaneous.
Mm 15 1 to 205 Portraits, topography.

In addition, other prints in the collection bearing inventory numbers besides those listed above have stamps which show that they come from the Banks collection. It is unlikely that the arrangement recorded above is entirely that of Sarah Banks herself. Much of the collection has by now been distributed among the main series, for example under portraits, historical prints, satires, engravings by Bartolozzi and so on. Some parts have, however, been kept together, often still as they were mounted by Miss Banks on large sheets of paper annotated with her notes. The following list of these is very summary; a fuller handlist is available for consultation in the Department:

A British visiting cards

C 1 1 to 5345 In six boxes. There is a blue slip index by name of owner; there is no index by designer or engraver.

1	1–673	Cards of Dukes down to Barons, by order of precedence.
2	674–1675	British alphabetical A to O.
3	1676–2469	British alphabetical P to Z, plus supplements.
4	2470–3419	By types of border, both British and foreign.
5	3420–4383	By types of border, both British and foreign.
6	4384–5345	By types of border; invitation cards; cards of thanks; plus appendix to foreign visiting cards.

B Foreign visiting cards

D 1 1 to 1482 In two boxes. There is a blue slip index, as for the British cards, without cross-references to engraver.

1	1–949	Miscellaneous; Corps Diplomatique; America to Italy.
2	950–1482	Italy (cont.) to Switzerland; English Ministers abroad; (for appendix see C 1.5025 to 5343 above).

C Admission tickets

C 2 1 to 1804, **C 3** 2 to 195, **J 8** 1 to 388, **J 9** 171 to 655. In six boxes and one volume. There is a blue slip index by function. Some of the contents are not really admission tickets.

1	C2 1–428	By function. Apothecaries Co. to Clubs.
2	429–944	Commemorations to Fêtes.
3	945–1384	Fêtes (cont.) to Lectures.
4	1385–1804	Opera to Vauxhall.
5	J 8.1–388	Invitations to Anniversaries.
6	J 9.171–	Various: balls, guilds, concerts, societies.

Volume C 3 2 to 195 Various admission tickets, mostly engraved by Bartolozzi.

D Miscellaneous

In four boxes. No index of any kind.

1 D 3 1 to 432 Book tickets, bankers' cards and bank notes, election prints, E&O notes, frontispieces, Handel commemoration, lottery tickets, Montem tickets.

2 D 3 433 to 700 Passes, post office, raffles, receipts, documents on the Royal Society, turnpike tickets, vignettes and title-pages.

3 C 2 1805 to 2011. Maps, funeral tickets, trade cards, invitations to balls.

	J 4	241 to 243 Various
	J 5	160 to 162 Various
	J 9	1 to 170 Tickets for the trials of Warren Hastings and Lord Neville.
	J 11	119 to 127 Puzzle portrait cards.
	Y 5	255 to 265 Tunbridge love letter, exhibition tickets.
	Y 7	24–29, 95–100, 104–120 Funeral tickets.
4	J 10	1 to 425 Prints and visiting cards relating to the Congresses of 1814 and 1815.

E Trade cards

D 2 1 to 4392 The main Banks series, into which other cards from the Franks and other collections have been incorporated, is described in the separate entry on Trade Cards and Shop Bills. The original arrangement of Miss Banks was lost when the cards were lifted and remounted on individual cards in the 1950s. Various items from D 2 were, however, not remounted, and about 100 items remain in a single solander box.

Printed ephemera from collections other than Sarah Banks's have been arranged in a parallel series to the Banks series. It is described here in the entry on the Franks collection, from which most of it comes.

Bartolozzi, Francesco (1728–1815)

There is a large collection of Bartolozzi's works arranged in eight portfolios in the order of A. de Vesme and A. Calabi's catalogue *Francesco Bartolozzi* of 1928. It is, however, not complete and a number of other engravings by him will be found in the master series, or in the Banks and Franks (qq.v.) series of admission tickets. De Vesme and Calabi has only been marked off with the prints in the main series. 503 items are listed in the inventory under S.5–8. The Department possesses on loan from the British Library an uncoloured copy of John Chamberlaine, *Imitations of Original Drawings by Hans Holbein in the collection of His Majesty*, 1792, which contains his engravings from the Holbein heads at Windsor. Coloured impressions of these prints will be found in the Marx Pennant.

Baxter, George (1804–1867)

A large group of works by George Baxter, the inventor of a method of printing in oil colours, and of his licensees, was bequeathed by Miss Winifred Mary Oliver Jones in 1936 as part of a collection of colour printing (q.v.) of the xixc. (1936–11–16–40 to 2124, list.) The Baxter collection has been mounted in seven boxes in the order of the catalogue in C. T. Courtney Lewis, *George Baxter, the picture printer*, 1924: the Departmental copy has been marked off with the holdings. The rest is arranged in a number of portfolios according to the name of the licensee.

Bellini, Jacopo (c.1400–1470/1)

Two albums of drawings by Jacopo Bellini survive, one in the Louvre and one in this Department (197* c.1; 1855–8–11–1 to 98). The British Museum volume has been published twice in facsimile. See Corrado Ricci, *Jacopo Bellini e i suoi libri di disegni, II Il libro del British Museum*, Florence (Alinari) 1908 (176* a.1), and V. Goloubew, *Les Dessins de Jacopo Bellini au Louvre et au British Museum, I Le livre d'esquisses de Londres*, Brussels 1908 (176* a.2; the Louvre album, published in 1912, is placed at 176* a.3). New publications of the book are expected at the time of writing by B. Degenhardt and A. Schmitt, and in America by Colin Eisler. Both will make use of new ultra-violet photographs. In view of the delicacy of the original album, permission to view it is only given by special request to the Keeper.

Bewick Family

In 1882 Miss Isabella Bewick gave to the Department a large collection of drawings and proofs of wood-engravings by her father Thomas Bewick and other members of the family, notably his brother John Bewick, and son Robert Elliott Bewick (1882–3–11–1243 to 5558, no list). It joined a significant collection already in the Department with which it was integrated. The drawings are kept with the mounted British drawings in the order of Binyon's catalogue, while the main series of book illustrations was mounted in order of the title of the books from which they came in nine royal solanders. The remaining material, which includes much ephemeral commercial engraving as well as a number of duplicates, was left unmounted in one solander and one album (247* a.5), labelled respectively 'Woodcuts by Bewick' vols I and II.

The Isabella Bewick gift consisted of:

1 **Thomas Bewick** (1753–1828). 227 drawings and watercolours, mainly for *A History of British Birds* 1826, and a few for *A General History of Quadrupeds* 1791. These are described in Binyon's catalogue, I pp. 108–21; see also Iain Bain, *The watercolours and drawings by Thomas Bewick and his workshop apprentices*, 1981. In addition there are 2787 proofs of his wood-engravings, including some examples hand-coloured by the artist. The Department also possesses etchings, engravings and a lithograph by him, eight wood blocks, his bookplate of William Thomas, and copies of many of his illustrated books (mostly shelved in case 1*).

2 **John Bewick** (1760–95). A collection of 30 drawings and watercolours including three views in Hornsey and a portrait design for his bookplate. See Binyon I, pp. 99–101. Also 1183 wood-engravings executed by him or by Robert Elliott Bewick.

3 **Robert Elliott Bewick** (1788–1849).

A collection of 151 drawings and watercolours, including 76 for the *History of British Fishes* (not completed), designs for *Aesop's Fables* 1818, and a sketch of his father. See Binyon I, pp. 101–8. Also 1183 wood-engravings executed by him or John Bewick.

Besides the Isabella Bewick gift, other Bewick prints were included in a collection assembled by W. J. Palmer and given by Herbert P. Horne in 1900. It was called 'A Century of Wood Engraving in England 1780–1880', and included 642 prints by Bewick, Clennell, Linton, Nesbitt and others (1900–6–13–67 to 708, list, now distributed).

Blake, William (1757–1827)

The very large collection of drawings, watercolours, miniatures, albums, prints, illuminated books, reproductions, plates and woodblocks in the Department is listed in full in the *Blake Newsletter*, Spring 1972, pp. 224–58. The most important subsequent additions are the preparatory drawing for the 'Canterbury Pilgrims' (1983–12–10–25) and the second state of the engraving of 'Mirth' (1985–7–13–45). A later issue of the *Blake Newsletter* for Summer 1975 gives a checklist of Blake slides. The manuscript of Blake's 'Notebook' (the Rossetti manuscript) is in the Department of Manuscripts of the British Library (Add. Mss. 49460).

The illuminated books are among the most important items. Most were acquired in the XIXc., and the rest were transferred from the Library in 1953. The numbers of the copies refer to G. L. Keynes and E. Wolf: *William Blake's Illustrated Books, a Census*, 1953.

1 There is no natural religion, ?1788. Copy A.

2 The Book of Thel, 1789. Copy D.
3 Visions of the Daughters of Albion,
   1793. Copies A, B, O.
4 America, a prophecy, 1793.
   Copies F, H.
5 Songs of Innocence and Experience,
   1794. Copies A, B, T.
6 The first book of Urizen, 1794.
   Copy D.
7 Europe, a prophecy, 1794. Copies a
   (mounted), D.
8 Small and large book of designs. Copy
   A (mounted).
9 The Song of Los, 1795. Copies A, D.
10 The Book of Los, 1795. Copy A.
11 Milton, a poem, 1804–8. Copy A.
12 Jerusalem, 1804–20. Copy A.

See s.v. Plates, Blocks, etc. for a note of
the Blake woodblocks and copper plates in
the Department. Microfilms are
commercially available of many of the
illuminated books.
See also exhibition 1957.

Blockbooks

The Department contains 12 single pages
from blockbooks, and one almost complete
one. This is 38 pages of 40 of Schreiber's
first edition of the *Biblia Pauperum*,
produced in the Netherlands *c.*1460–5
(1845–8–9–1 to 38); they have been
mounted with the single sheets. For a
complete catalogue see C. Dodgson,
*Catalogue of Early German and Flemish
Woodcuts in the British Museum*, I 1903, pp.
209–12. The main collection of blockbooks
is in the Department of Printed Books of
the British Library, and has been
catalogued in Part 1 of the *Catalogue of
Books printed in the XVth century now in the
British Museum*, 1908 (by A. W. Pollard).

Bookplates

The Department contains a very large
number of bookplates. This is made up of
three individual collections (Franks,
Rosenheim and Viner) in addition to the
general Department collection. These four
groups are kept separately, and are here
described in turn:

1 Sir Augustus Wollaston Franks The
Franks collection, bequeathed in 1897,
contains both British and foreign plates.
The British collection was largely built up
by Franks himself; the Continental plates
are for the most part an amalgamation of
the de Rozière and Bilco collections which
Franks had purchased en bloc.

a BRITISH AND AMERICAN PLATES
   There are 35,098 in total, mounted in 58
   albums. The arrangement is in the first
   place alphabetically by owner; then
   follow plates of Royalty; Universities,
   Colleges and Schools; School prizes;
   Ecclesiastical, Parochial and Public
   Libraries; Naval and Military; Legal and
   Medical; City Companies; Public
   Offices; Booksellers and Circulating
   Libraries. The group of 640 plates from
   the pattern book of a late XVIIc.
   engraver, possibly John Sturt, known as
   the Brighton plates from their place of
   purchase, is kept in one album. The
   entire collection is catalogued by E. R. J.
   Gambier Howe, *Catalogue of British and
   American Book Plates bequeathed to the . . .
   British Museum by Sir Augustus Wollaston
   Franks*, 3 volumes, 1903–4.

b GERMAN There are 4752 plates
   mounted in 10 albums and 2 folders,
   with an additional volume of late XVIIIc.
   armorial plates. All the plates have been
   marked off by Franks in his own
   interleaved and annotated copy of
   F. Warnecke, *Die deutschen Bücherzeichen*

Ex-Libris, Berlin 1890.

c FRENCH 8908 plates in 38 folders. These, and all the following plates of sections d to h, are described and numbered by Franks in a series of bound manuscript catalogues.

d ITALIAN 952 plates in 7 folders.

e SWISS 1327 plates in 5 folders.

f DUTCH 693 plates in 3 folders.

g SCANDINAVIAN (115), Spanish and Portuguese (94), South American (6); a total of 215 plates in 1 folder.

h RUSSIAN, POLISH, BULGARIAN, GREEK 147 plates in 1 folder.

2 Max Rosenheim Presented by Mrs T. Rosenheim in 1932. It contains some 11,000 foreign plates, many of which are duplicates of the Franks collection. There is no catalogue or listing, but the plates are mounted on cards in boxes by country as follows: England (1 box); France (24, plus 9 armorial); Germany (28); Italy (6); Netherlands (3); Russia, Poland, Greece, Hungary, China, Siam (1); Scandinavia (2); Spain, Portugal, Brazil, Mexico, Peru, Haiti (1); Switzerland (4). The Swiss plates have been marked off in Rosenheim's own copy of L. Gerster, *Die schweizerischen Bibliothekzeichen (Ex-libris)*, Kappelen 1898. References to Warnecke have been written on the mounts of the German plates.

3 George Heath Viner Given in 1950. This collection contains more than 8000 British plates, and was acquired with the intention of supplementing the Franks collection, and no duplicates were accepted. Some 5500 of the plates are earlier than 1800, among them two of major interest: those of Sir Nicholas Bacon of 1585 (now placed in Franks album 2) and of Joseph Holand (Holland) of 1585 (in a heraldic manuscript). (A third early plate, of Sir Thomas Tresame (Tresham),

is in the Franks collection.) Some 4700 of the plates are alphabetically arranged by the name of the owner in 7 volumes; another section is kept according to the designer or engraver, A. J. Downey (3 boxes), G. W. Eve (8), E. D. French (2), G. T. Friend (3), H. S. Marks and others (7); and the remainder by types and subjects (e.g. landscape, armorial, pictorial, etc.).

4 The main Departmental collection has been assembled in an unsystematic way over the years. Dodgson made great efforts to build up the collection of plates by modern engravers. In more recent years no attempts have been made at regular acquisition. It is arranged as follows:

a OWNER SERIES British and American, arranged alphabetically in 2 portfolios. All other countries in 1 portfolio.

b ARTIST SERIES American, various (2 boxes), Australian, various (1 envelope), H. J. F. Badeley (1 box), F. von Bayrus (1 box), Paul Boesch (1 album), A. J. Downey (1 box), English, various (4 boxes), G. W. Eve (5 boxes), Foreign, various (1 box), E. D. French (1 box), D. L. Galbreath (1 volume), German, various (2 boxes), S. Harrod (1 box), W. H. Hooper (1 box), W. F. Hopson (3 boxes), G. Johnston (1 volume), E. W. Oldham (1 box), R. Osmond (1 box), H. Soane (1 volume), C. W. Sherborn (15 boxes), S. L. Smith (1 box), L. Titz (1 box), J. Vinycomb (1 volume).

Finally there is a small group of bookplates among the miscellaneous ephemera assembled by Sarah Banks (q.v.). They were inventoried as D 3.2 to 179, and are kept in the Banks series. Two albums of original designs for bookplates by G. W. Eve are placed with the collection of sketchbooks: 199 a.5*, 5**; 1937–2–26–1(1–125), 2(1–140).

Boydell, John (1719–1804)

The great print publisher and Lord Mayor
of London. He began as an engraver, and a
reprint of his own early plates is in
*A Collection of views in England and Wales
drawn and engraved by John Boydell*, 1790
(172* b.1; 1859–5–14–6 to 178). After
1755 he turned to publishing, and his
subsequent progress can be followed in a
series of catalogues issued from 1764 to
1803 (see *Print Quarterly* I, 1984 pp.
14–15). His first major undertaking was
'a collection of prints from the most capital
paintings in England'. Of this there is no
copy in this Department or in the British
Library. His most famous project was the
commissioning in 1786 of 100 paintings
from many different artists to be engraved
to accompany a new edition of
Shakespeare. The text was published in
1802 in nine volumes, and was
accompanied by 95 small-size prints *not*
taken from the new paintings (no copy in
this Department; copies in the British
Library 685 k.8; 76 i.1–9). The 100
large-size engravings were published in
parts, and bound in one or two volumes
with 'A collection of prints from pictures
painted for the purposes of illustrating the
dramatic works of Shakespeare' on the
title-page and the date 1803. The
Department's copy has been broken up and
the plates distributed in the master series;
the remaining prefatory text is at Oo 7.6.
The British Library possesses two
complete copies at Tab 599c and 4 Tab 57.

Brass-rubbings

In the xixc. the Department held a large
collection of brass-rubbings (described in
Fagan's Handbook), but this was long ago
transferred to the Department of
Manuscripts of the British Library. There
are now no rubbings in this Department.

British Museum

A collection of some 280 prints, drawings
and photographs of exterior and interior
views of Montagu House and the new
British Museum and Reading Room, is
kept together for convenience in what is
known as the British Museum portfolio. It
contains some items of special interest such
as an anonymous watercolour of Montagu
House and its gardens from the north-east
of *c.*1800 (1929–7–14–2), and designs for
the new building in pencil, ink and
watercolour washes by Sir Robert Smirke
(1919–4–15–835 to 845, list). Most
architectural drawings relating to the
building will, however, be found in the
Central Archives, and many departments
possess their own photographic records of
their own galleries. A series of photographs
of the galleries of the Museum taken in the
late 1870s is also in the Central Archives;
a set of recent copies of these is boxed in
the Department library (166 c.47). The
Department also contains an album
including photographs of British Museum
officials, collected by Robert Cowtan
*c.*1850–60 (210* b.11; 1943–11–15–1,
no list).

An album in the Department library
contains a miscellaneous group of
engravings of antiquities in the galleries of
the British Museum, views of the buildings
and galleries, portraits of persons
connected with the Museum, and various
obituaries and press-cuttings (242 c.1).
Another album contains Sir Charles
Barry's 1857 proposals for extending the
Museum, together with the comments on
them by the then keeper, W. H. Carpenter
(244 b.7).

The Department's collection also
contains many drawings and watercolours
of the Museum buildings which have been
placed under the names of the artists in the
series of drawings. The most important are

by George Scharf (1788–1860) (q.v.), who made a record of old Montagu House and the new building in the course of construction during the years 1828–50 (1862–6–14–612 to 644, list). Other notable drawings are as follows:

1 Marcellus Laroon the younger (1679–1772): A concert at Montagu House (with an inscription by Horace Walpole). 1848–7–8–207 (Binyon III p. 36).

2 John Vardy (d.1765): Design for the British Museum, elevation and plan, probably intended for a site in Whitehall 1754. 1984–1–21–1.

3 Michael Angelo Rooker (1743–1801): Porch of Montagu House, looking along Great Russell Street, 1778. 1868–3–28–334 (Binyon III p. 242).

4 Samuel Hieronymus Grimm (1733–94): The encampment outside Montagu House in 1780. 1984–5–12–4.

5 George Saunders (1762–1839): Plan and section, elevation and ground plan for a proposed new wing of the British Museum c.1802–4. 1984–1–21–2 (1 to 3).

6 Thomas Hosmer Shepherd (1793–1864): The British Museum Reading Room c.1817–40. 1938–11–12–1.

7 Edward William Cooke (1811–80): An album of drawings showing the moving of colossal Egyptian statues within the British Museum in 1834. 1914–2–6–1 to 22 (list).

8 J. W. Archer (1808–64): Views of the gateway and courtyard of Montagu House c.1842. 1874–3–14–438 to 444; 1914–2–6–23; 1939–3–10–1 (Binyon I p. 54).

9 T. H. Shepherd: Montagu House during the demolition 1850. 1977–4–2–4.

10 L. W. Collmann (1816–81): The decoration of the entrance hall and staircase of the British Museum (the figures are drawn by Alfred Stevens). 1902–1–29–1.

11 Sir Richard Westmacott (1775–1856): The Progress of Civilisation, design for the pediment of the British Museum. 1887–5–2–1 (rolled).

12 Frederick Mackenzie (1787–1854): Front of the British Museum (lithograph touched with pencil and white, with an alternative drawing of the foreground on a separate piece of paper). 1901–5–8–1.

13 Alfred Stevens (1818–75): Design for the decoration of the British Museum Reading Room. 1909–9–29–1.

14 D. Fox Pitt (d.1929): Interior of the Reading Room of the British Museum. 1912–6–8–1.

15 Muirhead Bone (1876–1953): The Egyptian Saloon, and Scaffolding on the staircase of the British Museum. 1907–1–24–1, 2.

16 Eric Gill (1882–1940): Design for the British Museum War Memorial, 1922. 1973–1–20–24.

17 See also admission tickets to the British Museum (Banks J 8).

18 See also three items listed s.v. Paintings.

British Museum Society

Since its foundation in 1968, the British Museum Society has made a number of notable gifts to the Department, as well as helping it in other ways. A short list of these gifts is given here:

1 Urs Graf, *Vita Almi Confessoris et Anachoreta Beati Batteni*, Basel (Adam Petri), 1511. 36 c.15; 1974–2–23–29(1–17).

2 Max Beckmann, Self-portrait (plate I of

Jahrmarkt), drypoint 1921.
1979–5–12–1.
3 Otto Lange, Head of Christ, colour
   woodcut 1916. 1982–7–24–24.
4 A fund was established in 1984–6 for
   the purchase of contemporary drawings
   by artists working in Britain.
5 In 1985 the Society gave funds to put
   together a collection of British prints
   which was exchanged with the National
   Gallery in Prague for a collection of xxc.
   Czech prints. The Czech collection was
   registered as 1985–11–9–25 to 123 (see
   exhibitions 1986).

Broadsheets

The Department possesses no collection of
broadsheets as such. A large number will,
however, be found in the Foreign History
series. Most of these have been marked off
in the Department's copies of Frederick
Muller, *De Nederlandsche Geschiedenis in
Platen*, 1863–82, and in G. van Rijn and C.
van Ommeren, *Katalogus der Historie, Spot-
en Zinneprenten . . . versameld door A. van
Stolk*, 1895–1908. Some others occur in
British History, among the Satires, in the
Banks and Franks collections, and in the
portfolio of Popular Prints.

Brocklebank, Mrs Petrena
(d.1937)

The Brocklebank collection, bequeathed to
the British Museum, consists of
photographs and other reproductions,
drawn from many sources, of historical
portraits. There are some 4000 items,
arranged in 60 albums in their own special
case. Mrs Brocklebank's interest was in the
genealogy of British and Continental royal
and ruling houses. The collection is
therefore arranged according to family and
house: for example, the Medici and other

Italian families; the Valois and Bourbons;
the Hapsburgs; the Plantagenets, Tudors,
Stuarts, and houses of Hanover and
Windsor. It is accompanied by genealogical
notes and an alphabetical index.
1937–10–8–166 to 226 (for the 60 albums;
no list).

Browning, Robert (1812–1889)

A collection of some 300 photographs
formed by Professor W. Hall Griffin in
order to illustrate the life and poetical
works of Browning (1812–89). It is housed
in four box files (250 a.14–17):

1, 2   The Ring and the Book.
3   Pippa Passes, La Saisiaz, Andrea del
       Sarto, Fra Lippo Lippi, The Pied
       Piper of Hamelin.
4   Manuscripts, Personalia,
       Miscellanea. 1937–12–23–2 to 11
       (no list).

Buckler Collection

This is kept in the Department of
Manuscripts of the British Library, and
consists of drawings of British topography
made by three generations of members of
the Buckler family: John Buckler, his sons
John Chessell and George, and grandson
Charles Alban. The collection was
acquired in different groups at different
times, but now consists of 144 volumes or
boxes, containing over 12,000 drawings or
watercolours. For a fuller description, see
M. W. Barley, *A guide to British
topographical collections*, 1974, pp. 62–3.
The Department of Prints and Drawings
only possesses, apart from a handful of
mounted drawings, an album of finished
watercolours by John and John Chessell
Buckler of the ruins of Wenlock Abbey,
Shropshire (197* d.5; 1948–2–14–6 to
27).

Burney, Dr Charles (1757–1817)

In 1818 the library of Dr Charles Burney, the famous classical scholar (son of Charles Burney, the historian of music), was acquired by Parliament for £13,500 and deposited in the British Museum. In the library were thirteen volumes of prints and drawings of theatrical interest, which were transferred to this Department. They are as follows:

1–10 Portraits of actors, often in their stage roles, and of others connected with the theatre, arranged in alphabetical order of sitter. The engravings are included in the *Catalogue of Engraved British Portraits*, and the references to them are noted on the blue slip index to portraits. The volumes contain 59 watercolour portraits by James Roberts for Bell's British Theatre (see Binyon III pp. 232–8). Volume 9 includes at the letter 'Th' a group of prints of interior and exterior views of theatres. Inventory K 57 to 66 (no list).

11 David Garrick. This volume no longer exists as such, but used to contain 300 engraved portraits and 5 watercolours by James Roberts, all of David Garrick. These have all now been incorporated with the rest of the Department's collection in a separate portfolio of Garrick portraits. Inventory Ee 3 (no list).

12 So-called 'Garrick topography'. Contains 164 views of theatres, buildings, hotels, busts and other subjects of theatrical interest; most are engravings, but there are a few watercolours 175 b.1; inventory Ee 12 (no list).

13 Scenes from plays. Contains 88 engravings of scenes from plays, arranged in a portfolio in alphabetical order of the actors and actresses appearing in them. Inventory R 10 (no list).

Although the volumes of the inventory itself contain no full listing of the collection, this is supplied by a separate manuscript volume, placed with the Index of Artists, which describes each item of the collection in the order that it appears, giving the title, artist and engraver. There is, however, no index. The Department library also contains Burney's own manuscript catalogue of the collection, drawn up around 1807, but this is much less complete (Pp. 6. 62–4; the portraits are further listed in S 3. 22).

Calendars and Almanacs

There are two xvc. German calendars, described by Dodgson as his numbers A 126(a, b) (Calendar of Magister Johannes de Gamundia), and A 127 (Fragment, with New Year wishes). Some later calendars and almanacs can be traced through the Book Index. A modern calendar is the *Calendarium Londinense* (1903–80) with etchings by British artists (167 c.19). The main collection of calendars and almanacs is in the British Library.

Calligraphy

The major collection of written and engraved calligraphy is in the British Library, and there are only a few random specimens in the Department. Of calligraphic handwriting there are two examples of note: the prefatory poem to the album of flower drawings by Le Moyne (q.v.), which is thought to be by John de Beauchesne (1962–7–14–1(1)), and the text by Marian Marsh that accompanies the Marx Pennant (see pp. 58–9). For engraved calligraphy, see George Bickham's engravings for Abraham Nicholas, *The Compleat Writing Master*, 1722 (166 a.35). The Department does not possess a copy of Bickham's *Universal Penman*, 1743.

There are a few calligraphic portraits. The most remarkable is a portrait of Louis-Philippe dated 1849, composed of thousands of letters, drawn by V. Touche, after an engraving by Thomson from a painting by E. Dubusse (1956–2–11–18). There are two very similar pairs of portraits of Louis XVI and Marie-Antoinette composed of script flourishes: the first pair is by Marie-Jeanne Bernard (1889–8–6–8,9), and the second by Joseph Bernard of 1786–7 (1889–8–6–10, 11). In the series of engraved portraits is one of Louis XVI in script flourishes by Beaublé (1889–8–6–13), and a group portrait of the writing masters of London by George Bickham (O'Donoghue V p. 81). There is also a volume engraved by J. P. Hemm, *Portraits of the Royal Family in Penmanship*, 1831 (230 b.2).

A group of 20 engraved calligraphic samplers is in the Arts and Sciences portfolio (q.v.), and there is a set of 52 German playing cards of 1769 on 7 sheets, consisting of military figures engraved in flourishes (Schreiber G53).

Callot Figures

In the early XVIII c. a type of figure derived from the 'Gobbi' of Jacques Callot (Lieure 407–26; Meaume 748–67) had a remarkable vogue throughout Europe. On the Continent they were usually known under the title 'Il Callotto resuscitato', while in England they were known as 'Lilliputian' figures. The following list gives all the examples in the Department, arranged in order of publication:

1 *Il Callotto resuscitato oder Neu eingerichtes Zwerchen Cabinet*, ?Augsburg 1715. 62 plates (12 Months and 50 single figures). 159* b.9; 1938–6–17–12(1–62).

2 *Il Callotto resuscitato . . .*, Amsterdam (W. Koning) 1716, engraved by Folkema and others. 78 plates. 157 c.30; 1938–6–17–13(1–78). Another copy with only 55 plates, 157 c.29; 1878–12–14–756 to 810.

3 Sutton Nicholls, engraver: series of the Months, copied from (1) above. 167 a.25; 1931–5–11–26(1–12).

4 Henry Overton, publisher: The Lilliputian Humorists drawn as big as the life (by) Signor Prettyprint, London 1730. 10 engravings, with 2 figures to a plate. 298* a.1; 1868–8–8–13793 to 13802.

5 John Bowles, publisher: Set of the months represented by Callot figures. 1874–2–14–1 to 12; in Authorities for Artists III.

6 Pigmy Revels or all alive at Lilliput, anonymous satires 1800. Set of 8 plates; George 9635–42. 282 b.8 ff.54–65.

Cards (Birthday, Christmas, New Year, Greeting, Valentines)

Although the Department has never attempted to collect Christmas or other cards in a systematic way, a number of groups of cards has come to it by gift or bequest. The collection does not contain the first Christmas Card, designed by J. C. Horsley for Sir Henry Cole; an example is in the Department of Prints in the Victoria and Albert Museum (inventory 20717). An early Christmas card in this Department is that dated 1848 by W. M. Egley; it is in the Cannan collection (1931–11–14–194). Two XV c. German New Year cards are catalogued by Dodgson as A 124 and 127.

1 Queen Mary's collection of Christmas Cards. Mounted in 31 albums dated 1872–1952. The collection contains all the cards sent to Queen Mary and George v, as well as some sent to other members of the Royal Family. Permission to consult this has to be obtained from the Royal Librarian at Windsor Castle. Case 187*.

2 Two boxes of Christmas and other cards, mostly woodcuts, sent to Campbell Dodgson. Most belong to the 1920s and 1930s. Arranged under the name of the artist. 188 a.5, 6.

3 A folder of cards designed by Barnett Freedman, mostly 1930s. 188 a.4; 1953–11–7–1(1–10).

4 Cards etched by Frank Paton, 1880–1909. 190* a.30.

5 A general portfolio of miscellaneous cards from many sources; including a selection by Alfred de Holeny Holinski, handmade cards of the 1960s, a collection of cards sent to Princess Louise, Duchess of Argyle, some by Queen Victoria.

6 Two boxes containing 64 mounted Valentines, mostly elaborate, from various sources.

See also s.v. Trade and Visiting Cards.

Caricature

The Department possesses very large numbers of works that might be classified under this heading. An extremely useful narrative account of the history of the genre and its representation in the Department is in the 16-page *Guide to an exhibition of caricature* which accompanied an exhibition held in 1939 (Cc 3.38(5)). 36 caricature drawings are described in the catalogue of the 1974 exhibition of Portrait Drawings, nos 224–59. A list of 42 items has been drawn up by Paul Goldman for a slide lecture on 'The Story of Caricature' in 1977; a copy is in the Departmental library (Am 7.12(16)). Books of engraved caricatures can be traced through the Book Index under the heading Caricature; the cards have been arranged by country. The following list mentions some of the more interesting items or groups of material in the collection, concentrating particularly on drawings, arranged according to period and type:

Italian caricature drawings

1 There are one or more drawings by the following artists: Leonardo da Vinci, Annibale and Agostino Carracci, il Guercino, Pierfrancesco Mola, Carlo Maratta, Lieven Mehus, Antonio Maria Zanetti.

2 Pier Leone Ghezzi: In addition to two mounted drawings, there are two albums of caricatures by him of contemporary figures in Rome. 197 d.4, 5; 1859–8–6–91 to 302 and 1871–8–12–818 to 1129. Neither has an index of sitters, but for the second (only) there is a list of the contents in the register.

British caricature XVIIIc.–c.1832

The main series of engraved satires and caricatures is described above, pp. 49–51. To the Departmental publications there mentioned may be added the catalogue compiled by Paul Goldman for an exhibition of Gillray's caricatures circulated by the Museum in 1985–7. See also s.v. Cruikshank. The collection contains drawings by virtually all the leading British caricaturists from George, Marquess Townsend onwards.

British caricature XIX–XXc.

a PUNCH DRAWINGS AND SIMILAR
There are mounted drawings by
H. M. Bateman, George Belcher,
George Du Maurier, Harry Furniss,
Sir Francis Carruthers Gould, Charles
Keene, John Leech, Phil May, Bernard
Partridge, Leonard Raven-Hill,
George Sala, E. L. Sambourne and Sir
John Tenniel. In addition there are two
albums:

3 Album in which various drawings by
   Furniss, Tenniel, Du Maurier and
   others have been mounted. 200* c.13;
   various register numbers.

4 Album of drawings by Sir Francis
   Carruthers Gould. 198* a.9;
   1946–5–30–1 to 33.

b NONSENSE DRAWINGS AND
HUMOROUS DOODLES BY SERIOUS
ARTISTS

5 Edward Lear: 21 comic drawings made
   in Italy in 1842 when on a tour with his
   servant Giorgio Kokoli
   (1970–4–11–24 to 44, mounted royal).
   Also a first edition of his *Nonsense songs,
   stories, botany and alphabets*, 1871
   (298* b.36).

6 Sir Edward Burne-Jones and Dante
   Gabriel Rossetti: album of humorous
   drawings. 200 b.3*; 1939–5–13–1 to
   56.

7 Sir Edward Burne-Jones: Letters to
   Katie. Illustrated with numerous
   drawings. 199 b.13;
   1960–10–14–2(1–101).

8 Richard Doyle: Dick Doyle's Journal of
   1840. Manuscript with text and
   illustrations. 201 a.3;
   1885–11–14–102.

9 Sir William Orpen: A collection of
   illustrated letters. 201 b.5**;
   1921–11–14–27 to 42.

10 Henry Tonks: various caricatures,
    mounted royal.

c THE PORTRAIT CHARGÉ
TRADITION

11 See s.v. Vanity Fair.

12 Charles Wirgman: Album of portrait
    caricatures. 200 a.16; 1938–11–29–6
    to 35.

13 See also mounted drawings by Sir Max
    Beerbohm, Alfred Edward Chalon,
    Carlo Pellegrini, Sir Leslie Ward.

d MODERN NEWSPAPER CARTOONS
There are original drawings for
cartoons by Wally Fawkes (Trog),
Michael Ffolkes, Leslie Illingworth,
JAK (Raymond Jackson), David Low,
Dominic Poelsma (Clive), Ronald
Searle, Reg Smythe.

Two oddments are an album of
anonymous Russian portraits and
caricatures from the collection of Count
Nesselrode of *c*.1820–50 (197* d.6;
1939–7–11–3(1–63)), and an album of
Italian drawings for caricatures of
c.1848–51 relating to *Don Pirlone*
(1948–10–9–20 to 125, list).

Cartoons

The Department possesses a number of
full-size drawings preparatory to paintings
or frescoes, as well as a few fragments. The
following are kept framed or apart from the
rest of the collection:

1 Michelangelo Buonarroti (1475–1564):
   'Epifania'. (Wilde 75; 1895–9–15–518*;
   in the exhibition gallery).

2 Raphael (1483–1520): The Virgin and
   Child (for the Mackintosh Madonna).
   (Pouncey and Gere 36; 1894–7–21–1).

3 Raphael: The Virgin and Child with St
   Elizabeth (for the Madonna del Divino
   Amore). (Pouncey and Gere 51;
   1926–4–12–1).

4 Polidoro da Caravaggio
   (1490/1500–1543?): Lamentation over

the dead Christ. (Pouncey and Gere 202; 1944–7–8–16).

5 John Michael Rysbrack (1694–1770): Cartoon of a sacrificial scene for the relief over the chimney piece at Houghton Hall, Norfolk. (1952–10–11–1).

Cf. s.v. Framed Works.

Catlin, George (1796–1872)

The Department possesses none of his original drawings of Indian tribes and life. There are, however, a number in the Department of Ethnography (Museum of Mankind), as follows:

1 Mandan O-Kee-Pa religious ceremony. 8 watercolours bound in a book, c.1850.
2 North American Indian portfolio of 25 coloured lithographs, published 1844.
3 Souvenir of North American Indians. 159 pencil drawings of 1861 bound in two volumes.
4 A selection of Indian pipes. 23 works in oil on paper of 1852 bound in one volume.

The Department of Prints and Drawings does possess four lithographs made after his paintings by J. M'Gahey Chester. These show Catlin shooting buffalo with Colt's revolving rifle, and pistol; and Catlin on the Rio Trombutos, and relieving his companions from 'an unpleasant predicament' in Brazil (1939–7–14–29 to 32, list).

Cavendish Album

The Department purchased in 1952, with the aid of a substantial contribution from the National Art-Collections Fund (q.v.), an album of 90 drawings assembled by Lord James Cavendish (d.1741), the second son of William, 2nd Duke of Devonshire. The drawings date from the late XVc. to XVIIIc., and include works by Dürer, Claude Lorrain, Vellert, Fra Bartolommeo, Annibale Carracci, Veronese and others. Many of the drawings have been taken out and mounted in the main series. Case 202; 1952–1–21–1 to 90 (list).

Ceremonies

Single-sheet engravings of such subjects are to be found scattered through the series of historical prints, as well as under the names of the designers or engravers. Books of prints are entered in the Book Index under the subject heading Ceremonies, and subdivided by types such as coronations, embassies, festivals, fireworks, funerals, processions, receptions, etc. There are 81 such books listed in total, covering the period 1515 to 1885. The countries represented are Austria, Britain, China, Denmark, France, Germany, India, Italy, Netherlands, Norway and Spain.

Cheylesmore, William 2nd Baron (1843–1902)

William Meriton Eaton was the second son of a wealthy silk broker, and spent most of his life assembling a collection of British mezzotints. On his death he bequeathed to the British Museum all the portrait mezzotints in his possession; most of the subject mezzotints remained with his family. The collection is registered under the numbers 1902–10–11–1 to 10776, and in the following order:

British Portraits
1–6843   British engravers, in alphabetical order of engraver.
6844–7504   Anonymous British engravers.

7505–7905　Foreign engravers, in alphabetical order.

7906–7969　Anonymous foreign engravers.

7970–7995　Not portraits, but subject pictures.

7996–8060　Not mezzotints, but portraits.

Royal Portraits and Historical Prints

8061–8474　Prior to Queen Victoria.

8475–9933　Queen Victoria.

9934–10776　Queen Victoria's family and contemporary Royalty.

A duplicate copy of the register is placed with the Index of Artists, and has been marked with the locations of the prints. The collection has also been marked off against Chaloner Smith's catalogue *British Mezzotinto Portraits*. Some of the British portraits have been mounted and placed in the series of select mezzotints. The remainder has been kept separate from the rest of the collection in 37 portfolios. The portraits of Queen Victoria have been incorporated with the rest of the Department's collection and placed in 9 portfolios. See further above, pp. 35, 41–3. See exhibitions 1905.

China and Western Prints

There are various sets of engravings in the British Museum which link China and Western artists:

1　36 Views of the Summer Palace at Jehol drawn by Shen Yu and engraved by the Jesuit, Father Matteo Ripa, in China, 1711–13. In the Department of Oriental Antiquities (OA 1955.1–12.01(1–34); 1968.2–12.027, 028).

2　*Les Conquêtes de l'Empereur de la Chine*, a set of 16 engravings made in Paris to the order of the Qianlong (Chien Lung) Emperor, 1767–74, under the direction

of C. N. Cochin fils, after paintings by the Jesuit Giuseppe Castiglione. One set in the Department of Oriental Antiquities with ms annotations by the Qianlong Emperor (OA 1928.8–15.09(2) and (5); 1938.1–29.01 to 017). Two sets in Prints and Drawings, one bound (243 b.34), the other distributed in the engraver series (1932–7–15–46 to 59).

3　Reduced copies of the above, engraved under the direction of Helman in the 1780s. (243 a.2; 1877–7–14–1505 to 1526).

4　European buildings in the Yuan Ming Yuan, a set of 20 engravings by Chinese artists of buildings in the Summer Palace built from designs of Castiglione and Benoit c.1783. In the Department of Oriental Antiquities (13 plates only) (OA 1916.2–14.01 to 04; 1924.5–23.013 to 021, bound).

Chinoiserie

There are several examples of Chinoiserie in the collection:

1　Jean Pillement (1727–1808): *Oeuvre de Jean Pillement*, in two volumes containing various sets of plates (161* b.6 and 168 c.1).

2　Antoine Watteau (q.v.): the Recueil Jullienne contains relevant items.

3　William Chambers: *Designs of Chinese buildings, dresses, furniture etc.*, 1757 (243 b.37).

4　Fans in the Schreiber collection. See Cust numbers 38–9, 311–32.

5　Four designs in pen and ink of figures with decorative borders. In album of cut paper in case 35; 1957–11–29–53 to 56.

6　Views of Ranelagh Gardens, including the Chinese House. Crace XIII 72–9.

Circus

A selection of 51 prints and drawings of circus and fairground material from the Department's collection was chosen by Paul Goldman for an exhibition in the Cockpit Gallery in London in 1976. The complete list is available in the Departmental library at Ar 6.1(16).

Claude Lorrain (1600–82)

The Department possesses the largest collection of the drawings of Claude in the world. There are 323 individual drawings by or attributed to him, of which 273 were bequeathed by Richard Payne Knight in 1824. These are arranged in the order of the catalogue by A. M. Hind, *Catalogue of the Drawings of Claude Lorrain in the Department of Prints and Drawings in the British Museum*, published on the occasion of an exhibition in 1926. In 1957 the Department further acquired in lieu of death duties from the collection of the Dukes of Devonshire at Chatsworth the Liber Veritatis, Claude's own record of the paintings which he had made throughout his career. It was published by Michael Kitson, *Claude Lorrain: Liber Veritatis*, 1978 (1957–12–14–6 to 206).

Clichés-verre

A cliché-verre is a photographic print made from a negative which has been drawn by hand by the artist. The only clichés-verre in the Department are the forty reprints from the Cuvelier collection published in 1921 under the title *Quarante clichés-glace* (161* b.21; 1922–4–10–213 to 248) which contains work by Corot, Daubigny, Delacroix, Millet and Rousseau. There is also one early printing of Corot's Saltarelle (Delteil 75; 1949–4–11–2401). The Department also possesses the original glass negative of Corot's Landscape with Rider (Delteil 46; 1925–1–20–4).

Coffee Houses

Coffee was introduced to England in 1652, and there are a number of drawings and satirical prints in the collection relating to it:

1 Anon. English *c.* 1705: Interior of a coffee house, bodycolour. 1931–6–13–2.
2 A description of the Calve's Head Club, 1710. Satire 1517.
3 The Westminster Calf's Head Club, 1710. Satire 1518.
4 The Coffehous mob, 1710. Satire 1539.
5 Jonathan's Coffee House, 1763. Satire 4091.
6 The Coffee-House Patriots; or news from St Eustatia, 1781. Satire 5923 (by H. Bunbury).
7 Midnight. Tom and Jerry at a coffee shop near the Olympic, 1820. Reid 1006, by I. R. and G. Cruikshank (184 c.7).
8 Portrait of Mr W. Howell (1784–1810), master at Garraways Coffee House for twenty years (not in O'Donoghue).
9 Three drawings by George Scharf: Cleveland Street Coffee House (1862–6–14–721), Steam cooking apparatus at Sanders Coffee House, Newgate Street, 1828 (1862–6–14–722), Exterior of Sanders Coffee House 1820 (1862–6–14–723).
10 Views of Button's and Tom's Coffee Houses in Russell Street are to be found in the Crace collection XVIII 106–8.
11 See also Trade Cards under Inns,

London for the following coffee houses: Bank, Leopard, City, Newcastle, St Pauls Churchyard, Goodwin's (all Heal collection); and Covent Garden, Turtle, Kinsey's, Grafton Street (all Banks collection).

Colour Printing

Italian chiaroscuro woodcuts are kept in the order of Bartsch XII. The complete holdings of the Department have been marked off in an annotated copy of Caroline Karpinski's 1971 volume in the series of *Le Peintre-Graveur Illustré*. The works of Hercules Segers and J. C. Le Blon are kept under the names of those engravers. An album contains 185 engravings printed in colour by Johannes Teyler under the title *Opus Typo-Chromaticum* (191* b.1; 1871–12–9–5003 to 5186).

There are separate mounted series of xviiic. British and Foreign engravings printed in colour (see above pp. 36, 37). For the xixc. see s.v. Baxter and Oleographs. In addition there is an extra portfolio of the works of the Baxter licensees (J. M. Kronheim, J. Mansell, Myers and Co., Le Blond). A special collection of the work of William Dickes was bequeathed by Mr A. Docker through the NACF in 1931. The list in the register (1931–2–13–1 to 1379) was arranged according to the order of the catalogue of Dickes's work compiled by Docker himself. The material has been placed in two portfolios and two albums (199* b.16, 17): the albums have all the preparatory drawings mounted with impressions of the corresponding prints, while the portfolios contain the remaining prints. There are also two portfolios containing other examples of British xixc. and xxc. colour printing given by Miss Winifred

Jones (1936–11–16–40 to 2124).

Another portfolio contains xixc. colour prints from France, Germany, Italy and the Netherlands. An album contains 25 states of a chromolithographic portrait of Maharajah Dhuleep Singh of 1854, by M. & N. Hanhart after Winterhalter (1912–10–12–5(1 to 25); 230* c.15).

Commedia dell'Arte

Among the works on this subject in the Department are the following:

1 Jean Bérain (1640–1711), attributed: 8 coloured drawings of figures. Croft-Murray I pp. 405–7 as Laroon.
2 François Joullain (1697–1779): A set of 16 unmounted engravings of figures. 1866–5–12–3010 to 3025 (list). (See B. Populus, *Claude Gillot*, 1930 p. 248 no. IV.)
3 Nicolas Bonnart, publisher: 12 engravings of figures. 170 b.21; 1938–3–11–6(204–215).
4 G. M. Mitelli (1634–1718): four figures, etching. (B.XIX 284.37).
5 Jacques Callot (1592–1635): Balli di Sfessania, etchings. (Meaume 641–664) and others.
6 Antoine Watteau (1684–1721), after: Les Jaloux, engraving. (Oeuvres II p. 9), and others.

See further the illustrations in Pierre Louis Duchartre, *The Italian Comedy*, 1929.

Conservation

The earliest records of conservation treatment applied to parts of the Department's collections belong to the period when they were stored in the Townley Galleries. At that time it was the Keeper himself who did whatever was necessary. By 1850 W. H. Carpenter reported that he had two attendants working for him: 'one cleans prints most skilfully and the other mounts the drawings'. In 1927 Dodgson had four members of staff whom he described as mounters and restorers. A major change occurred in 1968–9 when the staff was regraded as Conservation Officers, and another in 1975, when the conservation staff of all departments were transferred to a newly created Department of Conservation and Technical Services. On conservation techniques, see two publications by members of staff of the Museum: E. G. Harding, *The Mounting of Prints and Drawings*, 1972, and A. D. Baynes-Cope, *Caring for Books and Documents*, 1981.

Contemporary Art Society

The Contemporary Art Society was founded in 1910 with the aim of presenting modern works of art to national and provincial museums. In 1919 it established a separate fund for the purchase of British and foreign prints and drawings by living or recently deceased artists; this survived until after the Second World War when it was integrated into the main fund. During its existence the fund was administered and the purchases chosen by Dodgson and then Hind. The works purchased remained for a time in the hands of the Society, and were lent to interested galleries around Britain. They were then given to a number of national and provincial collections, with the lion's share, about 75%, going to the British Museum. Between 1922 (the date of the first distribution) and 1945, all acquisitions of XXc. works by the Department were made from this fund or other gifts, since the regular purchase grant was reserved for works from earlier centuries.

Since the late 1940s the Department has continued to benefit from the generosity of the CAS. Distributions take place every three to four years, and usually one to three works are allocated here.

Cook, Captain James (1728–1779)

Captain Cook made three voyages to the South Pacific: on the *Endeavour* 1768–71, on the *Resolution* and *Adventure* 1772–5, and on the *Resolution* and *Discovery* 1776–80 (during which he was killed). The Department possesses a few drawings made on these voyages, although a far greater number is now in the Department of Manuscripts of the British Library (to which some were transferred from Prints and Drawings during the XIXc.) and in the Natural History Museum at South Kensington:

In the British Museum

2ND VOYAGE: all by William Hodges. View at Otaheite 1773 (1890–5–12–107) and Man on the Island of Mallicolo (1868–12–12–340*)(Binyon 1 and 2); 9 miscellaneous drawings in an album of drawings from the estate of P. J. de Loutherbourg (201 c.5, ff.87–88; items 272 to 277, 279, 282, 283). (Number 271 in this album belongs to the 1st Voyage.)

3RD VOYAGE: all by John Webber. Album of fish and birds (199* b.2; 1914–5–20–358 to 403; from the collection of Sir Joseph Banks). 5 miscellaneous drawings: a view in the Nootka Sound (1859–7–9–102; Binyon 11), a Chinese boat (1909–7–3–2), a hippopotamus and a giraffe (1914–5–20–689, 692) and a view in the South Seas (1957–7–5–54).

The Department does not possess any of the narrative publications of the voyages, but does have a broken-up set of the plates to Captain Cook's voyages, after Hodges and others, distributed under the names of the master (1868–12–12–299 to 397) as well as a collection of proofs of Woollett's contributions, in addition to a large group of Webber's own etchings of South Sea scenes (all case 6*). These fall into three groups: the 16 hand-coloured etchings published 1787–8; the reworked states of some of these plates with aquatint added by M. C. Prestel; and a new set of plates of 1788–92 in soft-ground etching, in full colour and two colour editions. Other impressions of the second and third of these groups are bound in 246* a.2; 1917–12–8–13(2–20).

In the British Library

1ST VOYAGE: Add. Mss 7085, 25 charts and plans. Add. Mss 9345, 75 drawings by S. Parkinson. Add. Mss 15508, drawings of ethnographic interest by various hands. Add. Mss 23920–1, drawings and engravings relating to the official publications of the voyages. 2ND VOYAGE: Add. Mss 15743, 10 drawings by William Hodges. 3RD VOYAGE: Add. Mss 15513–4, drawings by John Webber. Add. Mss 17277, drawings by John Webber, including many preparatory sketches for Add.Mss 15513–4.

See also the book by R. A. Skelton, *Captain Cook After Two Hundred Years*, 1969, and the catalogues of the exhibitions *Captain Cook's First Voyage Round the World*, held in the King's Library in 1968, and of *Cook's Voyages and Peoples of the Pacific*, held in the Museum of Mankind in 1979.

The information above is drawn from the complete listings contained in Rüdiger Joppien and Bernard Smith, *The Art of Captain Cook's Voyages*, I and II 1985, III forthcoming 1988.

Copyright

Copyright deposit Although English law (unlike French) has never established any copyright deposit for prints, a number of prints were presented to the Department in the 1880s and recorded as having been acquired under the Copyright Act. These prints were registered in groups. Some of the most notable are:

1883–8–11–251 to 282	French prints, mostly photogravures and oleographs.
1883–8–11–283 to 337	Christmas and New Year cards.
1884–11–8–21 to 67	Prints after various masters, French colour prints.
1885–3–14–123 to 175	French prints, mostly military costumes and portraits.
1886–2–16–43 to 80	Prints after French masters.

Copyright and the collection The ownership of works of art by the Museum confers no copyright. The copyright remains with the copyright owner in accordance with the terms of the Copyright Acts:

DRAWINGS The copyright belongs to the artist or whoever is granted or sold it by the artist until 50 years after the artist's death.
PRINTS The copyright for commercial undertakings, when a plate is made to order, belongs to whoever commissioned the work. The copyright continues for 50 years from the year of publication.
PORTRAITS The copyright belongs to whoever commissioned the work, and continues for 50 years after the artist's death.

The Museum does, however, control access to the collections, and does own copyright in photographs it supplies of items in the collection. Permission has to be granted before any such photograph may be reproduced, and a fee may be charged for this.

See Museums Association Information Sheet 7: *Copyright law concerning works of art*, by Charles H. Gibbs-Smith.

Coronations

See the catalogue of an exhibition held in the King's Library in 1937. Numbers 124–174 record 51 prints and drawings of the subject, covering the years from 1547 to 1838, which are at present kept in various places in the collection. See also the Banks, Franks and Guest (qq.v.) collections, for printed programmes of coronations. See also s.v. Ceremonies.

Costume

The main series of costume prints is described above (pp. 52–3, Authorities for Artists), where some indications are also given on the whereabouts of other plates of costume. See also the entries on Cries, Lloyd, Rubens (for his Costume book), Talman, Theatrical, Topography and Trades; military costume is described in the entry Military. The present entry contains notes on a few other collections or groups of costume prints and drawings kept in the Department:

General and British

1   The so-called Queen's Costume books. This is the collection of Sir William Augustus Fraser, Bart (1826–98), bequeathed by him to HRH the Princess of Wales and to successive Princesses of Wales thereafter. It was deposited on permanent loan in the British Museum by HRH Alexandra, Princess of Wales in 1899. It is therefore not registered or catalogued, but is kept together in case 171. It contains a total of 74 bound volumes of costume plates, most of which are runs of the leading fashion periodicals of their day. They are arranged in the following groups: Paris 1785–93, 1788–98, 1797–1823, 1831–84 (60 volumes); Paris and London 1824–6, 1828–30 (6 volumes); Paris, Vienna and London 1827 (1 volume); England 1809–26, 1828–30 (4 volumes); London 1892–4 (3 volumes).

2   The Sarah Banks collection contains two bound volumes with costume plates. The first is a collection of English costume from 1760–1817 taken from pocket books, etc., mounted on 129 pages (170 b.4; C 4.1 to 468, list). The other is a series of coloured etchings of Danish costume with a ms index (170 a.1; Mm 2.153 to 245).

3   The bequest by F. W. Fairholt (1818–66) includes among other material three made-up volumes with the manuscript title 'A collection of prints and literary scraps illustrating costume'; it includes numerous plates in colour, satires, plates from the Lady's Magazine, the work of Hollar and Bickham, and cuttings from magazines. Most of the prints are British, but a few are foreign. (169* c.12 to 14; 1866–5–12–1779 to 2950, no list).

4   See also A. Racinet, *Le Costume Historique*, Paris 1888. Six volumes containing nearly 500 colour lithographs of costumes of most countries (169* a.2 to 7).

5 Richard Cook, Sketches of costume VIII–XVc. An album and portfolio of drawings copied from manuscripts etc. 198 c.4,4*; 1857–6–6–53 to 114.

6 Mary Hamilton, Mrs Siddons's dresses and attitudes in various characters 1802–3. Bodycolour. 201 b.10; 1876–5–10–816 to 896.

7 The British Library possesses an interesting collection of prints illustrating the costume of different nations from the XV–XVIIc. BL 146 i.10.

French

8 Two made-up albums with a manuscript title 'Recueil de vues de Versailles, Paris etc. et de portraits et de costume' contain numerous late XVIIc. and early XVIIIc. French costume prints by Bonnart, Deshayes, Arnoult, St Jean, etc. (170 b.21–2; 1938–3–11–5(1 to 213) and 6(1 to 243).

9 Another similar album has the manuscript title 'Figures emblematiques', and contains more late XVIIc. costume prints by the Bonnarts, in which the figures are allegories of the seasons, the elements and so on (170 c.11; 1922–4–10–143 to 208).

10 The Monument du Costume, the series of XVIIIc. French engravings after gouaches by S. Freudenberger and J. M. Moreau le jeune, is kept mounted in two boxes (1894–6–11–4 to 11, 15 to 19; 1925–1–14–1 to 41); the Neuwied reprints of 1789 are in one bound volume (170 c.2; 1866–5–26–514 to 539).

Russian

11 The collection of etchings and aquatints by Jean Baptiste Le Prince (1734–81) includes a large number of prints showing Russian costume and daily life. See 1853–12–10–663 to 797 (list).

12 A. Orlowski, an album of drawings with portraits and caricatures of Russian types. 197 c.15; 1887–5–2–114(1–20).

Swiss

13 Apart from the enormous numbers of prints and drawings of Swiss costume in the Lloyd bequest (q.v.), there is an album entitled 'Costumes Suisses vers l'an 1800' with watercolours by D. A. Schmid. 197 d.10; 1876–7–8–1406 to 1430.

Turkish

14 60 woodcuts of Turkish and Levantine costume, taken from Nicolas de Nicolay, *Les quatre premiers livres des navigations et pérégrinations orientales*, are kept with Foreign History 1568 (1927–2–10–31 to 90, no list).

15 Amadeo Preziosi, an album with watercolours of costume of Constantinople dated 1844. 197 b.15; 1921–6–14–29 to 58.

Cotman, John Sell (1782–1842)

There is no complete catalogue of the Department's outstanding collection of the work of Cotman. Those drawings acquired before 1898 are listed in Binyon, and a selection of 82 watercolours and drawings is reproduced in Adele M. Holcomb, *John Sell Cotman*, 1978.

The first acquisitions of his work were made with the purchase in 1859 of part of the Dawson Turner (q.v.) collection (1859–5–28–1 to 146), which included watercolours of *Croyland Abbey, St Mary Redcliffe* and others (1859–5–28–115 to 122). In 1885 two drawings were purchased from another source: a portrait of Crome and a pastoral scene

(1885–5–9–1399,1400). The largest group, comprising 348 drawings and watercolours, came with the Reeve (q.v.) collection (1902–5–14–7 to 355). The remainder of the collection of his drawings is made up of: *Gormrie Lake, Yorkshire, Mont St Michel*, and *Mount and Fort of St Marion* from the Lloyd (q.v.) bequest (1958–7–12–329 to 331); drawings of Normandy and Norfolk given by Mrs Rowland Barker and since mounted into an album (200 c.4*; 1937–2–13–9 to 62); *Cottage with pigs* and *House on Colnebrook Moor* bequeathed by E. W. Meyerstein (1953–4–11–3,4); and the *Window of Greyfriars Church Norwich* presented by Dr Joan Evans (1967–2–11–5).

There is a full collection of the etchings, including the following bound volumes:

1 *Ancient Buildings in various parts of England*, 1811. 166 d.21.
2 *Grand Festival at Great Yarmouth*, 1814. One copy acquired 1882 (165 a.15), the other purchased from Reeve in 1905 (165 a.16).
3 *Etchings in soft ground, for the most part unpublished*, 1814–17. From the Palgrave collection, with ms title-page and a letter from Mary Anne Turner to F. T. Palgrave (165 a.24).
4 *Architectural Antiquities of Norfolk*, 1818. From the Dawson Turner collection, with letter from Cotman to Turner and impressions of each state of every etching (166 d.22, 23).
5 *Antiquities of St Mary's Chapel*, 1819. From the Dawson Turner collection, with additional proofs of the plates (165 b.20).
6 *Architectural Antiquities of Normandy*, 1822. From the Dawson Turner collection, including letter from Cotman to Mrs Turner and impressions of each state of every etching (166 d.24 to 27).
7 *Liber Studiorum*, 1838. One copy from the Dawson Turner collection (165 b.21), the other, which had been given by Cotman to J. J. Cotman, from the Reeve collection (165 a.15).
8 *Sepulchral Brasses of Norfolk and Suffolk*, 1839. 166 d.28, 29.
9 *Eight original etchings by the late John Sell Cotman, now first published*, 1846. 166 d.30.

Crace, Frederick (1779–1859)

One of the famous family of interior decorators, and later Commissioner of Sewers. His collection of drawings and prints of London topography was mainly put together between 1829–59, and was purchased from J. G. Crace, his son, in 1880 for £3000 with funds raised by an auction of duplicate prints. The collection is arranged in a topographical sequence on sheets in 38 portfolios; a few of the more important drawings and watercolours have been extracted and mounted. A further 19 portfolios containing maps and plans that originally formed the first part of the collection were transferred to the Map Room of the British Library in 1933. There is a published catalogue: *A catalogue of maps, plans and views of London, Westminster and Southwark, collected and arranged by Frederick Crace, edited by his son John Gregory Crace*, 1878; the Department copy has a topographical index bound in. The register takes the form of a numbered copy of this catalogue: 1880–11–13–1 to 6166. References to items in the Crace collection should include the portfolio, sheet and sub-numbers. There is a microfilm of the entire collection and the so-called 'Crace supplement', which is simply the rest of the Department's collection of London topography arranged in the same order as the Crace collection.

Cracherode, the Rev. Clayton Mordaunt (1730–1799)

A wealthy recluse who assembled a most remarkable collection of books, engraved gems, coins and prints and drawings which he bequeathed to the British Museum, of which he was a trustee from 1784. An amusing account of his habits will be found in the *Dictionary of National Biography*; to it should be added the fact that he was one of the main subscribers to the fund established to support J. R. Cozens during the last years of his insanity. There is a manuscript catalogue of the drawings made in 1845 by Carpenter before most of the albums containing them were broken up and their contents mounted. There were 848 drawings in all, including works by Dürer, Claude, Holbein, Rembrandt, Rubens and van Dyck; they have the inventory numbers Ff, Gg 1 to 3, Ll 2 and 3, and At (an album of drawings by Grimaldi). The prints were stamped, rearranged and incorporated with the rest of the collection in 1808, but unfortunately no catalogue was ever made. Thus prints from the Cracherode collection can only be identified by the embossed stamp placed on them while in the Museum. The strengths of the print collection are the great series of Rembrandt etchings, and of Italian engravings and etchings from the XVIc. to XVIIIc.

Cries (Street Cries, Cries of London)

In this entry are described series of prints of street vendors. Prints showing the actual processes of manufacture are described in the entry for Trades. A complete catalogue of prints on this subject is given by Karen F. Beall, *Kaufrufe und Strassenhändler (Cries and Itinerant Trades)*, Hamburg 1975. This notes locations for the items included. The most important prints in the collection are as follows:

Cries of London

1 Five XVIIc. broadsheets kept in the Authorities for Artists series. See Corbett and Norton's third volume of Hind's Engraving in England, pp. 366–9, nos 80–4.

2 After Marcellus Laroon I: The cryes of the City of London 1711, etchings with texts in three languages. 170* a.10; 1972 U.370(1–73).

3 Copies of the above published by P. Tempest. 169 b.3; 1856–7–12–545 to 565.

4 Paul Sandby: Cries of London, c.1760, unmounted etchings. Set of 12 incomplete.

5 After Francis Wheatley: Thirteen Cries of London, 1793–7, stipple engravings. Uncoloured impressions, mounted (1871–12–9–594 to 606); impressions printed in colour, bound as frontispieces to the volumes of the Marx Pennant.

6 J. T. Smith: The cries of London 1839, etchings. 170* a.11; 1852–12–11–262 to 292.

7 Thomas Rowlandson: Characteristic sketches of the lower orders, in Samuel Leigh's *New Picture of London*, 1823. Coloured etchings. 298 a.7.

8 H. Merke after Thomas Rowlandson, set of aquatints. George 9474–80.

Other Cities

9 Nicolas Bonnart: various etchings in an album of costume prints. 170 b.22; 1938–8–11–6(106 to 140).

10 G. Valck (publisher): copies after the Larmessin set of vendors wearing fantastic costumes composed of items of their trade. I 7–185 to 205 (with Authorities for Artists).

11 Edme Bouchardon: Études prises dans le bas peuple, ou les Cris de Paris, 1734–42. 162 c.32; another copy containing the original drawings 197 c.8 (1857–6–13–672 to 793).

12 The Cries of Bologna, title-page and 40 plates etched by G. M. Mitelli after Annibale Carracci. Bartsch XIX 301.117–157.

13 G. M. Mitelli, street vendors in Bologna 1700, 27 figures etched on one plate. 1852–6–12–576.

14 Annibale Carracci: Le Arti di Bologna, 1740. 164 b.22; 1942–5–14–3(1–81).

15 Jean-Baptiste Le Prince: three sets of etchings of Cries of Russia, 1764–8, each with 6 plates.

16 Gaetano Zompini: Le arti che vanno per le via nella città di Venezia, 1785. 164 b.23; 1972 U.383(1–61).

17 Carle Vernet: Cris de Paris. 170* a.19; 1854–12–11–301 to 400.

Crookshank, Lt-Col. C. de W.

The author of the standard catalogue of *Prints of British Military Operations . . . covering the period from the Norman Conquest to the campaign in Abyssinia*, 1921. Most but not all of these prints were in his own collection which he bequeathed to the Trusteeship of the Secretary of State of War. Originally housed in the Royal United Services Institution in Whitehall, the collection was transferred to the British Museum in 1944 and registered as 1944–5–13–1 to 553. When the new National Army Museum in Royal Hospital Road, Chelsea was opened in 1971, the collection was transferred there by the Trustees of the British Museum. It therefore no longer forms part of the Department.

Cruikshank, George (1792–1878)

A descriptive catalogue of the works of George Cruikshank, etchings, woodcuts, lithographs and glyphographs with a list of books illustrated by him, was published in 1871 by G. W. Reid, the Keeper of the Department of Prints and Drawings. Although it is often thought to be a catalogue of the Museum's collection, it is not, being based on a number of private collections. The catalogue contains 5265 items and covers the years 1803–70. Reid consulted Cruikshank in compiling the catalogue, and included in it work that was carried out by George in collaboration with his father Isaac, or with his brother Isaac Robert.

It was not until 4 August 1884, by a codicil to her will, that the artist's widow, Mrs Eliza Cruikshank, bequeathed to the Museum 'tracings of his works, sketches, India and other proof etchings and prints of any kind whatever . . . to be called the George Cruikshank Collection'. It was registered as 1891–11–16–179, but at the time no list was made. It consisted of 4260 etchings, 4065 drawings and 2637 prints by other artists. Most of it has subsequently been included in the new 'U' register as 1974 U.1 to 2664, 1975 U.1 to 728, 1079 to 1570, with a few further items being in the 1978 U register.

The Reid catalogue has been used to mark off the prints and books. Most of the prints are kept in a separate series of 15 portfolios in Reid's order, while the books are in the Departmental library and included in the card index. The satires were later included in the George catalogue, but are still kept in the Reid series rather than the George series. 3869 drawings have been included in Binyon's catalogue, volume I pp. 280–349, and the remainder, which he omitted, have been listed in a typescript inventory compiled in

1974–5. Almost all the drawings catalogued by Binyon have been mounted in 10 albums in his order, which follows that of Reid's catalogue (199 c.1–10); impressions of the related finished prints have been mounted next to the drawings. Two sketchbooks have been placed as 201 a.1*,1**, while another album (200 b.5) contains the drawings by Captain Marryat which served as the basis for the 'Life of a Midshipman' (Binyon 24–34), The drawings omitted by Binyon are kept unmounted.

Cut Paper

The Department has never attempted to collect examples of paper cutting, but possesses a few specimens. These have been mounted in an album (case 35), which now contains: 54 by anonymous artists of portraits and other compositions (1878–9–14–104 to 157), 3 by Amelia Blackburn (1956–3–14–1 to 3), and 2 by HRH Princess Mary dated 1788 (1857–5–20–75, 6). The album also contains a pricked paper version of a Carrington Bowles mezzotint (1937–11–9–1). There is also a volume of reproductions after Marcus Behmer, *Zehn Scherenschnitte*, 1930 (168 a.24). See also s.v. Delany and Silhouettes.

Dal Pozzo-Albani Collection

Cassiano dal Pozzo (1588–1657), the famous Roman collector and antiquarian, assembled a collection of drawings of sculpture and other antiquities. This was acquired by Pope Clement XI (Albani) in about 1703, and the bulk of the drawings were purchased from his heirs by George III in 1762. These albums are now at Windsor Castle. A number of other drawings which had remained with the Albani family were presented to the British Museum in 1903 by Sir Charles Hercules Read; they are now bound in two albums and kept in the Department of Greek and Roman Antiquities. They were published by C. C. Vermeule in *Transactions of the American Philosophical Society*, vol 50, part 5 (1960), pp. 5–78. The same author had previously published an article on the whole collection in *Art Bulletin*, 38 (1956), pp. 31–46; see also John Fleming, 'Cardinal Albani's drawings at Windsor', *Connoisseur* CXLII (1958), pp. 164–9.

Dalziel Brothers

The Dalziel brothers, of whom the most notable were Edward, George and Gilbert, ran the most important wood-engraving workshop of the mid-XIXc. in England. Being very conscious of their posthumous reputation, they saw that the Department acquired the bulk of the records of their output. In order of acquisition these were:

1 Complete set of 829 proofs from designs by Sir John Gilbert to illustrate Routledge's edition of Shakespeare, 1859–60. Purchased from Messrs Dalziel. 248 b.1–3; 1898–5–20–212 to 1040 (list).

2 513 proofs for five publications: Sir John Gilbert, *Longfellow's Poetical Works*, 1856 (248 b.4); Sir John Tenniel, *Lalla Rookh*, 1861 (248 b.5); J. D. Watson, *Pilgrim's Progress*, 1861 (248 b.7); J. D. Watson, *Robinson Crusoe*, 1864 (248 b.8); G. J. Pinwell, *Goldsmith's Works*, 1865 (248 b.9). Purchased from Charles Dalziel; 1905–10–19–215 to 727 (list).

3 A complete set in 49 volumes of the production of the Dalziel workshop 1839–93, comprising some 54,000 impressions. Each proof was pasted in as it was made, and the albums therefore

are invaluable as a document both to the chronology and the variety of its output which ranged from the highly 'artistic' to the utterly banal. Purchased from Gilbert Dalziel. Each volume is listed in a general way under 1913–4–15–163 to 210, and some of the volumes have contents lists at the front. In these cases references have also been transferred to the Index of Artists. But a complete index remains a desideratum. Two items in the albums are the proofs to Tenniel's illustrations to the Alice books. Those to *Alice in Wonderland*, 1865, will be found in volume XX, folios 77 ff. (others are kept loose in the series of wood-engravings after English masters). Those to *Alice Through the Looking-Glass*, 1872, are in volume XXVIII, folios 145 ff.

Davy Collection

In 1852 the Department of Manuscripts acquired 37 volumes of materials assembled by David Elisha Davy, son of David Davy, of Rumburgh Hill, Suffolk, with a view to writing a parochial history of Suffolk (Add. Mss. 19077 to 19113). Certain parts of these collections were transferred to this Department:

1 Three volumes of engraved views of Suffolk arranged alphabetically from Aldeburgh to Yoxford, including some maps. (173 c.9–11; 1853–1–12–335 to 846, list).
2 Brass rubbings. These were later transferred back to Manuscripts (1853–1–12–847 to 1337).
3 Portraits of persons connected with Suffolk (1853–1–12–1338 to 2246, list. These are now distributed in the portrait series).
4 Prints of Suffolk topography

(1853–1–12–2247 to 2335, list. These are distributed in the topography series).

The Department library also contains copies made in 1864 of two catalogues compiled in 1849 by Henry Davy: one of engraved portraits of persons connected with the county of Suffolk (Add. Mss. 19174), the other of engravings of castles, churches, seats, etc. illustrating the antiquities and topography of Suffolk (Add. Mss. 19175). There is also a large collection, mounted in four solanders, of etchings by Henry Davy of antiquities of Suffolk (1865–7–8–775 to 784; 1870–5–14–1489 to 1548; 1871–8–12–2933 to 3070).

Delany, Mrs Mary (1700–1788)

The Department possesses most of the surviving work of Mary Delany, the famous diarist, in the medium she made her own, the 'Paper Mosaic' or 'Plant Collage'. The method was to cut the petals and leaves from coloured paper, and paste them on to a background of black paper. Some unusual tints were created from paper on which the colours had run, and occasionally she added touches of watercolour. Mrs Delany began her paper cuts at the age of 72, and intended to make a set of 1000 specimens. George III and Queen Charlotte gave instructions 'that any curious or beautiful plants should be transmitted to Mrs Delany when in blossom'. The collection was bequeathed to the Department in 1897 by Lady Llanover, the editress of Mrs Delany's letters. They are mounted in the original 10 albums, in which are inserted detailed lists of the plants in the writing of the Rev. John Lightfoot. A number of specimens have since been extracted and mounted for exhibition. For a full list see the register 1897–5–5–1 to 974, and note the monograph by Ruth Hayden, *Mrs Delany, her Life and her Flowers*, 1980.

Dickens, Charles (1812–1870)

The collection of the work of Dickens formed by John Furber Dexter was purchased from his estate by the Library in 1969. Three volumes from the collection, Dexter numbers 322–4, were transferred to this Department. They contain 54 drawings and watercolours by George Cruikshank, Hablot K. Browne, John Leech and others; the subjects include actors and actresses in characters by Dickens, illustrations of his works, a portrait of him, and two signatures of George Cruikshank. 200* c.10–12; 1969–9–22–1 to 3 (list).

There are also two portfolios containing illustrations to his works. The contents include a collection of prints transferred from the Library in 1910 (1910–7–5–1 to 500, list), and others from the bequest of H. S. Ashbee with many watercolours by J. Clayton Clarke (1900–12–13–3299 to 3702, list).

See also s.v. Landells.

Dighton, Robert (?1752–1814)

Caricaturist and etcher, who finds his place in this handbook as the greatest thief in the Department's history. In 1806 it was discovered that he had been systematically stealing the Cracherode Rembrandts, on which he had then stamped his own collector's mark (Lugt 727). The full extent of his depredations could not be ascertained as there was no inventory against which to check. A deal seems to have been agreed that in return for not being prosecuted, Dighton would allow the Museum to remove all the prints in his possession that might have been abstracted from it.

Dodgson, Campbell (1867–1948)

Keeper of the Department of Prints and Drawings 1912–32. During his life he made countless gifts to the Department, and on his death in 1948 he bequeathed to it his entire collection of prints and a few drawings. It included some 30 early printed books with woodcut illustrations and 20 early single-sheet woodcuts. The bulk of the collection, however, was of modern prints: about 2500 British, 1580 French and 1000 of other schools. 1949–4–11–1 to 5241. Some additional items were later registered as 1951–5–1–1 to 132. See exhibitions 1933, 1967 and 1978 (French Lithographs). See also pp. 93, 140.

Don Quixote

There is a separate portfolio of illustrations to *Don Quixote*, all from the H. S. Ashbee bequest (see s.v. Illustrations to Authors). For a complete list see 1900–12–31–5429 to 5630. The major items are colour aquatints by Jazet, engravings after Henry Alken, etchings by Bartolommeo Pinelli, and prints after Charles Coypel. Apart from this portfolio, there are an album of drawings by John Vanderbank (1694–1739) made in *c.*1726–30 (197* d.14; 1862–10–14–803 to 889, list; Binyon IV pp. 252–5); an album of drawings by Francis Hayman (1708–76) to illustrate Smollett's edition of 1755 (201 b.4; 1859–6–11–331 to 358; Binyon II pp. 278–80), and five drawings by Jean Honoré Fragonard (1732–1806) from the well-known series (1907–11–6–1; 1908–4–14–1 to 4). A single watercolour by Henry Liverseege (1803–32) shows

Don Quixote in a panelled room with a sword and Mambrino's helmet (Binyon 1; 1900–8–24–522).

Dotted Prints

These are relief prints taken from metal plates, of which the surface has been covered with punched dots to produce a decorative effect. The method was popular in the xvc., and is sometimes known by the French term 'manière criblée'. The collection in the department was catalogued by Dodgson in his *Catalogue of Early German and Flemish Woodcuts*, volume I pp. 152–208, under the numbers B 1 to 35. There have been two important acquisitions since 1903:

1 *Regula Beatissimi Monarchorum Patris Benedicti*, 1460, a manuscript with two dotted prints pasted inside the covers of Sts John the Baptist and Christopher. (159* b.3*; 1918–7–13–2 and 3).
2 Thomas à Kempis, *De Imitatione Christi*, Ulm 1487, with two dotted prints by Master Bartholomeus pasted inside the covers. (36 a.7; 1972–2–26–1 and 2).

Downman, John (1750–1824)

Downman made up four series, each consisting of several bound volumes, of his preparatory drawings under the title 'First sketches of portraits of distinguished persons'. The Department possesses various volumes of or relating to this sequence (cf E. Croft-Murray, BMQ XIV, 1940 pp. 60–6):

FIRST SERIES: consisted of eight volumes, of which 1, 3 are in the Fitzwilliam, while the others were broken up. The Department possesses Downman's manuscript catalogue with introduction to this series. 166 c.31; 1950–2–11–3.

SECOND SERIES: all in the Fitzwilliam.
THIRD SERIES: four volumes, all in this Department from the bequest of E. G. Millar. 240 b.5; 1967–10–14–181 (no sub-numbers).
FOURTH SERIES: six volumes, of which 1–4 and 6 are in this Department. 240 b.6, 7; 1936–11–16–27 to 31. The fifth part is not in the collection, but is represented by a set of photographs.

Complete sets of photographs of the third and fourth series are bound at 240 b.9, 10.

In addition to the above, the Department possesses a number of individually mounted drawings, mostly from the Millar (q.v.) bequest (1967–10–14–162 to 207); a bound collection of 'sketches and first ideas collected by his daughter Isabella' (240 b.8; 1884–4–26–1 to 49); and the remains of an album of drawings collected together in 1825, and subsequently partly dismembered (240 b.11; 1967–10–14–202(1–11).

Drawing Books

There are 105 drawing books in the Departmental collection, mostly housed in case 167*. The contents include landscape, proportions of the human body, caricature, flowers, animals, trees, sporting subjects, etc. They come from Britain, France, Germany, Italy and the Netherlands and range from the xvi–xixc. Many have texts as well as plates and many are in colour.

Ducerceau, Jacques Androuet (active 1545–1585)

Two albums containing 122 architectural drawings of French châteaux in pen and ink on vellum from the collection of

George III were transferred from the Library on 8 December 1886, and have since been mounted in eight antiquarian solanders. They were not registered at the time, but have since been allocated the numbers 1972 U. 793 to 910. Most of the drawings are related to the engraved plates in Ducerceau's *Les plus excellents bastiments de France*, 1576 and 1579 (of which the Department owns no copy, although the British Library has an edition of two parts with 30 plates). A finding list is kept with the drawings which gives a concordance both with the facsimile edition of *Les plus excellents bastiments de France* by H. Destailleur, two vols 1868, 70 (168 b.1, 2), and with the edition of a selection of the drawings by W. H. Ward, *French châteaux and gardens of the XVI century: a series of reproductions of contemporary drawings hitherto unpublished . . .*, 1909. The Department also possesses a number of sets of ornament prints by members of the Ducerceau family.

Duplicates

The first record of the sale of duplicate prints from the collection is in the Minutes of the Committee of Trustees on 20 April 1787. According to this there was a sale of printed books and coins, which must also have included prints, since Lugt (304) notes a duplicate stamp bearing that date. The sale was held by Leigh and Sotheby, but no catalogue seems to survive.

It was followed by a sale for which the catalogue does survive: *A Catalogue of the prints and books of prints, duplicates of the British Museum . . . which will be sold by auction May 8 1811* etc. The sale was conducted by T. Philipe, who had been entrusted by the Trustees with the task of rearranging the collection of prints

between 1808 and 1810. It included works by Marcantonio, Dürer, van Meckenem, Rembrandt and others. There is a marked copy in the Department library with prices and the names of the purchasers.

In 1880 another sale was held to raise funds to pay for the acquisition of the Crace collection: *A Catalogue of duplicate prints and etchings, the property of the Trustees of the British Museum . . . which will be sold by auction . . . the 21st day of April 1880* etc. The sale was held, curiously, in the Department itself, but was conducted by Sotheby, Wilkinson and Hodge. It contained 93 lots of Netherlandish and Italian prints only, and realised £2153 9s.

A fourth sale took place in 1924 in collaboration with the Albertina, at Boerner's in Leipzig: *Kostbare Kupferstiche des XV–XVIII Jahrhunderts. Dubletten des Britischen Museums und der Albertina [and of other owners], 14–15 November 1924.* There were 887 lots, but the catalogue does not reveal (though Department records do) which lots belonged to which owner.

A minor sale took place at Puttick and Simpson on 2 June 1938: *Catalogue of engravings, drawings and pictures, Baxter and Le Blond colour prints, modern etchings etc.* Lots 15–27 consisted of duplicate Baxter and other colour prints from the Winifred M. Oliver Jones bequest; these duplicates, however, were never registered.

The most recent sale was held at Sotheby's on 26 June 1986 (lots 648–672) to raise funds for the purchase of a monotype by Castiglione from the collection at Chatsworth. The 25 lots raised a total of £95,350.

Besides these five recorded auctions, there has been a constant process of exchanging duplicates directly with the trade or other museums in exchange for new acquisitions. The numbers of prints exchanged in this way must greatly exceed the numbers disposed of by auction. Every duplicate released from the collection will bear on its verso both its original acquisition stamp, and a special duplicate stamp (Lugt 305) which will bear in its centre the initials of the Keeper who authorised its disposal. The Department registers also carry full records of these transactions.

Only prints which were purchased have been regarded as alienable duplicates. If the duplicates were given or bequeathed, they have been placed in a separate series of inalienable duplicates. It is from this series that most of the loan collection was put together (see s.v. Loans).

Dürer, Albrecht (1471–1528)

The foundation of the Department's collection of Dürer's drawings is the Sloane album 5218; this now only contains a small residue since the Dürer drawings have been extracted and mounted. Two other Dürer drawings come from Sloane 5261. The Dürer manuscripts contained in Sloane 5228 to 5231 remain in the Department of Manuscripts of the British Library.

The collection of drawings is at present arranged in the order given by John Rowlands in the 1971 exhibition catalogue of Dürer's work. The engravings are in the order of Campbell Dodgson's 1926 catalogue *Albrecht Dürer* (in the series 'The Masters of Engraving and Etching'). The woodcuts are in the order of Dodgson's 1903 official catalogue of German and Flemish woodcuts. The Department also possesses the original woodblocks for the Martyrdom of the Ten Thousand and the so-called 'Ercules' (presented by Junius S. Morgan; 1919–11–11–1,2) and for 35 of the 37 plates of the Little Passion

(1839–6–8–3(1 to 35), lacking plates 16 and 21). The Triumphal Arch of Emperor Maximilian is kept framed (E 2.334–353). See exhibitions 1928 and 1971.

Dyck, Sir Anthony van (1599–1641)

The drawings by van Dyck in the Department were catalogued by A. M. Hind in volume II of the *Catalogue of Drawings by Dutch and Flemish Artists*, 1923. He included 87 drawings which he thought to be by van Dyck himself, and 24 more in an appendix of school drawings and copies. In 1957 the so-called 'Italian sketchbook' was acquired from Chatsworth in lieu of Estate Duty. It contains drawings made during his travels in Italy 1621–7, mostly copies of other works of art (case 203; 1957–12–14–207(1–121), list). It had been published by Lionel Cust in 1902; a new edition by Christopher Brown is currently being prepared.

The 190 plates of the series known as the Iconography is mounted in a single sequence of 24 volumes in the order of the catalogue by F. Wibiral, *L'Iconographie d'Antoine van Dyck*, 1877. The 18 plates etched by van Dyck himself occupy the first four volumes; his three other etchings are in the first volume. The 1759 reprinted edition of the Iconography (Amsterdam, Arkstee & Merkus) is at 158* c.6; 1935–12–13–1(1–125).

There are two portfolios of unmounted prints after his compositions. Many are listed in the inventory under the numbers R1a, R1b, and R2 (537 items).

Egypt

There are some interesting drawings of Egyptian antiquities, life and topography:

1 Baron Dominique Vivant-Denon (1747–1825), two solanders containing unmounted drawings made during the French expedition to Egypt, including views, plans, daily life, temples, sculpture, mummies, etc. Cc 4.1–206, list (= 1836–1–9–1 to 206). Many of these drawings were for plates in the following:

2 *Description de l'Égypte*, 1809–13, made by the scholars on Napoleon's expedition. Text 173* a.9–13; plates 174 c.13–19.

3 William Alexander (1767–1816), drawings made for the publication *Egyptian Monuments in the British Museum*, 1805–7. 200 c.1; A 13.1–37 (no list); Binyon I pp. 26–7.

4 Edward William Cooke (1811–80), drawings showing the removal of the colossal Egyptian sculpture in the British Museum, May–June 1834. 198 b.4; 1914–2–6–1 to 22 (list).

5 C. Laver, album of drawings made in Assiout and Cairo, *c.*1828–30. 198 c.9; 1879–10–11–various; Binyon III pp. 37–9.

6 O. B. Carter (1806–59), album of drawings for Robert Hay's *Illustrations of Cairo*, 1840. 198 c.2; 1879–10–11–various; Binyon I pp. 199–201.

7 Robert Hay, drawings and plans of his house in Cairo. 199* b.10; 1879–10–11–1492 to 1517.

The Department also possesses a copy of the first three volumes (bound in four) of David Roberts, *The Holy Land*, 1842–9, containing colour lithographs by Louis Haghe after watercolours by Roberts (175 e.18–21; 1915–7–6–1 to 123; the order of the plates differs from that in the Abbey bibliography). These three volumes cover Palestine and Syria; they do not include the views of Egypt published in three further volumes as *Egypt and Nubia* in 1846–9.

Elgin Marbles

There are various drawings in the Department related to this subject:

1 Archibald Archer (1789/90–1848): The temporary Elgin Room in the British Museum 1816–31. Oil-painting, now hanging outside the Trustees' board room.

2 Benjamin Robert Haydon (1786–1846): Album of studies after the marbles, made in 1808–11 when still in the possession of Lord Elgin. Binyon II, pp. 277–8.

3 John Flaxman (1755–1826): Book of sketches based on the Elgin marbles, together with other drawings. 197 a.9; 1943–12–3–1(1 to 17).

4 Henry Corbould (1787–1844): A portfolio of drawings made to the commission of the Trustees for 'Ancient Marbles'. Binyon I, pp. 248–55.

5 Thomas Bruce, 7th Earl of Elgin (1766–1841): drawing by G. P. Harding (d.1853), 1898–2–15–28.

6 William Henry Prior (active 1833–57): The temporary Elgin Room in the British Museum. Sepia with figures in watercolour; 1838–1–13–1.

7 James Stephanoff (1788–1874): The Elgin Marbles in an idealised setting 1833. Watercolour, 1934–1–13–1.

Other material is in the British Museum portfolio (see s.v. British Museum), and in the Department of Greek and Roman Antiquities.

Facsimiles

The Department published between 1888 and 1894 a series entitled *Reproductions of Drawings by Old Masters in the British Museum*. The series was divided into four portfolios with both text and plates. A parallel series was entitled *Reproductions of Prints in the British Museum*. This was divided into a number of portfolios of varying size (all case 245*):

1ST SERIES, PARTS I–III: 1882–4. Italian and German Prints XV–XVIc.
2ND SERIES, PARTS I–XV: 1886–1906. Early Italian and German; German, Dutch, Italian prints; Early mezzotints; Germany, Netherlands 1530–1620; School of Rubens and van Dyck; French 1580–1680; Early English; English, French, Italian, German XVIIIc.
3RD SERIES, PARTS I–VII: 1907–13. German 1475–1575; Italian 1525–50; French 1620–70; Flemish 1520–1650; Dutch 1615–50; Rembrandt, Lievens, Bol 1630–80; Later Dutch masters 1640–1700.

The Department library also contains among others the following series of facsimiles of prints, listed here in order of publication:

1 William Young Ottley, *A collection of 129 facsimiles of scarce and curious prints by the early masters*, London 1828. 180 b.1.
2 *Héliogravure Amand-Durand. Eaux-fortes et gravures des maîtres anciens . . . Notes par Georges Duplessis*, Paris 1872–8. 179 c.1–10.
3 Imperial Press Berlin. *Engravings and Woodcuts by Old Masters . . . by Dr Friedrich Lippmann*, London 1889–1900 (English edition). 179 c.11–20.
4 Paul Heitz (editor), *Einblattdrücke des fünfzehnten Jahrhunderts*, Strassburg 1899–1942, in 100 volumes. Case 185.
5 Graphische Gesellschaft, Berlin (Bruno Cassirer). A run of publications from 1906. 180 b.13–36.
6 Max Geisberg, *Der deutsche Einblattholzschnitt in der ersten Hälfte des XVI Jahrhunderts*, 40 portfolios, 1923–42. Case 179*.

For reproductions of drawings, see above p. 40. Note also The Vasari Society. *Reproductions of Drawings by Old Masters*, Oxford 1905–35. In 16 parts. Case 177*.

Fairholt, Frederick William (1818–1866)

Antiquarian draughtsman, who made a large bequest primarily of his own work. See 1866–5–12–1 to 4250.

1 1 to 1778. Reports of the Congresses of the British Archaeological Association 1844–9. Extra-illustrated with original drawings in three volumes (290 c.6–8).
2 1779 to 2950. Costume prints in three volumes (169* c.12–14; see s.v. Costume).
3 2951 to 4250. Drawings, etchings and woodcuts by Fairholt to illustrate numerous works. Most have been mounted in seven volumes, labelled The Archaeological Album, Illustrations of Coins, Halliwell's Shakespeare, Miscellanea Graphica, Country Houses, Up the Nile, and The Percy Society (290* a.1–7).

Fans

The Department has never attempted to build up a collection of fans. The best collection in the country is the Messel collection now in the Fitzwilliam Museum, and there is also a good group in the Victoria and Albert Museum. In 1891, however, Lady Charlotte Schreiber presented her collection, which was mainly restricted to printed examples collected with an eye primarily on their subject-matter. The greater part of it had already been reproduced photolithographically in two large folio volumes published by the collector herself in 1888 and 1890 under the titles *Fans and Fan-Leaves, English* and *Fans and Fan-Leaves, Foreign* (168 c.7–8). A condition of the gift was that a catalogue should be published, and this appeared in 1893, compiled by Lionel Cust: *Catalogue of the collection of fans and fan-leaves presented to the Trustees of the British Museum by the Lady Charlotte Schreiber*. The fans are catalogued in two sequences subdivided by country and subject: first mounted fans (1 to 337) and then unmounted (1 to 332). These are followed by the few painted fans (333 to 380), while a supplement lists the books, catalogues and manuscripts on the subject which came with the gift. There is an index of artists, publishers and subjects. The register contains a complete listing, 1891–7–13–58 to 745.

A few other drawn fans in the collection are:

1 Antoine Watteau: Design for a fan-leaf (1965–6–12–1).
2 Lelio Orsi (1511–87): Design for a fan-holder (Popham 45; 1860–6–16–17).
3 Francesco Salviati (1510–63): Design for a fan-holder (Popham 54 as Orsi; 1948–1–9–3).
4 Anon. English *c*.1730: St Bartholomew's Fair (1941–7–12–2; cf. Schreiber 104).
5 A separate portfolio contains 39

unmounted fan leaves including some etched by François Vivares *c*.1738 in a Chinoiserie style.
6 For fans in use, see s.v. Costume, Monument du Costume.

Fawkener, William

Nothing seems to be known about this collector, who bequeathed in 1769 a collection of prints and drawings contained in 39 volumes (see Trustees' minute of 21 April 1769). Four of these contained 386 drawings, mostly Italian, and were placed in the Department of Manuscripts with the numbers 5210–3. In the 1837 inventory they were described under the pressmark T 11–14, and the total number of drawings listed comes to 310. The full number of 386 is given by the manuscript catalogue of the Fawkener collection drawn up by Carpenter in 1845 (see pp. 8–9). What seems to have happened is that a number of Fawkener drawings, particularly those of the Northern schools, were remounted in the Sloane and Cracherode albums, and thus given different inventory numbers. They can, however, be recognised by the initials WF written on the versos of most of them. The other 35 volumes are not recorded in the records of the Department of Manuscripts, and must have been placed in Printed Books since they contained prints. They would have been rearranged in 1808 and there is now no record of what they contained.

For some reason the Fawkener drawings are now referred to by their manuscript numbers, and not by their 1837 inventory numbers (i.e. as 5211–56, not T 12–56).

Fenwick, T. Fitzroy (1856–1938)

Grandson of Sir Thomas Phillipps (1792–1872), the famous and eccentric collector of manuscripts, from whom he had inherited a group of drawings catalogued by A. E. Popham, *Catalogue of Drawings in the collection formed by Sir Thomas Phillipps Bart, FRS, now in the possession of his grandson T. Fitzroy Fenwick*, 1935. Most of the drawings had been acquired at the Woodburn sale of 1860, and came from the collection of Sir Thomas Lawrence. Almost all the collection was presented to the Museum in 1946 by an anonymous donor (Count Antoine Seilern); a few more important drawings came as the gift of the National Art-Collections Fund (q.v.), while a number of others were retained by Seilern, and now form part of his bequest to the Courtauld Institute. The group was registered as 1946–7–13–1 to 1277, and marked off against the Department's copy of Popham's catalogue. Some later arrivals were registered as 1951–2–8–1 to 35. In 1957 some more drawings from the collection were discovered by Messrs Robinson, who had acquired the remains of the Phillipps collection, and given to the Museum; only some of these had been included in Popham's catalogue. They were added to the previous drawings and registered as 1946–7–13–1278 to 1576.

Finberg, Alexander J. (1866–1939)

The compiler of the inventory of the Turner Bequest, published in 1906. His association with the Department became close following the transfer of the bequest to the British Museum in 1931. After his death his wife, the dealer Hilda Finberg of the Cotswold Gallery, presented to the Department two sketchbooks, four drawings and fourteen etchings by him (1939–12–9–2 to 19; 1939–10–14–8; 1951–3–21–5), as well as a large number of his manuscripts (see above p. 68).

Finiguerra, Maso (1426–1464)

Described by Vasari as the inventor of the art of engraving plates for printing. Documents show him to have been a leading Florentine goldsmith and engraver in niello (q.v.). However, no surviving niello or engraving is securely documented as by him. On grounds of quality, and backed by some circumstantial evidence, a niello pax of the Coronation of the Virgin in the Bargello has a good claim to be his. The Department possesses a sulphur cast of this (A. M. Hind, *Nielli . . . in the British Museum*, 1936, no.151). On the basis of this work, various other nielli have been attributed to him. Of the works in the British Museum, the most likely candidates are the sulphur of the Virgin and Child enthroned (Hind 152, of which there is also an impression on paper, Hind 154), and a similar nielloed plate of the Virgin and Child (Hind 1). No engravings from plates intended for printing can be attributed to him with any likelihood.

The Department possesses an album of finished drawings of *c*.1460–70 with scenes from Biblical, mythological and ancient history, known as the Florentine Picture Chronicle (197 d.3; 1889–5–27–1 to 95, with six folios added later; see Popham and Pouncey 274). This was published in facsimile by Sidney Colvin, *A Florentine Picture Chronicle*, 1898, with an attribution to Finiguerra, which cannot be sustained. More recently the drawings have been attributed to the same hand as the engravings of the Planets (Hind A III) and the Prophets and Sibyls (Hind C I, II), and this has then been speculatively identified as Baccio Baldini.

Flock Prints

The six known surviving impressions are listed by A. M. Hind, *An Introduction to a history of woodcut*, 1935, pp. 172–4. None is in the British Museum.

Florence, Henry Louis (1844–1916)

Benefactor who left a legacy to the Museum, of which the Trustees decided to devote the income to the Department of Prints and Drawings. At the time of writing, the income is a few hundreds of pounds a year. The first purchases were made in 1919, and most have been drawings and watercolours of the British school. All the items have had 'Purchased from the H. L. Florence Fund' stamped on their mounts, and a full list could be compiled from the bill books. Florence bequeathed his collection of objects to the Victoria and Albert Museum.

Forgeries

There are two boxes of forgeries and deceptive copies of the work of J. M. W. Turner, Sir Joshua Reynolds, J. B. C. Corot, John Singer Sargent, John Hoppner, Rembrandt, Leonardo, Goya and others. Many of these were exhibited in an exhibition entitled *Forgeries and Deceptive Copies*, held in the Department's galleries in 1961: the subjects included natural history, antiquities, coins and medals, graphic arts, literature, music, postage stamps, etc., from the British Museum and other public and private collections. There was a published guide to the exhibition, but no catalogue. The labels have been mounted into a volume in the Department library, together with press cuttings and photographs (Ee 6 12).

One other item of interest is an album of drawings in pen and brown ink, plus a few etchings, by Peter Thompson (fl.1835–63) which he passed off as by a supposed 'Captain John Eyre', who worked in the manner of Hollar. 200 c.7*; 1909–6–28–26 to 102.

In a different category is a large group of imitations of Rembrandt's etchings made by Captain Baillie and others. For some of these see the catalogue of the exhibition entitled *Rembrandt in Eighteenth-century England* held at the Yale Center for British Art, New Haven, 1983. The Department also possesses a drawing by Tom Keating in the manner of Samuel Palmer (1979–4–7–3), and an album of wood-engravings by Eric Hebborn (249 b.15; 1978–12–16–9(1–26)).

See also s.v. R. C. Lucas.

Fowler, William (1760–1832)

A complete collection of the principal mosaic pavements, stained glass, brasses, fonts, etc. drawn, engraved in colour and published by William Fowler. Contained in four portfolios of mounted prints; 1890–7–17–12 to 126 (list). The Department library contains certain notes on Fowler himself, drawn up in 1869.

Framed Works

Various outsize works are kept in frames. Many are listed elsewhere in the entries for Cartoons, Miniatures and Pastels. A list of the others is given here for convenience. It does not include any xxc. works, since too many modern prints and drawings are stored this way to be described in detail.

1 Andrea Andreani after Giambologna: The rape of the Sabines, chiaroscuro woodcut. B XII.94.4; 1895–6–17–87.

2 Andrea Andreani after Titian: The Triumph of Faith, woodcut. B XII 91.9.

3 Andrea Andreani after Alessandro Casolani: Pietà, chiaroscuro woodcut. Meyer 15; 1903–4–8–19.

4 Ludolf Backhuysen and Jan van Call I: Panorama of Amsterdam from the Y, with the yachts of Peter the Great and the City of Amsterdam, watercolour. Hind 43; 1847–3–26–1 to 3.

5 Jacopo de' Barbari: A bird's-eye view of Venice 1500, woodcut. 1895–1–22–1192 to 1197.

6 Charles Bentley: Fête Champêtre, watercolour. 1982–5–15–21.

7 Niccolo Boldrini after Titian: The conversion of St Paul, woodcut. Passavant VI.231.43; 1935–7–13–1.

8 British School, early xixc.: A Doric temple overlooking the sea, watercolour. 1977–6–11–3.

9 John Scarlett Davis: The library at Tottenham, the seat of B. G. Windus, Esq, watercolour. 1984–1–21–9.

10 Peter De Wint: Lincoln, Stone quarry with peasants driving cattle, two watercolours. 1958–7–12–341, 342.

11 Albrecht Dürer: The great column, drawing (Sloane 5218–87, 88) and woodcut (Dodgson 35).

12 Idem: The Triumphal Arch, woodcut. Dodgson 130; first edition. E 2.334–353 (Nollekens-Douce bequest).

13 Florentine c.1460/70: Two decorative panels with angels, drawings with watercolour stencilling to imitate damask. 1935–10–12–1, 2.

14 Felice Giani: A panel of ornament, pen and wash. 1981–3–28–3.

15 Samuel Hieronymus Grimm: The encampment in the grounds of Montagu House in 1780, watercolour. 1984–5–12–4.

16 Wenceslaus Hollar: Prospect of London and Westminster from Lambeth, etching. Parthey 1013; 1926–6–17–10(1–4).

17 Philip James de Loutherbourg: Summer, Winter, two polygraphs on canvas. 1982–6–19–1, 2.

18 Isaac de Moucheron: Gardens of a palace; A woodland glade, two watercolours. 1958–7–12–466, 467.

19 Peter Oliver: The penitent Magdalene, drawing. Croft-Murray 2; 1956–8–2–1.

20 Henry Overton, publisher: A view of the public fireworks in 1748, engraving. 1877–6–9–2060.

21 Giovanni Battista Piranesi: Trajan's column, The Antonine column, etchings. 1926–5–11–35, 36.

22 Paul Sandby: Two views of the Thames from the gardens of Somerset House, looking east and west, watercolours. Crowle XIII 30, 31.

23 Ferdinand Schmutzer: The Joachim Quartett, etching. W77; 1978–1–21–355.

24 After Titian: The crossing of the Red Sea, woodcut. B XII.25.6; 1980 U.9.

25 After Titian: The martyrdom of the 10,000, woodcut. 1866–7–14–53.

26 Arnold van Westerhout after Lenardi: Thesis of Emericus Czaky dedicated to Pope Innocent XII in 1695, engraving. 1985–12–14–1.

Franks, Sir Augustus Wollaston (1826–1897)

Keeper of the Department of Antiquities and Ethnography 1866–96, and perhaps the greatest benefactor in the history of the Museum. His gifts to this Department, although much smaller than those to other departments, are not insignificant. In 1895 he presented a group of portraits, mostly woodcuts from books (1895–4–18–1 to 251) and title-pages (q.v.). On his death he bequeathed his collection of bookplates with his records and notebooks about it, as well as his collection of printed ephemera, which seems to have been designed to complement the Banks collection. The bequest was given a block entry as 1897–12–31.

It is now kept in three different series:

A BOOKPLATES See separate entry.

B TRADE CARDS See separate entry, section headed 'Banks'.

C THE REMAINDER is kept in five boxes arranged in roughly the same way as the Banks collection (q.v.). Whereas the Banks series consists exclusively of material from that collection, within the 'Franks' series is kept all similar printed ephemera from all non-Banks sources – of which the Franks bequest is by far the most important constituent. The following description is only summary; a fuller listing is available for consultation.

1 Admission tickets. Drawings, prints A–L.
2 Admission tickets. Prints M–Z.
3 Admission tickets. Bartolozzi and school, Royal occasions, foreign, blanks and modern impressions of invitation cards.
4 Shop bills, cards, and advertisements relating to British and foreign trades; British and foreign funeral cards; foreign marriage cards.
5 Banknotes and assignats, printed material, programmes, proposal sheets for British and foreign books, pamphlets, plans, menu cards, certificates and diplomas, material relating to book illustration.

Franks's collection of book-stamps, mostly heraldic, is in the British Library (LR 406 i.9).

Freemasonry

There are several items on this subject in the collection:

1 A geometrical view of the grand procession of the scald miserable masons in the Strand, 1742, engraving (Satire cat. 2546). Crace XVII–101.
2 William Hogarth: Night, engraving 1738 (Paulson 155). Showing Sir Thomas de Veil (1684–1746) with the doorkeeper of his lodge.
3 Portraits of William Williams (1774–1839) and John George Lambton, 1st Earl of Durham (1792–1840) in masonic dress.
4 After G. B. Cipriani (1727–85): Set of masonic jewels, engraved by W. S. Leney. 1873–7–12–462 to 467.
5 After John Nixon: Freemason's Tavern in Great Queen Street 1811, engraving. 1875–7–10–5238.
6 Admission tickets to Freemasons' Grand Lodge and Freemasons' Hall. Banks collection, C 2 85, 565, 1029, 1035, 1113, 1331–2; J 9 482,490. Other masonic admission tickets are elsewhere in the Banks series as well as in the Franks series.
7 Satires: The Free masons surpriz'd, c.1760 (3796), and How to make a mason, 1804 (10340).
8 P. Lambert: Freemasonry 1787, series of six engravings. 1896–5–11–385(1–6).
9 David Allen: Laying the foundation stone, Edinburgh University, etching. 1868–3–28–604.
10 Freemason's bookplate. Franks 34460.
11 Freemason's Jubilee Medal 1887 by Kenning, London. Cheylesmore 9414.

Frost Fairs

The Crace collection (portfolio VIII, views of the Thames) contains a separate group of 78 prints of frost fairs (that is fairs held on frozen water) spanning the years 1683 to 1855. These are kept on sheets 78–91, and in a separate album, 172* b.3. Most of them are described in the Crace catalogue pp. 225–37. The album was bequeathed to John Crace in 1878 by a Mrs George, and includes some items which are not described in the Crace catalogue. Five other prints are to be found in the Crace supplement, and a number of satirical prints relating to the fair of 1814 are catalogued by George as numbers 12185, 12341–8. Cf s.v. Skating.

Games

In 1893 Lady Charlotte Schreiber presented a collection of 141 engraved games of Italian, French, German and British origin. Most are kept loose between the pages of one album arranged by country, but 23 of them take a three-dimensional form and are kept separately. 1893–3–31–1 to 141 (list).

Gavarni, Guillaume Sulpice Chevalier (1804–1866)

To the small group of Gavarni's lithographs already in the collection was added in 1980 the entire collection formed by R. E. Lewis of California. It includes many proofs, annotated impressions and unique states, as well as 35 complete sets. 1980–5–10–70 to 354 (list).

Gernsheim 'Corpus Photographicum'

The 'Corpus Photographicum' of drawings was founded by Dr Walter Gernsheim in 1936. The principle was that his photographic team would visit both public and private collections of old master drawings around the world, and distribute the photographs to subscribers. The project still continues under the direction of Dr Jutta Lauke, and in mid-1986, a total of over 111,500 photographs had been distributed. In 1986 the annual total was 3900 photographs, of which 600 were of modern periods. The only two subscribers to the series in the British Isles were this Department and the Department of Prints and Drawings in the Victoria and Albert Museum. The V&A discontinued their subscription in mid-1985, leaving the only complete series here.

The photographs have all been dry-mounted on to cards, and arranged in boxes alphabetically by artist within schools. The index sheets have been bound, and have been annotated with any new locations that have followed from new attributions. Both photographs and index volumes may be consulted by students in the Print Room. Note that the Gernsheim series is kept quite separate from the main series of reproductions of drawings which is described on p. 40 above.

Glass Painting

An album in the collection contains designs for glass painting by Swiss artists of the XVI–XVIIc., including Jost Amman, Nicolas Manuel Deutsch, Abraham and Samuel Sybolt, Daniel Lindtmayer and others. 197 d.11; 1899–1–20–1 to 91. Other drawings will be found among the Netherlandish and German works in the collection.

Glass Prints

Sometimes called glass transfer pictures.
The print is glued to a sheet of glass, the
paper rubbed away, and the back painted.
The only glass prints in the collection come
from the Cannan collection of skating
prints (q.v.). 1931–11–14–647 to 668 (list).

Goff, Colonel Robert C.
(1837–1922)

Gave a large collection of etchings made by
himself of English, Italian, Egyptian and
other scenery, and architecture, flowers,
leaves, etc., arranged in ten portfolios.
Case 255*; 1899–7–13–218 to 321;
1911–12–30–1 to 104; 1922–2–23–1 to 40
(list).

Goya, Francisco (1746–1828)

A complete listing of the eight drawings
and very large collection of Goya's prints in
the Department is given as an appendix to
the book by Juliet Wilson Bareau, *Goya's
Prints: The Tomás Harris Collection in the
British Museum*, published on the occasion
of an exhibition in 1981. The Harris
collection was acquired in lieu of estate
duty and registered as 1975–10–25–10 to
430. Its great strength is in the
completeness of its holdings of the
published editions of Goya's four main
series, and in the three albums of proof
copies which Goya gave to his friend Ceán
Bermúdez. A complete list of all the sets in
the Department follows:

LOS CAPRICHOS: trial proof before
corrections (Bermúdez), trial proof after
corrections (two sets, one mounted), 1st,
2nd, 3rd, 5th (two sets), 6th, 9th, 10th and
12th editions.

THE DISASTERS OF WAR: working proof
with manuscript titles (Bermúdez), 1st
(four sets, one mounted), 2nd, 3rd, 4th
(two sets), 5th and 7th (two sets) editions.
LA TAUROMAQUIA: 1st (Bermúdez album
plus another mounted), 2nd, 3rd, 4th (two
sets), 5th, 6th and 7th editions.
THE PROVERBIOS (or Disparates): proof
(mounted), 1st (mounted), 3rd (two
editions), 5th (two editions), between
5th and 6th, 6th, 7th, 8th and 9th
editions.

The rest of the collection is arranged in
the order of Harris's standard catalogue
published in 1964. See also exhibitions
1963: a bound volume in the Departmental
library (Ee 6.13) preserves all the labels as
well as a complete photographic record of
this exhibition.

Great Exhibition 1851

The Crystal Palace was built in Hyde Park
in 1851, dismantled the following year and
re-erected in Sydenham, where it was
destroyed by fire in 1936. The following
pictures will be found in the Department:

1 *Dickinson's comprehensive pictures of the
   Great Exhibition*, colour lithographs by
   Nash, Haghe and Roberts. 244*;
   1902–4–16–2 to 58 (list).
2 Crace collection, portfolio IX, numbers
   101–3; the Crace supplement contains
   28 photographs taken in Sydenham
   before and after the fire.
3 Dalziel collection, volume III, contains
   proofs of the illustrations of the special
   number of the Art Journal devoted to the
   Exhibition.
4 Baxter made a series of colour prints on
   the subject of which impressions are in
   the collection (Courtney Lewis numbers
   160–194).
5 Owen Jones (1809–74): View of the

Crystal Palace seen in perspective.
Binyon 1; 1899–4–27–1.

6 A design for converting the Crystal
Palace into a tower 1000 ft high. Colour
lithograph after C. Burton, published
1852. 1871–8–12–5378.

See further Christopher Hobhouse,
1851 and the Crystal Palace, 1937.

Gribelin, Simon (1661–1733)

The Department possesses an album of
engravings assembled by the artist himself
in 1722 which comes from the collection of
Thomas Dodd. 1859–6–25–121 to 645
(no list). It forms a pair to another album
from the collection of Horace Walpole,
now kept at Strawberry Hill; a microfilm of
this is in the Department. See Sheila
O'Connell in *Print Quarterly*, II 1985,
pp. 27–37.

Guest, Montague (1839–1909)

Guest was the third son of Lady Charlotte
Schreiber by her first marriage, and
brother-in-law to Sir Austen Henry
Layard. He presented in 1906 a collection
of printed ephemera. This was not
registered but was stamped with his name
and the date. One box was put under
embargo, and not opened until 1973.
A small part was then registered as
1974–1–31–1 to 5; another part was
transferred to the Department of
Manuscripts where it forms Add. Mss.
57934–41; the final part was disposed of.
The whole collection is kept separately,
and comprises the following:

1 Admission tickets, mostly XIXc. but with
some XVIIIc., in eight boxes. The events
covered include theatrical and public
occasions, Coronations, funerals, and
memorial cards.

2 Invitations, the earliest dated 1863,
many dated 1906–9, in six packets.
Covering private and official occasions.

3 Printed Coronation programmes,
covering the coronations of George III,
George IV (including a book of
admission tickets), William IV, Queen
Victoria and Edward VII.

Guest's collection of badges and tokens
was presented to the Department of British
and Medieval (now Medieval and Later)
Antiquities in 1907. See *Catalogue of the
Montague Guest collection of badges, tokens
and passes*, 1930.

Hall, Chambers (1786–1855)

A wealthy collector, who shortly before his
death presented to the British Museum
various antiquities and works on paper.
There were 95 of the latter, registered as
1855–2–14–1 to 95:

1 Raphael, Composition study for
the Borghese Entombment,
drawing in pen and ink (Pouncey
and Gere 12).

2–67 Watercolours and drawings by
Thomas Girtin.

68–73 Etchings by van Dyck, being early
states of the Iconography.

74–85 Etchings by Parmigianino.

86–90 Etchings by Annibale Carracci.

91–95 Various other etchings.

The rest of his collections were given at
the same time to the Ashmolean Museum
at Oxford.

Harleian Manuscripts

The large collection of manuscripts
assembled by Robert Harley, 1st Earl of
Oxford (1661–1724), and his son Edward,
2nd Earl (1689–1741) was purchased from

the widow of the latter by Parliament in 1753 for £10,000 at the foundation of the British Museum, and are now in the Department of Manuscripts of the British Library. The only Harleian manuscript in the Department is the treatise with drawings of a variety of machines for use in peace and war by Francesco di Giorgio, formerly Ms 3281. It is now at 197 b.21; 1947–1–17–2(1–84), Popham and Pouncey 55. Cf Bagford collection.

Hauke, César Mange de (1900–1965)

A French dealer and scholar, who was educated at an English preparatory school, and spent the early part of his career in America. In 1965 he bequeathed to the Department 16 very important XIXc. French drawings. These were registered as 1968–2–10–16 to 31, and catalogued by P. H. Hulton on the occasion of the exhibition of the bequest held in June 1968.

Hawkins, Edward (1780–1867)

Keeper of the Department of Antiquities in the British Museum between 1826–60. He wrote extensively on coins and medals and compiled the material for his posthumously published *Medallic Illustrations of the History of Great Britain and Ireland*. His collection of medals was purchased by the Trustees in 1860, and his personal and political satires in 1868 after his death (1868–8–8–3207 to 13802).

Henderson, John (1797–1878)

A wealthy amateur and collector, whose father lived next door to Dr Monro, and himself lived at 3 Montague Street. Among many bequests to museums and galleries,

he left the British Museum his maiolica and Islamic pottery, his Venetian glass and other oriental works of art, and 170 works on paper. Almost all were drawings or watercolours: 4 by Canaletto, 6 by J. R. Cozens, 27 by Girtin, 13 by Turner, 42 by David Cox and 72 by W. J. Muller. In addition there were 3 drawings by himself and 5 by his father, and 3 prints. 1878–12–28–1 to 170 (list). See Binyon II.

Heraldry

A portfolio contains some 300 miscellaneous prints on the subject. Among them are a group of late XVIIIc. German armorial plates (1942–2–15–1(1–113)); the crest and badge of Henry VIII; Arms of Sir Thomas White 1553, Sir Walter Martyn, the Russell family (1868–6–12–1351 to 1362); arms of sponsors of Blome's Gentlemen's Recreation (1847–3–6–331 to 340); Hollar's illustrations to Ogilby's Entertainment of Charles II. Many of the remaining prints are pages extracted from books, and have been registered as 1983 U.914–1172. Items of interest kept in other places are:

1 Jorg Breu II: Arms of Maximilian I (1876–7–8–2634, 5 verso), Arms of Charles V (1876–7–8–2638, 9 verso), drawings on the versos of portraits of the two emperors.
2 Joseph Holland, compiler: An album of *c.*1585 with 1740 watercolours of English arms, including those of benefactors of Westminster Abbey. Viner collection; 215 a.13; 1950–5–20–382.
3 Marcus Gheraerts I: Procession of the Knights of the Garter 1576, etchings. 166 d.1 (Hind, *Engraving in England*, I pp. 104–21).

4 Jodocus Hondius: Talbot's Rose 1589, a record of Knights of the Garter 1486–1589, engraving. (Hind, I p. 177).
5 Sir Peter Lely: 16 drawings of Knights of the Garter. Croft-Murray I pp. 407–16.
6 John Pine: The installation of the Knights Companions of . . . Bath 1725, engraving. 165 c.1; 1870–5–14–2684 to 2724.
7 The arms of the peerage of the reign of George III, engravings. 290* b.1; 1928–1–30–18(1–197).
8 John Elmslie (1813–75): 197 proofs of engravings, chiefly bookplates or of heraldic and topographical subjects. 1912–10–11–11 to 207 (list).

See also the collection of bookplates and the Book Index s.v. Heraldry. Some material from this Department was included in the exhibition British Heraldry held jointly by the British Museum and British Library in 1978, and is reproduced in the catalogue.

Hill, Sir George Francis (1867–1948)

The distinguished authority on medals and Keeper of the Department of Coins and Medals. To assist him in his corpus of Italian medals of the Renaissance he assembled a collection of reproductions, mostly photographs of Italian portraits of the xv–xvic. taken from paintings, frescoes, drawings, coins and medals. This he presented to the Department before his death. It is kept separately as follows: 22 boxes in alphabetical order of sitter, including separate boxes for the Sforza and Medici families, plus a separate box for Popes; unidentified sitters arranged by artist within schools in 12 other boxes, with male and female sitters kept separately. There is a card index in 7 drawers.

Hills, Robert (1769–1844)

A very large collection of his etchings presented by Mrs Garle in 1861 is mounted into ten volumes as follows:

1   Early works, Red deer.
2   Fallow deer, Roe bucks, Goats.
3, 4   Cows, Oxen.
5   Sheep, Swine.
6   Horses.
7   Asses, Mules, Dogs.
8   Cattle in groups.
9, 10   Touched proofs.

See 1861–2–9–364 to 1604 (list).

History

The main series of British and Foreign historical prints has been described above on pp. 46–7, as has the series of Satirical prints on pp. 49–51. There is a separate entry for Naval History. The Book Index has under the heading History references to 263 books of historical prints, divided according to country: America, Belgium, Britain, China, Europe, France, Germany, Greece, Holland, Hungary, India, Italy, Poland, Scandinavia, Spain, Turkey. The purpose of this entry is to refer to other groups of historical prints and drawings kept elsewhere in the collection, which will be found useful for particular enquiries.

British History

1 See playing cards for historical events such as the Spanish Armada, the Popish Plot, the Rump Parliament, Monmouth's Rebellion and the Sacheverell trial (Willshire E 185–195; O'Donoghue E 57–65).
2 See the Grangerised volumes of Clarendon's *History* and Whitelock's *Memorials* (p. 55) for xviic. subjects.
3 See Cheylesmore collection, catalogue

numbers 8475–9933, for the part which covers the lives of Queen Victoria and Prince Albert.

Continental History

4 An album contains etchings and woodcuts by Jean Perrissin and Jacques Tortorel with the general title *Tableaux des guerres, massacres, troubles et autres événements remarquables advenus en France de 1559 à 1570*. See Robert-Dumesnil XI pp. 256–81. 1855–4–14–179 to 223; 1920–4–27–1 to 24 (lists).

5 See s.v. Topography (Netherlands) for the Beudeker Atlas in the Map Room of the British Library, which contains a large number of historical prints.

6 Two volumes in the King's Library of the British Library labelled 'Popish Ceremonies' (C.134 g.10) contain many historical prints of the XVI–XVIIc., not entirely relating to the Catholic Church.

7 An album of prints after Adam François van der Meulen contains views of the victories of Louis XIV. 1869–4–10–1879 to 1980 (list).

8 *Batailles gagnées par le . . . Prince Eugène de Savoye sur les ennemies de la Foi . . . dépeintes et gravées . . . par J. Huchtenberg*, 1725, contains views of events between 1697–1717. 250 a.2; 1891–4–4–9(1–16), no list.

9 Moreau le Jeune, *Figures de l'histoire de France dessinés par Moreau le jeune et gravées sous sa direction, avec le discours de M. l'abbé Garnier*, 1785. Four volumes containing the preparatory drawings with proofs of the plates. 197 c.9–12; 1868–8–22–7903 to 8232.

10 Jean Duplessi-Bertaux, Album of 60 drawings and 60 etchings of scenes from the French Revolution. 197 c.13; 1865–6–10–126 to 185.

The collection contains drawings of historical events by F. Barlow, J. S. Copley, H. Singleton, B. West and R. Westall. See also s.v. War Artists.

Hogarth, William (1697–1764)

The main series of prints by Hogarth has been mounted in nineteen portfolios, with additional items placed in a supplementary portfolio. A copy of Paulson's catalogue has been marked with the locations. Many of Hogarth's satirical prints were included in Stephens's volumes of the catalogue of Personal and Political Satires. A complete checklist of impressions of Hogarth prints in the Department, which gives full references to locations, in the order of Paulson's catalogue has been compiled by Sheila O'Connell; a copy of the unpublished typescript has been bound in the Department library. For Hogarth drawings in the collection, see Binyon II pp. 316–26; the most important more recent acquisitions are the remainder of the surviving original drawings for the Industry and Idleness series. The manuscript of Hogarth's Peregrination of 1732 is at 201 a.6; 1847–3–20–1 to 10. See also exhibitions 1964 and 1983.

Holbein, Hans II (1497/8–1543)

The Holbein drawings in the Department have been catalogued twice; the first time by Binyon (as British drawings), the second as a list by Christopher White in the appendix to Croft-Murray of drawings by foreign artists working in England (pp. 557–71). The famous series of portrait drawings is in the Royal collection at Windsor Castle. They were, however, engraved by Bartolozzi (q.v.) in *Imitations of original Drawings by Hans Holbein in the collection of His Majesty for the Portraits of illustrious persons of the Court of Henry VIII,* 1792. A copy of this publication with impressions in monochrome is in the Department; many impressions printed in colour will be found as extra-illustrations to the Marx Pennant. See also p. 167.

Hollar, Wenceslaus (1607–1677)

The 51 drawings in the collection are catalogued by Croft-Murray pp. 345–68. Very full records of the collection of etchings will be found in the catalogue raisonné of the prints published in 1982 by Richard Pennington. This follows the numbering established in Parthey's catalogue of 1853. 1218 items came from Sir Hans Sloane, and were included in the 1837 inventory as Q 4 to 6. The prints have been mounted into 18 albums according to their subject matter, with additional boxes of supplementary and outsize material. The items extracted for the exhibition held in 1983 have been kept mounted in 5 royal solanders. A finding list gives the locations by Parthey/Pennington numbers. The Department also possesses a copy of the microfiche of the Windsor Hollar collection, which can be used as a quick visual reference for the British Museum collection. See exhibitions 1983.

Huth, Alfred Henry (1850–1910)

A great bibliophile, who in his will allowed the British Museum to select any 50 items it wanted from his library. A catalogue of these was published: *Catalogue of the fifty manuscripts and printed books bequeathed to the British Museum by Alfred H. Huth,* 1912. One of these items (p. 13, number 10) was a Dutch manuscript of the Hours of the Blessed Virgin Mary, which had pasted into it 21 engravings, 17 by the Master of the Berlin Passion, 3 by the Master of the Blumenrahmen and 1 by the Master of the Dutuit Mount of Olives. Originally entered as Add. Mss. 38123, it was transferred to this Department in 1912 (158* b.1; 1912–10–22–1(1 to 21)).

At the Huth sale in 1911, the Department succeeded in acquiring 31 lots. A complete list is given in the register (1911–7–8–1 to 151). Many were single sheet woodcuts or engravings of the xvc. The most important were the Wittenberg Heiligthumsbuch of 1509 with illustrations by Cranach, a set of proofs of illustrations to the Theuerdank, and a volume of woodcuts of the Apocalypse by Matthias Gerung (see Dodgson II p. 213; 158 c.1). Two later acquisitions which came from the Huth collection were a dotted print of St Oswald and St Notburga (Schreiber 2717; 1915–5–8–1) and a set of engravings from a passion series by the Master of the Blumenrahmen copied after the Master of the Berlin Passion (158* b.4; Lehrs 12–23, 25–38; 1915–5–8–2 to 27).

Illuminated Manuscripts

There are a few xvc. manuscripts in the collection that have prints taking the place of illuminations. In addition to the Book of Hours described in the entry for the Huth bequest, and the volume described in the entry for dotted prints, there are four prayer books:

1 Dutch mid-xvc. with 3 drawings, 4 miniatures, 2 engravings (not in Lehrs) and one later woodcut. 158* b.32; 1934–4–3–1(1–10) (Malcolm Add. 83).
2 German, Nuremberg before 1461. With 34 woodcuts, Dodgson A 142(1–34). 158* b.3; 1890–10–13–54(1–35).
3 German, Cologne 1490/1500 Rosenkrantz Marien. With 3 engravings by the Monogrammist PW (Lehrs VII

267.3, 5, 8b). 158* b.2; 1890–1–18–11
to 14.

4 Franco-Flemish, late xvc. Officium
Beatae Mariae Virginis. With the set of
12 engravings of the Passion by Israhel
van Meckenem (Lehrs 142–153). 158
b.1*; 1897–1–3–1 to 12 (Sloane ms
3981).

Ordinary manuscript material has been
described on pp. 66–71.

Illustrated Books

See the remarks in the Introduction
p. 5 on the scope of the collection of
illustrated books, and pp. 53–4 on their
arrangement. There is also a portfolio
containing odd fragments of illustration cut
from books. It includes headpieces,
tailpieces, vignettes, initials and title pages
(for the last two see entries in this Index).
There is a separate series of illustrations
cut from xvc. books. It has been
catalogued by Dodgson I pp. 213–38.
More initial letters, tailpieces and
cartouches will be found in a volume of
woodcuts by Jean-Michel Papillon (161*
a.2*; 1878–7–13–2790 to 4138, no list).

Illustrations to Authors

Henry Spencer Ashbee (1834–1900), the
great bibliophile, bequeathed a large
number of books to the Library, and to the
Department a large collection of loose
prints assembled with a view to using them
to extra-illustrate editions of his favourite
authors. Apart from a few portraits and
topographical prints, most were
illustrations and proofs of illustrations for
numerous books. Most of these have been
placed in the main series under the master
or engraver. But a large number have been
kept in individual portfolios under the
name of the author they were intended to
illustrate. Thus there are portfolios of
illustrations to Cervantes, Dickens (2),
Fielding, Goldsmith, La Fontaine, Le
Sage, Molière (5), Richardson,
Shakespeare, Sterne and Voltaire. See for
the entire bequest 1900–12–31–1 to 6572.
Ashbee's watercolours went to the Victoria
and Albert Museum. See also s.v.
Browning for the Hall Griffin collection.

India

British artists working in India
See the article by Sir William Foster
'British artists in India', *The Walpole
Society*, XIX 1931, pp. 1–88, and its
supplement, XXI 1933, pp. 8–9. The list
of artists on p. 88 has been marked to show
those represented in the collection. Among
them are two works by a draughtsman
working for the East India Company, a
Lieutenant Robert H. Colebrooke:
Seringapatam, and Mausoleum of Hyder
Aly Khan at Laulbaug, both watercolours
of 1792 (Binyon I p. 222). The major
collection, however, is in the India Office
Library, now part of the British Library;
see Mildred Archer, *British Drawings in the
India Office Library*, 1969.

Indian artists employed by the East India Company
Works of this type are not kept in this
Department, but in the Department of
Oriental Antiquities or in the British
Library. For botanical illustrations,
see the chapter on Company artists in
P. H. Hulton and L. Smith, *Flowers in Art
from East and West*, 1979 pp. 45–50.

See also s.v. Topography.

Industrial Imagery

The Department has a marked copy of
F. D. Klingender, *Art and the Industrial
Revolution* 1947, which gives the locations
of the works that are to be found in the
collection. Some further references will be
found in the 1958 exhibition catalogue
Eight Centuries of Landscape . . ., pp. 29–30.
Other works are:

1 Samuel Bough (1822–78): View of a
   manufacturing town, watercolour.
   1886–6–7–9; Binyon I p. 136.
2 J. L. A. T. Géricault (1791–1824): The
   coal waggon, watercolour.
   1968–2–10–28.
3 idem: Coal waggon; Entrance to Adelphi
   Wharf, lithographs. Delteil 36, 40.
4 George Walker, *The Costume of
   Yorkshire*, 1814 (170* a.13;
   1906–10–16–2(1–82)). Plate 3 shows a
   steam engine.
5 Etchings after drawings by T. H. Hair,
   *c.*1842, of collieries and colliers. 1978
   U.662–7 (list).
6 Graham Sutherland (1903–80):
   Sketchbook of tin miners, 1942. 240 a.8;
   1980–10–11–157(1–71).
7 Henry Moore (1898–1986): Five
   drawings of coal miners, being pages
   from a wartime sketchbook.
   1975–1–18–1 to 5.

Institute of Contemporary Arts

The ICA visitors' book covering the period
1950–65 was presented by an anonymous
donor in 1975 (200 b.9;
1975–7–26–4(1–78)). It contains 79 sheets
drawn on by visiting artists, among them (in
order of appearance): Picasso, Sutherland,
Moore, Kokoschka, Steinberg, Topolski,
Dubuffet, Chagall, Tzara, Man Ray,
Guttuso, Masson, Maréchal, Shahn,
Mathieu, Baj, Ernst, Sidney Nolan,
Reinhardt, Miró, Tapiès, Saura.

Irving, Sir Henry (1835–1905)

A bequest of portraits from Richard Henry
Bath in 1933 included six volumes
containing portraits, theatre programmes
and tickets, press cuttings, menus,
invitations and other items relating to the
famous actor. 209* b.13–18;
1933–10–14–642 to 644 (no list).

Jones, Inigo (1573–1652)

There is a portfolio containing 23 drawings
from the workshop of Inigo Jones
(1848–8–5–1 to 23). Of these 8 are
thought to be by Jones himself, and have
been catalogued by Croft-Murray as such
(I pp. 377–81, nos 11–18): 5 are elevations
and plans for Whitehall Palace, while 3 are
plans for a large ideal palace. In addition,
there are 10 other drawings attributed to
him in the collection (Croft-Murray nos
1–10). The masque designs by him are all
in the possession of the Dukes of
Devonshire at Chatsworth.

Kaye, the Very Rev. Sir Richard

In 1810 he bequeathed to the British
Museum twelve volumes of drawings made
for him by Samuel Hieronymus Grimm
(1733–94) of English antiquities and
topography. These were originally placed
in the Print Room, and were included in
the 1837 inventory under the Qq
shelfmark. They were still in the
Department when they were catalogued in
the 1844 *Catalogue of the Manuscript Maps,
Charts and Plans, and of the Topographical
Drawings in the British Museum*, but in the
following year they were transferred to the
Department of Manuscripts as Add. Mss.
15537–15548, where they remain.

Kelmscott Press

The collection includes a number of items relating to the Kelmscott Press:

1 422 woodblocks cut by W. H. Hooper (1834–1912) from designs by William Morris, Sir Edward Burne-Jones and Walter Crane to illustrate the edition of Chaucer and other works printed at the Press. 1897–11–17–35 to 132; 1898–3–5–1 to 4; 1897–12–28–1 to 323. Presented by the executors of William Morris.
2 Proofs of illustrations to the Kelmscott Chaucer designed by Burne-Jones and cut by W. H. Hooper in 1896. 248 a.3; 1912–6–12–308 to 392.
3 Proofs on vellum of 5 illustrations to A Dream of John Ball, and A King's Lesson by Morris, designed by Burne-Jones and cut by Hooper. 247* a.9; 1905–10–12–9 to 13.
4 46 proofs of woodcut initials and ornaments designed by Morris for the Kelmscott Press. 248 a.4; 1905–10–12–14 to 46.
5 See also the Index of Artists under Hooper for a large collection of miscellaneous work.

Kirkall, Elisha (c.1682–1742)

An album from the Sloane collection contains a large number of his mixed-media chiaroscuro prints and mezzotints printed in colours. It includes copies of 6 plates of Hogarth's Harlot's Progress, 3 coloured engravings of Augustus's Bath, mezzotints after Jacob van Huysum for the Catalogus Plantarum published by a Society of Gardeners, and a receipt for one guinea to Sir Hans Sloane for 12 prints. See X 6.87–143 (list) and the article by Edward Hodnett in the Book Collector of 1976 on his white-line relief engravings.

Knight, Richard Payne (1751–1824)

On Payne Knight's life and works, see The Arrogant Connoisseur, edited by Michael Clarke and Nicholas Penny in 1982. His bequest enriched many departments of the British Museum. This Department was left 1144 drawings, including no less than 273 by Claude. They were inventoried as Oo 1 to 11, and Pp 1 to 5. A manuscript catalogue was drawn up by Carpenter in 1845 before most of the albums were broken up. The arrangement was as follows: Oo 1 John Hamilton Mortimer; 2 Gainsborough; 3–4 Various; 5 English; 6–8 Claude; 9–11 Dutch and Flemish; Pp 1–5 all Italian. The most famous portrait of him is that by Sir Thomas Lawrence, now in the Whitworth Art Gallery. A copy of this by Mrs M. S. Carpenter is hanging in the Trustees' board room together with a bust of him by John Bacon.

Landells, Ebenezer (1808–1860)

A volume contains proofs of woodcuts by Landells and others for various publications of the period 1842–3, including Punch, The Old Curiosity Shop, Barnaby Rudge and others, 248 b.3*; 1857–2–17–167 (no list).

Lawrence, Sir Thomas (1769–1830)

There are 26 drawings of the royal size. The main series of prints after his paintings are arranged in six albums, in alphabetical order of sitter, in the order royalty, male, groups and ladies. In addition, there are two outsize albums; to these there is a manuscript catalogue. Kept separately are another album with a set of reproductions of his drawings presented by their engraver F. C. Lewis in 1836, 1890–12–9 (24 to 47) list, and a volume published by Henry Graves of *Engravings from the choicest works of Sir Thomas Lawrence* containing mezzotints by a number of engravers (1911–5–17–26(1–48)).

The Department failed to purchase Lawrence's superb collection of old master drawings in 1838 for £18,000 (see Popham's Handbook, pp. 122,130–1). But three later groups of acquisitions consisted almost entirely of items from his collection. Two were from the sales of the dealer Samuel Woodburn who was responsible for dispersing the collection: one in June 1854 (see 1854–6–28–1 to 117), the other in June 1860 (see 1860–6–16–1 to 139). For the third, see s.v. Fenwick. See also pp. 69, 71.

Le Moyne de Morgues, Jacques
(*c*.1533–1588)

A French draughtsman who accompanied Laudonnière's expedition to Florida in 1564–6, and later settled in England. His chief surviving works are two albums of flower drawings, one in the Victoria and Albert Museum and the other in the British Museum (1962–7–14–1(1–51) now broken up and mounted royal, the empty original binding being placed at 197 d.15), and a book with hand-coloured woodcuts of animals, birds, fruit, flowers, etc. entitled *La Clef des Champs*, London 1586 (162 a.25; 1952–5–22–1(1 to 48)). See Paul Hulton and others, *The Work of Jacques Le Moyne de Morgues, a Huguenot Artist in France, Florida and England*, two vols 1977, which includes a complete catalogue of his work.

Leonardo da Vinci (1452–1519)

For the 34 drawings by or after Leonardo in the collection, see Popham and Pouncey nos 95–128. For the engravings of the school of Leonardo, see A. M. Hind, *Early Italian Engraving*, 1948, pp. 83–95. The Departmental library also possesses a number of facsimiles of Leonardo manuscripts and drawings, besides the individual items placed in the general series of reproductions of drawings. In the following list the series published by the Reale Commissione Vinciana is abbreviated R CV:

1 Institut de France, Mss A to M, and Ashburnham Mss 2037,8: 270 b.9–14 (Éditions Ravaisson-Mollien); also Mss A, B only 186 a.11, 13a (RCV 1936,41).

2 Windsor, Anatomical Mss A, B: 270 a.15–16 (ed. Sabachnikoff 1898, 1901).

3 Windsor, Quaderni d'Anatomia (Ms C): 186 a.1–6 (ed. Vangenstein et alii 1911–16).

4 British Library, Arundel Ms 263: 186 a.7–10 (RCV 1923–30); and 270 a.10–13 (ed. Rouvèyre 1901).

5 Milan Ambrosian Library, Codex Atlanticus: 270 c.1–9 (ed. R. Accademia dei Lincei 1894–1904).

6 Turin Biblioteca, Flight of Birds Ms: 186 a.14 (RCV 1926) and 270 a.14 (ed. Sabachnikoff 1893).

7 Victoria and Albert Museum, Forster Mss: 270 a.1–3 (ed. Rouvèyre 1901) and 186 b.1–3 (RCV 1930–6).

8 Leicester (now Hammer) Ms: 270 b.15 (ed. Calvi 1909).

9 Milan Castello Sforzesco, Codex Trivulzianus: 270 b.1 (ed Beltrami 1891).

10 Drawings in various collections: 186 c.1–7 (RCV 1928–52).

11 Windsor, Geographical portfolio: 186 c.8 (RCV 1941).

12 Drawings in the Venice Accademia: 186 c.9 (ed. Heydenreich 1949).

13 Drawings at Windsor: 270 a.4–9 and 270 b.2–8 (ed. Rouvèyre 1901).

Letters and Alphabets

A general portfolio of fragments taken from illustrated books includes a number of initial letters. Among them is a group purchased from Daniell (1870–10–8–1254 to 1317). Besides these there are:

1 A collection of engraved and woodcut letters mounted into four volumes, arranged by country of origin: Italian; French; German, Bohemian, Austrian; Swiss, Dutch, English, Icelandic. 244 a.4–7. This is probably the collection formed by Michael Caspari; 1881–11–12–378 to 1317.

2 Another similar collection, but much less methodical, being more decoratively arranged and giving no indication of the source of the letters; the manuscript title-page runs 'Miscellaneous matters relative to printing for collecting specimens of blooming letters'. It contains 5014 items, and was purchased in four lots at the Wellesley sale in 1866. 250 b.2; 1866–12–8–633 to 636.

3 An alphabet dated 1464 containing letters composed of human figures was presented by Sir George Beaumont in the early 1820s (inventory B10) and published by Campbell Dodgson in 1899, *A Grotesque Alphabet of 1464*. This series lacks the letter S, and has only fragments of A, T, V. It was mounted and described as A 131 in Dodgson's 1903 catalogue of woodcuts. In 1910 another complete series was discovered,

and later presented to the Department by C. W. Dyson Perrins. This volume also contains a second early alphabet with interlace characters. 36 a.6; 1947–7–24–1 to 19.

4 Other early woodcut alphabets can be found under the heading Alphabets in the Book Index; the Holbein alphabets are not kept in book form but as single prints.

5 An album of woodcuts by J. M. Papillon (1712–60) contains many decorated letters. 161* b.2*; 1878–7–13–3352 to 3806 (list).

6 A 'Hierogliphisch Alphabeth' produced in Haarlem in 1751 is contained in the Dirk de Bray album, no.556 (see s.v. Merchants' Marks).

A collection formed by Joseph Ames is in the British Library, 463 h.11.

Lloyd, Robert Wylie (1868–1958)

Chairman of Christie's, the auctioneers, and an enthusiastic Alpine climber. He bequeathed to the Museum his collections of Japanese swords, Chinese lacquer and of watercolours and Swiss prints of costume and Alpine views. By the terms of the will no items may be lent. His bequest was registered as 1958–7–12–318 to 3149 and divides as follows:

318–472 18 Continental and 137 British drawings and watercolours, including 16 by John 'Warwick' Smith and 61 by J. M. W. Turner. By the terms of the bequest the watercolours are kept separately from the rest of the Department's collection in 8 royal, 2 imperial and 1 antiquarian box. The original stipulation, before the construction of the new exhibition gallery, was that they might only be exhibited to the public for two weeks in February, this being the month in which natural light is at its weakest.

473–2974 Swiss prints, mostly Alpine views, but with many sets of costumes of Swiss cantons, arranged alphabetically by artist. There are also a few drawings, mostly of costume but with a special group by Gottfried Mind, the 'Raphael of cats'. The names are entered in the Index of Artists, and there is a finding list to the contents of the boxes: 44 royal and imperial (with continuous numbering), 6 atlas and 1 antiquarian. By the terms of the bequest the collection has to be kept in the same cabinets as Lloyd himself used.

2975–3149 Books of prints of Swiss costume and views. These are all housed in cases 266*, 267* and 268*. All can be found through the Book Index. There is also a handlist arranged by author/engraver.

See exhibitions 1959, 1963, 1966, 1969.

Loans

The earliest records of items being lent from the collection are in the late XIXc. By 1932 such loans had been placed on a regular footing, and the Trustees published a *List of Duplicate Prints available for loan from the Department of Prints and Drawings with regulations for their use*. Loans were limited to duplicate objects, and selections of prints were circulated to provincial museums and galleries. Such circulating exhibitions lapsed in the Second World War, and were not revived; but some of the items in the duplicate collection were lent between the late 1950s and about 1970 to the Circulation Department of the Victoria and Albert Museum.

A special case was the Turner Bequest, which was never legally part of the Department's collection. Loans were made regularly from the 1930s to provincial museums and galleries, and occasionally under British Council auspices abroad. After 1945 loans of items from the main collection that were not duplicates were allowed to other institutions in the United Kingdom, but it was not until the British Museum Act of 1963 that the Trustees were empowered to lend items abroad from any part of the collection. In 1985 the Department lent to 33 centres in the United Kingdom, and 26 abroad. Circulating exhibitions under the Museum's own auspices were restarted in 1981, when a selection from the 1978 exhibition 'From Manet to Toulouse-Lautrec' was toured to four centres in the United Kingdom.

London

The main collection of London topography is the Crace collection and the so-called Crace supplement (q.v.). Important additional material is contained in the Grangerised editions of Pennant compiled by Crowle and Marx (see pp. 55, 58–9), in the National Photographic Record (q.v.) and in Sir Ambrose Heal's research material (see s.v. Trade Cards). See also prints by Hollar and drawings by Archer and Scharf (qq.v.), The Book Index gives references to 48 books of prints: on this see also the invaluable listings and indices in Bernard Adams, *London Illustrated 1604–1851*, 1983. There is a blue slip index to the contents of the Crace collection, Crace supplement and some of the more obvious books of prints (the Pennants have their own indices); it is arranged both by topography and by artist/engraver. Other material can be traced through the blue slip index to the British drawings.

In 1927 the Department was bequeathed 29 volumes of photographs, maps, portraits, prints, cuttings, etc. formed by George Potter of the topography of North London, with special reference to Hampstead and Highgate. There is a typed index volume. 1927–11–26–1 (no list).

Most of the panoramic views of London are to be found in the Crace collection, volumes I, II, III and XXXVI, and in the Crowle Pennant XIII (kept in a separate portfolio). Among the most notable long views in the Department are:

1   Claes Jansz. Visscher, Long view from the south 1616, engraving. Crace I 16; 1880–11–13–1124(1–4). Another impression is in the Map Room of the British Library (C 5 a.6); it also possesses a crudely coloured impression of an early copy of the Visscher view – the so-called 'Pepys' version (162.0.1).
2   Wenceslaus Hollar, Long view from Bankside 1647, etching. Two impressions, one mounted in six pieces (1880–11–13–1126), the other joined together into a continuous strip (Crowle Pennant XIII 25).
3   Robert Barker, London from Blackfriars Bridge 1792, aquatint. 1880–11–13–1200 (Crace III 92).

The following are kept with other large rolled works:

4   H. Vizetelly, View of London c.1844, wood-engraving. 1942–7–2–1.
5   H. Vizetelly, View of the north bank of the Thames c.1844, wood-engraving. 1940–1–10–3.
6   Edwin Edwards, London from Greenwich Observatory, etching. 1889–5–8–296.
7   Edmund Hort New, View of the city and port of London from the south bank 1917, pencil. 1924–5–10–1 (in three sections).
8   Adrian Berrington, Waterloo Bridge, etching. 1925–10–13–1.

Among the drawings of London in the collection will be found Thomas Girtin's watercolours of 1797–8 for a panorama (Binyon 31–6), and Charles François Daubigny's chalk drawing of the construction of the Thames Embankment in 1866 (1908–6–16–47). See also a sketchbook of drawings made during the summer of 1810 in north London and surrounds by J. C. Nattes (198* a.4; 1898–10–14–1(1–56), Binyon 5).

There are also fine collections of topographical views of London to be found in the Museum of London, the Guildhall Library, the Westminster Public Library (and other local authority archives), and the Yale Center for British Art in New Haven.

Lucas Collection

In 1917 Baroness Lucas and Dingwell gave a group of 4651 prints in memory of her brother who had been killed in action in 1916. They came from the collection at Wrest Park, Bedfordshire, which had been begun by Henry Grey, Duke of Kent (d.1741), but largely formed by Thomas Philip, 2nd Earl de Grey (1781–1859). There is a complete list in the register (1917–12–8–1 to 4651), which is arranged by school and type: reproductive prints, portraits, historical, costume and topographical. A typescript volume in the Departmental library supplies an index to masters and engravers (Cc 7.20). Each print has been given a special Lucas stamp (Lugt 1696). The rest of the collection was sold at auction in 1918–19.

Lucas, David (1802–1881)

The main collection of the mezzotints by Lucas after Constable is kept unmounted in a large box in the order of the Wedmore catalogue. From this a small number was selected for mounting in the 1950s, and is now kept in three royal solanders. Apart from these, a fine group of impressions will be found in an extra-illustrated copy of Leslie's *Memoirs of the life of John Constable*, 1843 (167 c.13), while the Department library also contains a set of the English Landscape Scenery in its original parts presented to Peter De Wint (166 d.32; 1913–5–24–326(1–22)). See Andrew Wilton, *Constable's 'English Landscape Scenery'*, 1979.

Lucas, Richard Cockle
(1800–1883)

There are two volumes containing prints, drawings and photographs of the work of Lucas, who is better known as the maker of a statue Flora, which after his death was acquired by the Berlin Museum as a work by Leonardo da Vinci. The first volume contains etchings, mostly landscape, and a portrait photograph of the artist (1859–8–6–946 to 1218, no list). The second contains 654 drawings, etchings and photographs inscribed on the cover 'My Monument'. Among them are studies of leaves, portraits and photographs of his sculpture with manuscript notes (1919–8–5–1).

Malcolm, John (1805–1893)

His great collection of Old Master drawings was formed on the advice of Sir John Charles Robinson, who compiled the catalogue: *Descriptive Catalogue of drawings by the old masters forming the collection of John Malcolm of Poltalloch*, 1869 (2nd edition 1876). The entire collection was purchased from his son, Colonel John Wingfield Malcolm, for £25,000 and registered as 1895–9–15–1 to 1448. The first 436 items are prints, the rest drawings entered in the

order of Robinson's catalogue. The Department copy of the catalogue has been marked with the register numbers. A number of the prints have been sold or exchanged as duplicates. The items acquired with the proceeds have been allocated in addition to their register numbers a so-called 'Malcolm addition' number in order to record their origin. On Malcolm see Lugt 1489. See also exhibitions 1894.

Maps

The Department has never collected maps, and many that were here have been transferred in the past to the main national collection which is that in the British Library. Manuscript maps are in the Department of Manuscripts, while printed maps are in the Map Room. See the *Catalogue of the manuscript maps, charts and plans and of the topographical drawings* [in the British Library], 3 vols, 1844–61; and the *Catalogue of printed maps, charts and plans* [in the British Library], 15 vols, 1967 (complete to end of 1964; a supplement for the years 1965–74 was published in 1978). There are also a few important maps in the Department, collected partly by accident and partly as examples of engraving.

Bound volumes

1 Claudius Ptolomy, *Cosmographia*, Bologna 1462 [i.e. 1477]. 163 b.2; 1845–8–25–492 to 517.
2 Francesco Berlinghieri, *Geographia*, Florence? 1481 [1482]. 163 b.1; 1845–8–25–552 to 582 (no list).
3 Claudius Ptolomy, *Cosmographia*, Rome 1508. 163 b.3; 1845–8–25–518 to 551.
4 Christopher Saxton, *Atlas of England and Wales* (with frontispiece portrait of Elizabeth I). 172 d.4; 1888–12–21–9(1 to 38).

5 Nicolas de Fer, *L'Atlas curieux ou le monde représenté dans les cartes générales et particulières*, Paris 1705. 174* a.1 6–17; 1861–10–12–982 to 1167.

6 Popple's map of North America, showing the British, French and Spanish settlements. 243 a.26(2); 1861–5–18–328. The same album also has bound in three other items: Covens and Mortier's map of the seat of war in Bavaria, in four sheets; Foster's map of the seat of war in the West Indies 1739; and a plan of the harbour, town and forts of Porto Bello, by Toms after Lieut. P. Durell, 1739.

7 Richard Blome, *England exactly described or a guide to travellers in a complete set of the counties of England*, London 1715. 172 a.26; 1864–11–14–1 to 32.

Single sheets

1 A large number will be found bound into the extra-illustrated volumes of Clarendon, Whitelocke and the Crowle and Marx Pennants (pp. 55, 58–9). See their individual indices. Particularly noteworthy are the contents of Crowle volume XIII, which include sixteen large-scale maps of London from the XVI–XVIIIC.

2 The section of maps in the Crace collection was transferred to the Map Room in 1933. But there are some others in the Crace supplement, kept in the order of the Crace catalogue.

3 A unique XVIC. woodcut map of the world entitled *Tuto il Mondo Tereno* by Giovanni Andrea Vavassore (called Guadagnino) is pasted together with a map of Italy, also by Vavassore, to the back of the woodcut by Matteo Pagani of the procession of the Doge. 1860–4–14–167.

4 Hans Holbein II (attrib.), *World Map*, woodcut, Basle 1532. 1895–1–22–1113 (Passavant III pp. 382–3).

5 Albrecht Dürer, Terrestial and Celestial Globes, woodcuts 1515. Dodgson I nos 126–8.

6 Impressions of most of Wenceslas Hollar's maps will be found, including the unique impression of the West Central district of London (Pennington 1002; 1982 U.2243).

7 Series of nine coloured pocket maps in illustrated cardboard cases engraved by Matthias Seutter; they include Great Britain, Italy, France, etc. 175* c.2; 1890–3–14–28 to 36 (list).

8 A zoological map of the world, engraved by Joseph Marianus after E. A. W. Zimmermann. 1914–5–20–677.

9 The Schreiber collection of fans includes a map of England (unmounted nos 193–4), and a map of Warwickshire (mounted no.74).

10 The collection of trade cards contains as section 82 the cards of map and chart sellers.

11 There are many sets of geographical playing cards. See Schreiber E44–51, 139–42, G267, 353, I27–31, 105–8, F123–7,173–4, D11–13, R3, S150 and Willshire F74–5, E178–9. The only complete set of the most famous English geographical cards, signed WB of 1590, is placed as Willshire 178B (1938–7–9–57; see Hind I p. 182).

Martin, Henry W.

In 1861 gave a large number of French satires, costume and history prints, including book illustrations by Gavarni. All have been given a special Martin stamp (Lugt 1799). 1861–10–12–1 to 2219 (list: 1–873 are single sheet prints, the remainder books of prints).

Mary, Queen of Scots
(1542–1587)

A collection of 1331 items assembled by
Joseph Cecil of Northampton was
purchased from his widow in 1885
(1885–5–9–52 to 1382, no list). It is now
mounted into five albums arranged as
follows:

1, 2 Portraits of her and her connections,
      including facsimiles of the warrant for
      her execution (I pp. 16,22) and prints
      of her execution (II p. 46).
3, 4 Scottish and English topography
      related to her life.
5   Foreign topography related to her life.

An early drawing of her execution is in
the Department of Manuscripts of the
British Library (Add. Mss 48027).

Medical Illustrations

There is no separate collection, although
many relevant items are to be found. Much
better collections exist in the Wellcome
Institute library in London, in the Science
Museum, and in the Ars Medica collection
in the Philadelphia Museum of Art (from
which various catalogues have been
published). Satirical prints can be traced
through the heading Medicine in the
subject index to the George catalogue.
Portrayals of London hospitals can be
found through the various indices listed in
the entry for London. Portrait prints have
been catalogued by Renate Burgess,
*Portraits of Doctors and Scientists in the
Wellcome Institute*, 1973. Many of these are
also in the Department's collection.
Some individual examples are listed:

1 A xvic. Italian manuscript from the
  Sloane collection (Ms 5281), containing
  drawings of surgical operations and

medicinal herbs. 197* d.2;
1928–3–10–94(1–205).
2 *Ein nützlich Regiment der Gesundtheyt*,
  1521, containing woodcuts by Hans
  Weiditz, including the treatment of
  abscesses and venesection. 158* a.3;
  1870–10–8–2100 to 2105.
3 *Caii Plinii Secundi des Weitberumbten
  Hochgelehrten alten Philosophi . . . Bücher
  und Schriften von Natur* 1584, containing
  on pp. 70–8 illustrations by Jost Amman
  of medical treatment and surgery. 159
  a.9; 1870–10–8–1941(1–13).
4 Abraham Bosse, Phlebotomy, etching
  1635. 1868–6–12–83; Duplessis 1391.
5 Barbara Hepworth, A theatre sister,
  drawn during an operation for the
  fenestration of the ear, 1948.
  1972–9–16–1.
6 Ceri Richards, sketchbook drawn in
  Westminster Hospital in 1952. 199 a.18;
  1973–4–14–29(1–75).

See also s.v. Anatomy.

Merchants' Marks

An xviiic. album labelled 'Dirk de Bray
woodcuts' contains, besides a number of
woodcuts by de Bray (all marked off in
Blokhuyzen's catalogue), a large number of
anonymous Dutch woodcuts which include
many Merchants' marks, mostly from
Haarlem and Amsterdam, printed in
Dutch, French and English. They are
remarkable for the variety of subjects
portrayed, such as initial letters (557–65),
trades and pastimes (400–12), flowers and
fruit (205–26, 586–92), trees (182–201),
cats and dogs (568–71) and birds, animals,
fishes and insects (27–92, 413–14, 461–9,
599–609). 1976 U.117–810.

Michelangelo Buonarroti
(1475–1564)

The Department's collection of drawings
by Michelangelo has been catalogued by
Johannes Wilde, *Michelangelo and his
Studio*, 1953. Numbers 1–84 are drawings
by him, 85–93 copies from his drawings,
94–8 copies from his frescoes, and 99–104
copies from his sculptures. The only later
addition is a sheet of studies for figures in
the fresco of the Last Judgement, accepted
from HM Treasury in lieu of Capital
Transfer Tax from the estate of the 4th
Lord Methuen and allocated to the British
Museum in accordance with his wishes
(1980–10–11–46). The drawing known as
'Epiphania' is kept on permanent display
(Wilde 75; 1895–9–15–518*). Prints after
Michelangelo are kept in one portfolio. See
also exhibitions 1953, 1964, 1975, 1986.

Military

Unlike naval history, there is no separate
series of prints of military events. Those
that are in the collection are kept in the
main history series, or under the names of
the artist or engraver. The Crookshank
collection (q.v.) used to be kept in the
Department but was transferred to the
National Army Museum in 1971. About
twenty books will be found under the
heading Military in the Book Index of the
Departmental library; they cover scenes
from British, French and German history.

The main series of prints of military
costume is kept in two boxes of the
Authorities for Artists series. The British
box contains some 112 lithographs,
photographs and other reproductions of
army and navy costumes. The Foreign box
has some 190 sheets, mostly colour
lithographs, including:

AUSTRIA 19, of which 11 are of costumes
of 1849 (1899–4–6–1 to 11, list).
FRANCE 110, including uniforms by
F. H. Lalaisse (1925–4–9–1 to 41, list),
F. Sicard's *Histoire des Institutions Militaires
des Français*, 1834 (1939–6–5–12 to 144),
and battle scenes by N. Cochin of *c.* 1650
(X 4.305–12). There are also prints of
military subjects by Callot and Stefano
della Bella (being duplicates of impressions
in the engraver series).
GERMANY 46 prints of Prussian military
uniform by L. Burger (1926–7–28–1 to
46).

The rest are of Mexican, Portuguese,
Spanish and Russian costumes.

Other prints of military costume can be
traced through the Book Index, in which
39 titles are described under the heading
Costume, Military. They cover costume of
Austria, Bengal, Eastern Europe, France,
Germany, Great Britain, Hungary, Poland,
Russia and Spain. *The Cloathing Book* of
1742 is not in the Department, but is in the
British Library. See also the *Index to
Military Costume Prints 1500–1914*,
published by the Army Museums' Ogilby
Trust in 1972. A collection of books of
military costume brought back from the
Hanover Military Library after 1945 was
for many years kept in the Department and
registered in 1960 (1960–4–9–1 to 112); it
was transferred to the National Army
Museum in 1977.

Individual items of interest are:

1 Thomas Cockson: Drill postures 1636,
   engraving. Y 5–215 (Hind I p. 255).
2 K. Cofield: Cannon taken at Quebec
   1760, indian ink. 1873–5–10–1736
   (Binyon I p. 222).
3 After Edward Dayes: Foot Guards and
   Line 1792–3, set of coloured aquatints.
   1859–7–9–116 to 130 (list).

4 Sir John Steele: Design for a memorial plaque to officers, men, women and children of the 78th Highland Regiment who died from malaria in India 1845–6, drawing. 1976–1–31–5.

5 G. Rottmann: Uniforms of the Prussian Army, late xviiic., bodycolour. 1917–12–8–4140. Also an album of drawings of similar subject-matter: 199* a.17.

6 P. J. de Loutherbourg: A collection of sketches mounted in an album, including many of naval and military costume. 201 c.5; 1868–3–28–1 to 299 (Binyon III pp. 69–77).

See also drawings by Paul Sandby for items of military interest drawn in Scotland; and drawings and prints by and after Thomas Rowlandson for military personnel, costume and scenes.

Millar, Eric George
(1887–1966)

Keeper of the Department of Manuscripts 1944–7. In 1967 he bequeathed some important manuscripts to the Library, and some drawings to this Department (1967–10–14–34 to 207, list). Of items 34 to 161, most were made for illustration, and included works by Arthur Rackham, Edmund Dulac and artists working for *Punch*. Items 162 to 207 were drawings by John Downman (q.v.). See the commemorative volume of the *British Museum Quarterly* (XXXIII 1–2), published in 1968 to coincide with an exhibition held in the Department's galleries in July–September 1968, which includes an article by Andrew Wilton on the drawings (pp. 85–9).

Miniatures

Forty-two portrait miniatures that used to be in the collection were transferred to the Victoria and Albert Museum and the National Portrait Gallery in 1938–9. A complete list of these is kept in a bound volume placed with the Department registers. The only British miniatures now in the collection are:

1 William Blake: Three portraits of the Butts family (Mr and Mrs Thomas Butts, and their son, also called Thomas). 1942–10–10–4 to 6.

2 Bernard Lens iii: Four portraits of Indian Chiefs who visited England in 1710. 1846–12–23–1 to 4. Also larger versions of three of these as 1840–12–12–33 to 35.

3 John Smart: Abdul Khalick and Mooiz Ud Din, sons of Tippoo, 1794. 1888–3–9–4, 5.

In addition, there are several continental works which are miniature-like in format or technique:

4 Jacob de Gheyn ii: A lady on her death-bed with a man beside her. 1865–6–10–1311; Popham 3.

5 Hendrik Goltzius: Portrait of an artist (1895–9–15–1020), and Self-portrait (1854–11–13–230). Popham 10, 12.

6 Adriaen van de Venne: Album containing scenes from everyday life. Case 196a; 1978–6–24–42(1–102). A monograph on this album by Martin Royalton-Kisch is forthcoming.

Mitchell, William (?–1908)

A wealthy Australian sheep farmer, who settled in London and from *c.*1860 began collecting prints and drawings. He was a close friend of John Malcolm. His collection of drawings was sold in Frankfurt in 1890, but he gave his superb collection of early woodcuts in 1895 to the Museum, where it was registered as 1895–1–22–1 to 1290. In 1904 he added his early illustrated books (1904–2–6–1 to 170). See Lugt 2638.

Modern Graphic Art Fund

This fund was created by the Trustees in 1967 in view of the perceived weakness of the modern collection, specifically to purchase xxc. works of art on paper. Originally it consisted of £2000 contributed equally by the Trustees of the British Museum and (between 1967–71) the C. G. and S. L. Bernstein Trust Funds. In the years between 1970–9 the Trustees raised the funding to £3000 a year. Since 1979 very considerable increases have been granted. The introduction to the catalogue of the exhibition of new acquisitions held in 1972 offers an account of the new policy and its historical background.

Moll, Carl Ehrenbert, Baron (1760–1838)

A physician by training, and a prominent figure in Bavarian politics. In 1808 he was president of the government in Munich. In 1818 he presented to the British Museum 10,977 engraved portraits of foreigners, mostly Germans. The inventory was compiled by Edward Carpenter in two volumes, and has the numbers Bb 1–17. The prints have now been distributed among the portrait collection, but are identifiable from the stamp placed on them (Lugt 1818).

Monotypes

The collection includes monotypes by the following artists:

1 Giovanni Benedetto Castiglione (1609–65): Theseus finding the arms of his father, c.1645. 1985–12–14–34.
2 William Blake (1757–1827): The lazar house of Milton 1795. 1885–5–9–1616.
3 Ascribed to Samuel Palmer (1805–81): Landscape with ploughman. 1929–4–16–7.
4 James Nasmyth (1808–90): nine prints, mostly marines and one view of Stonehenge dated 1876–7. 1928–10–16–21 to 27; 1930–10–31–1; 1960–6–20–1.
5 Edgar Degas (1834–1917): Five prints (Janis 135, 235, 271, 295, 302).
6 Camille Pissarro (1831–1903): Baigneuse. 1978–10–7–27.
7 Paul Gauguin (1848–1903): Studies with self-portrait, 1894 (1949–4–11–3675); Two Marquesans, c.1902 (1968–2–10–31). Field 19, 86.
8 Sir Hubert von Herkomer (1849–1914): 1905–3–27–1 to 6.
9 Walter Sickert (1860–1942): Le Mont de Neuville c.1899. 1981–3–28–5.

There are also xxc. monotypes by Prunella Clough, Robert Colquhoun, Benjamin Creme, Terry Frost, W. S. Graham, Jacob Kainen, Peter Lanyon, Joseph Solman and F. E. McWilliam.

Moore, Henry (1898–1986)

The collection contains 22 mounted drawings (15 royal, 6 imperial and 1 atlas). A few were purchased, but most were presented either by the artist himself or by Lord Clark. In addition Lady Clark bequeathed in 1977 the so-called Shelter sketchbook drawn in autumn 1940 (a second shelter sketchbook belongs to Irina Moore). The pages of this have now been individually mounted in 4 royal solanders (1977–4–2–13[1–67]). There is also a drawing in the visitors' book of the Institute of Contemporary Arts (q.v.).

A complete set of Moore's collographs of the early 1950s, plus working proofs, was presented by Mr and Mrs Bernhard Baer, former directors of Ganymed (1985–5–4–21 to 29; the rest of their gift, mostly of Ganymed material, is registered as 1985–5–4–30 to 84). The Department also possesses three of Moore's illustrated portfolios:

1 Goethe Prométhée, translated by André Gide, 1950. With 8 lithographs. 160 d.24; 1952–6–10–1(1–8).
2 Elephant Skull, 1970. With 28 etchings. Case 262; 1971–4–3–7(1–33).
3 Selections from poems by Auden, 1974. With 21 lithographs. Case 289; 1974–7–20–46.

The last formed the subject for an exhibition organised by Vera Russell and held in the Department's galleries in 1974 under the title Auden poems/Moore lithographs. An illustrated catalogue of 21 pages was published.

Morghen, Raphael (1758–1833)

In 1843 the Department acquired from Colnaghi's the large collection of Morghen's engravings formed by his friend, Signor Paruli of Venice. It came arranged in twelve portfolios of varying size, to which have been added other impressions acquired since. All are reproductive prints; included are a number of portraits and topographical views. There is a manuscript inventory in the library at Nn 1.1–17. 1843–5–13–591 to 1242 (list).

Morin, Jean (c.1590–1650)

Shortly before his death, Mr Osbert Barnard, director of the firm of print dealers Messrs Craddock and Barnard, gave the Department his outstanding collection of the etchings of Jean Morin. The gift came in two parts which were registered separately: the religious and landscape subjects (1985–1–19–40 to 64), and the portraits (1985–5–4–85 to 205). A large part of the gift was exhibited at the end of 1986 (no catalogue). The Department also possesses an early XVIIIc. album with the arms of the Vavasor family of Haslewood on the binding, which contains 50 of Morin's portrait etchings (208* a.7; 1887–8–1–1 to 50).

Mosmann, Nikolaus (1729–1787)

The Department possesses 291 drawings made by Mosmann in Rome after frescoes by Guido Reni and other artists for the Earl of Exeter. They are arranged in seven volumes, and described in a manuscript catalogue at Z 4.21. Inventory T 2–5 (list).

Music

There is no separate collection of items of musical interest, but there is an excellent guide to the musical resources of the British Library and the various departments of the British Museum compiled by A. Hyatt King, A Wealth of Music, 1983. Pages 137–54 are devoted to this Department, and extract the relevant playing cards, fans, and so on, as well as listing alphabetically under the names of artists and engravers items kept in the main series. This entry can therefore confine itself to mentioning the existence of a separate card index of engraved portraits of musicians, many of which will be found in the O'Donoghue and Hake catalogue; for a few drawn portraits, see nos 260–78 in the 1974 exhibition catalogue of *Portrait Drawings*. The collection of trade cards includes a special section (88) devoted to teachers of music and to performers and sellers of musical instruments. The last box of the Authorities for Artists has a section devoted to musical instruments.

A few outstanding items are:

1 A rehearsal of an oratorio (often wrongly called 'Handel conducting an oratorio'). Anonymous English etching *c*.1735. 1856–7–12–210.
2 Louis Carmontelle: Mozart at the harpsichord with his father and sister, watercolour. On loan from the National Gallery (NG 2911; 1972 U.653).
3 Thomas Gainsborough: A music party, red chalk. 1889–7–24–371.
4 After Hans Holbein: A band of wind players on a balcony, chalk. 1852–5–19–2 (Binyon 15).
5 Marcellus Laroon III: A concert in Montagu House, pencil. 1959–7–11–2.
6 Esaias van de Velde, attrib: Concert with singers and instruments, red chalk. Sloane 5226–59.
7 Hilda Wiener (d.1940): Album of pencil portraits of musicians, drawn at concerts in Brussels in the 1930s; each drawing is accompanied by the programme of the concert and is autographed by the musicians, among them Stravinsky, Milhaud, Mascagni, Lotte Lehmann, Respighi and Rachmaninov. 210 b.14; 1951–11–1–1 to 18.

Music Titles

A large group of XIXc. lithographed music title pages and sheet music covers was acquired in 1922. A few have been placed under portraits, but most are in two portfolios: one of British covers by British artists or by foreigners working in England (about 260 items), the other by French lithographers (about 113 items). Some are complete with their scores. The names of the artists have been entered in the Index of Artists. 1922–7–10–68 to 775 (list).

Many more sheet covers will be found in the Music Room of the British Library.

National Art-Collections Fund

Since its foundation in 1903, the NACF has given numerous prints and drawings to the Department. An account by Campbell Dodgson of the early gifts will be found in *Twenty-five Years of the National Art-Collections Fund 1903–1928*, edited by D. S. MacColl 1928, pp. 145–57. Later gifts have been equally important, especially in the years 1941–6 when no purchase grant was available. On his death in 1948, Campbell Dodgson bequeathed a small capital to the Fund to produce an income of about £120 a year which was to be used for this Department. Gifts from this source are described as being presented by the National Art Collections Fund (Dodgson Fund). A full account of all gifts is given in the NACF annual reports, and the Fund's archives contain details and photographs of all works so presented.

National Gallery

In 1935 the National Gallery deposited on indefinite loan in the Department fifteen drawings by Rubens and one by van Dyck, all from the Peel collection: see A. E. Popham in *British Museum Quarterly* X, 1935 pp. 10–18. They are:

NG853A–D	Rubens	The Fall of the Damned.
853E		The beheading of St Paul.

853F	Descent of the Holy Spirit.
853G	Calvary.
853H	Portrait of a boy aged 4.
853I	Portrait of an unknown woman, half-length.
853J	Portrait of an unknown woman, head and shoulders.
853 K & M	Design for base to Michelangelo's Last Judgement, by Perino del Vaga retouched by Rubens.
853L	Title-page for Torniellus, *Annales Sacri* 1620.
853M	Title-page for *Obsidio Bredana* 1626.
853N	Rear view of a lioness.
NG877A Van Dyck	Crucifixion.

After the Second World War a watercolour by Carmontelle of Mozart as a child with his father and sister was added to the loan (NG 2911; this had previously been included in Martin Davies's 1946 catalogue of the French paintings in the National Gallery).

National Photographic Record and Survey

The name given to a scheme devised by Sir John Benjamin Stone MP which aimed to produce an entire photographic survey of the British Isles at the turn of the century. It was begun by Stone himself, and in May 1898 he presented 200 platinotype photographs taken by himself the previous year, of the architecture and monuments of Westminster and of individual members of Parliament. This was followed by gifts from other contributors, which included the work of other photographers. The collection contains 3232 photographs, and is arranged in 91 boxes, according to place. There is an index on blue slips both to topography and to the few portraits. Most of the items are dated 1897–1904, although one item is dated 1853, two 1875, and a few after 1904, the latest being 1911. A selection was published in two volumes in *Sir Benjamin Stone's Pictures, Records of National Life and History*, (with notes by Michael MacDonagh), 1905, 6. (The Stone collection of albums of commercial prints, glass negatives and mounted prints is owned by the City of Birmingham Public Libraries.)

Natural History

The field covered by the term Natural History includes animals, birds, fishes, flowers, insects and shells. Many books of prints on these subjects will be found in the Book Index under these headings. A number of albums of drawings are listed below, but the most important (such as the albums by Merian, van Huysum and Robert) are described elsewhere in the Topic Index in the entries on Sir Joseph Banks, Mary Delany, Jacques Le Moyne de Morgues, Sir Hans Sloane and John White.

There is a portfolio labelled Natural History, which contains almost entirely the loose drawings and prints from Sir Joseph Banks's collection which were transferred from the Library in 1914. The contents are divided into wrappers of shells, birds, mammals, reptiles and fishes, plants, insects, horns and bones, butterflies.

The catalogue of an exhibition held in

1958 entitled *Eight Centuries of Landscape and Natural History in European Watercolour 1180–1920* contains a brief historical introduction and lists examples in the collection from the xv–xxc. Information on botanical prints and drawings can be found in the book that accompanied the 1979 exhibition *Flowers in Art from East and West* by Paul Hulton and Lawrence Smith, while the exhibition handlist gives references to the 57 exhibits that came from this Department's collections.

1 Alexander Marshall (1639?–82): Studies of flowers, watercolours over metalpoint on vellum. Croft-Murray p. 440, nos 1–33. Formerly in an album; now mounted. 1878–12–14–59 to 91, list.
2 S. Holzbecker (active *c.*1660): 73 flower drawings, on vellum. 197 c.7; 1888–12–11–1(1–74), no list.
3 Studies of shells by P. J. Redouté, J. C. Desève, Fossier and J. G. Prêtre. 290 a.11; 1877–10–13–2857 to 2928 (no list). (The three drawings by Redouté are the only works by him in the Department; others are in the Victoria and Albert Museum.)
4 Georg Dionysius Ehret (1708–70): Six plants, bodycolour on vellum. 1974–6–15–23 to 28 (mounted).
5 Margaretha B. Dietzsch (1726–84): Bird drawings in gouache. 201 b.12; 1948–2–24–1 to 10. Also two further mounted drawings.
6 Maria Emma Gray (1787–1876): Seven albums with 3608 tracings prepared for her four volumes of etchings *Figures of Molluscous Animals, selected from various authors*, London 1842–50. Case 102*; 1877–11–24–45 to 3652 (no list).
7 John Curtis (1791–1862), by and after:

One volume of engravings made for publications on natural history, including the *Transactions of the Linnean Society*, and Hooker and Taylor's *Museologia Britannica*; and five volumes of engravings for his *British Entomology* 1824–39. 290* a.8–13; 1871–12–9–3546 to 4458, list.
8 John Obadiah Westwood (1805–93): Album of watercolours of British insects. 201 b.9; 1877–10–13–2929 to 2940.
9 William Raddon (act. 1828–35): Album of watercolours of British insects. 200 b.6; 1877–10–13–2941 to 2957.
10 Elizabeth Emily Murray (b.1847): Studies of birds' wings, watercolours of 1870s. 1904–10–21–1 to 41, of which 9–41 have been mounted in an album, 199* a.8.
11 Flowers of the Holy Land. A small book containing nine compositions of pressed flowers. 35 b.1; 1949–4–11–5281(1–9).
12 Margaret Stones (b. 1920): Botanical studies, watercolours. 1974–2–23–9 to 11.

Naval History

There is a separate series of four portfolios containing prints showing scenes from British naval history. They are arranged in chronological order of the event depicted from 55BC to AD1849, and have been marked off in Harry Parker, *Naval Battles from the collection of prints formed and owned by Commander Sir Charles Leopold Cust*, 1911. The Cust collection was bequeathed to the Admiralty, and is now in the National Maritime Museum. The same museum also owns the McPherson collection, and has the best collection of prints on naval history in the country.

The portfolio of Shipping (q.v.) also contains relevant material, such as prints or reproductions of warships, and plans and sections of ships and flags. A set of 63 drawings by Thomas Mitchell (*fl.*1763–89), assistant surveyor of the Navy, of naval bases, has been divided between the mounted British drawings (Binyon III pp. 108–9) and the shipping portfolio (1882–10–14–1 to 63).

Prints and drawings of interest in the Department's collection kept elsewhere include:

1 The battle of Zonchio, August 1499, between a Turkish and two Venetian vessels, anonymous Venetian woodcut coloured by hand. 1932–7–9–1.
2 The *Ark Royal*, anonymous English woodcut *c*.1588. Showing Lord Howard of Effingham's flagship against the Spanish Armada. 1874–8–8–1367.
3 The Armada plates of 1588, being a set of 12 charts (title page and 11 plates) engraved by A. Ryther after designs by Robert Adams. 173 c.18; 1888–12–21–8(1–12); the last plate is mounted separately.
4 Engagements between the English and Spanish fleets in 1588, engraved by John Pine in 1739 after the tapestry hangings in the House of Lords. 243 a.26(1); 1861–5–18–305 to 327.
5 The *Soveraigne of the Seas* 1637, built for Charles I in 1635–7, engraved by John Payne. 1854–6–14–252.
6 147 drawings of ships and naval actions by the elder and younger Willem van de Velde acquired from various sources, among them Sloane 5214. Many drawings are connected with the Anglo-Dutch wars. They have been catalogued by Croft-Murray and Hulton, I pp. 486–534.
7 The bequest of Naval prints and drawings from Captain Walter Dasent, RN, with 35 drawings, among them 15 by the van de Veldes, and 77 prints mostly of actions 1743–1854. 1940–12–14–1 to 112 (list).
8 An album of studies by P. J. de Loutherbourg for the painting of Lord Howe's victory on the Glorious First of June 1794. 201 a.7; 1857–6–13–580 to 611 (Binyon III p. 77). For another similar de Loutherbourg album (201 c.5; Binyon 20), see s.v. Military.
9 A volume by Samuel Owen of drawings and prints of sea fights and naval engagements 1793–5. 198 a.16; 1904–10–18–1 to 24 (list).

See also the catalogue of the Nelson centenary exhibition held in the British Museum in 1905 (pp. 71–82) for a list of relevant items in this Department.

Nielli

Niello is a black metallic amalgam used by goldsmiths to fill the lines engraved on metalwork. Under this general heading comes a varied group of items in the Department's collection: both silver and copper plates inlaid with niello and sulphur casts or prints on paper taken from such plates before the addition of the niello. The impressions on paper have been mounted and are kept in five small solanders; the plates and casts are in display cases in the Print Room. All have been catalogued and fully illustrated by A. M. Hind, *Nielli chiefly Italian of the XV century, plates, sulphur casts and prints preserved in the British Museum*, 1936. Catalogue numbers 1–133 are plates (of which 107–133 are related items kept in the Department of Medieval and Later Antiquities), nos 134–152 are sulphur casts, and nos 153–324 are prints. The bulk of the collection was purchased, along with many other early Italian prints, from Messrs Smith in 1845 (1845–8–25–1 to

266), and was formed by William Coningham (1815–84). See also s.v. Finiguerra.

Nollekens, Joseph (1737–1823)

Nollekens, the sculptor, bequeathed to the Museum 'the book of all my prints by Albert Durer, together with the print of the Triumphal Arch of the Emperor Maximilian', subject to a life interest to his friend Francis Douce. It arrived in the Museum after Douce's death in 1834. The prints have the inventory numbers E 2 and E 5.

Nuremberg Chronicle

Hartmann Schedel's Nuremberg Chronicle (*Liber Chronicarum* or *Weltchronik* in the German edition) takes its name from the town of its publication in 1493. It contains woodcuts designed by Michel Wolgemut and Wilhelm Pleydenwurff, and possibly the young Dürer. The Department possesses a slightly imperfect copy of the Latin edition (36* b.1; 1870–10–8–1938: see Dodgson I pp. 246–8), as well as 28 cut-out prints (Dodgson I p. 228). Complete copies will be found in the British Library. Wolgemut's drawing for the frontispiece, showing God creating the world, is in the collection (1885–5–9–43). See Adrian Wilson, *The Making of the Nuremberg Chronicle*, 1976.

Oleographs

An oleograph is a lithograph printed in colours which has been varnished to simulate the appearance of an oil painting. A separate portfolio contains nineteen large oleographs which were acquired in the 1870s and 1880s. The prints are after the work of French, German, Russian and Swedish artists. Other oleographs have been placed in the master series. See also s.v. Colour Printing.

Ornament and Design

The national collection of designs for the applied arts and of engraved ornament is in the Victoria and Albert Museum. Drawings and prints of this type have never been deliberately collected by this Department. A number of drawings of ornament will be found scattered through the series of mounted drawings. See also s.v. Architecture. Besides these there are two interesting albums of designs:

1 A jeweller's pocket book of *c*.1550, apparently from South Germany. 240 a.6; 1978–12–16–14(1–172). Most of the pages are blank, but 15 have drawings on them. A further 42 drawings and prints were inserted loose between the pages; these have been registered and mounted separately as 1978–12–16–15 to 56.
2 A sketchbook of ornamental designs of the early xviic., perhaps English. 199 a.10; 1917–6–9–1 to 20.

The main series of mounted ornamental prints is described above pp. 51–2 Others will be traced under the heading Ornament in the Book Index. The most important of these are eight volumes bound together in the xviiic., with contemporary lists of contents at the beginning. They are classified by types, and the contemporary labels on the spines read: Dessins pour les maisons; Frises et panneaux d'ornemens; Orfèverie, Horloge, Graveur, Serrurer; Cheminées et portes; Ornemens pour les maisons; Dessins d'orfèverie et de serrurerie; Broderies, marques, chiffres; Fleurs, festons, trophées (161 c.18–26; 1937–9–15–442 to 449). A similar but unrelated volume contains garden plans and designs (161 c.27; 1938–3–11–7). From the xixc. the collection contains *The Grammar of Ornament* by Owen Jones, published in 1856. The text is bound separately, while the 100 plates are in two solanders (1859–7–9–1920(1–100)). See also s.v. Fowler.

Paintings

Although there are a few oil sketches on paper mounted among the collection of drawings, oil paintings on canvas form no part of the Museum's collection. Most of those that used to be here were transferred to other institutions in the xixc. (see p. 14). Nevertheless, various paintings have remained in the building, and for want of any more suitable custodians have been put in the curatorial care of this Department. A volume containing a complete record of these is kept with the registers; the following list is only a summary:

VIEWS OF THE MUSEUM The temporary Elgin Room 1816–31 by A. Archer; The entrance gate *c.*1840 by Percy Carpenter; The King's Library 1931 by F. H. Shepherd.
PORTRAITS CONNECTED WITH THE BM John Arnold, Sir F. A. Barnard, Sir Joseph Banks, Samuel Birch, Rev. T. Birch, Sir E. A. Bond, Taylor Combe, Sir John, Robert and Thomas Cotton, William Courten, Sir Henry Ellis, Sir John Forsdyke, George ii, Dr A. Gifford, Sir G. F. Hill, John Winter Jones, Gowin Knight, Richard Payne Knight, Sir Henry Austen Layard, Lady Layard, Miss M. P. Layard (the property of the British Museum Society), Sir Frederic Madden, Matthew Maty, Sir Charles Newton, Robert and Edward Harley Earls of Oxford, Sir Anthony Panizzi, Joseph Planta, Hormuzd Rassam, C. J. Rich, Dr A. Scott, Sir Hans Sloane, Sir E. Maunde Thompson, Humphrey Wanley, Sir John Wolfenden, J. T. Wood. Sir Frank Francis is portrayed in a drawing by John Ward; Sir John Pope-Hennessy is represented by a bust by Elizabeth Frink. There is no portrait of Sir Thomas Kendrick.
PORTRAITS UNCONNECTED WITH THE BM Ulysses Aldrovandi, Augustus of Poland, J. S. Bach, Joseph Brant, Pierre Corneille, Oliver Cromwell, Mary Davis, Frederick iii of Saxony, Johann Gutenberg, Harper and White, Henry viii, Innocent xi, Isabella of Austria, Martin Luther, Mary Tudor as Princess, Cosimo de' Medici with his secretary Bartolommeo Concini, Molière, Jean-Jacques Rousseau, Andreas Vesalius, Voltaire, St Teresa. There is also a painting by V. M. Bramley of a Cree Indian Healing Ceremony.

Panoramas

In 1866 the Department purchased from the dealer Daniell a collection of plates and accompanying texts describing some of the panoramic pictures and models that were exhibited in London between about 1812 and 1860. Most relate to the Panorama in Leicester Square, a few to that in the Strand and others outside London. The plates have been mounted into an album (168* b.2; 1866–11–14–18 to 117, plus a few later acquisitions). The texts have been bound together at X 7.7–9 (1866–11–14–118 to 216). Views of the entrance and a section of the rotunda of Burford's Panorama in Leicester Square are in the Crace collection (XVIII 21, 22).

Panoramic Scenes

The term is used here to cover not just landscapes, but any long scene designed to be viewed sequentially. The main series of panoramic prints and drawings is kept in 5 special panoramic-size solander boxes (20″ × 45″), which contain a total of 56 items. Among still larger items, which have to be kept separately, either folded or rolled, are the following:

Georg Glockendon, attrib: The Continents, c.1511, woodcut. 1957–7–5–55.
F. Kirchmaier: Long view of Regensburg, woodcut 1589. 1865–6–10–756.
Giovanni Guerra: Erection of the Obelisk in St Peter's Square, Rome in 1586, etching. 1947–3–19–26.
Hendrik Goltzius: Funeral of Prince William at Delft 1584, engraving. 1872–1–13–573.
Georg Gartner II: Funeral Procession of Georg Frederick Margrave of Brandenberg-Ansbach, 1603, engraving. 1924–4–15–21 incomplete; Andresen I 273.2.
Elias Holwein: Funeral procession of Duke Heinrich Julius of Braunschweig-Lüneberg on 4 October 1613, woodcut. 1980–6–28–3.
Anonymous Italian early XVIIc.: View of Naples with a procession. 1964–7–30–1.
Johannes Ronzonus: A long procession, etching. 1979–7–21–31.
Frankfurt am Main, etching published by Visscher after M. Merian.
Long view of Florence, anonymous etching mid-XVIIc. 1872–1–13–592*.
Romeyn de Hooghe: View of Rotterdam, etching. 1873–6–14–16.
Samuel Buck: View of London and Westminster 1749, pen and ink. 1886–4–10–24.
Funeral Procession of Queen Elizabeth from a drawing by William Camden, engraving late XVIIIc. 1885–7–11–138.
Anonymous English XVIIIc.: Hunting at Melton Mowbray, aquatint. 1906–4–19–157.

I. R. Cruikshank: The road to the fight, aquatint. 1894–3–14–7.
The British Forces in Egypt at camp near Alexandria, aquatint by F. C. Lewis after Captain Walker. 1872–7–13–610.
Coronation procession of George IV in 1822, aquatint. 1890–8–8–9.
Rome, aquatint by T. Sutherland after T. Shew, 1827. 1907–12–17–1.
Paris, lithograph by C. Motte. 1954–1–18–2.
Victor Adam: March of the Netherlandish Army towards Ostend in 1600 as re-enacted by the students of Utrecht High School in 1836, lithograph. 1955–2–12–4.
Temple of the East (Sciagraphicon), colour lithograph published by Alfred Essex. 1957–2–7–1.
Athens in 1841, lithograph by Miss Abbott after Arthur Abbott. 1922–8–4–1.
View of the Bosphorus, anonymous pencil drawing mid-XIXc. 1905–12–14–1.
The funeral procession of the Duke of Wellington in 1852, aquatint. 1902–10–18–53 (incomplete).
Sisters of Mercy in the Crimea, lithographed caricature in mock-medieval style by Albert Way(?). 1910–1–29–1.
Charles Meryon: San Francisco in 1856, etching. Delteil 73. states III, IV, V.
Edwin Edwards: View of Framlingham Castle, etching. 1889–5–8–297.

Many other panoramas will be found in the main collection; an example is a view of St Petersburg in four plates aquatinted by John Augustus Atkinson (1863–7–25–338 to 341). A few more are listed among the framed works. See also s.v. London for an account of panoramic views of London.

Pastels

This entry lists some of the more notable works on paper executed with pastel or in a highly finished pastel-like manner in the collection:

Eugène Delacroix (1798–1863): Landscape at sunset. 1975–3–1–34.
Johannes Dörflinger (b.1941): Bergblatt, 1982. 1983–10–1–41.
Sandra Fisher (b.1947): Sappho in old age, 1978. 1984–6–9–14.
Thomas Frye (1710–62): A girl holding a cat. 1975–12–6–1.
Thomas Gainsborough (1728–88): George, 1st Duke of Montagu. 1951–1–29–1.
Henri Gaudier-Brzeska (1891–1915): Head of a Japanese girl. 1971–2–27–1.
Duncan Grant (1885–1978): Edward Wolfe sketching at Vanessa Bell's flat, 1918. 1981–12–12–1.
John Greenhill (c.1640–76): Portrait of a girl. 1985–10–5–57.
John Greenhill: Two portraits of Sir Thomas and Lady Twisden. 1986–3–1–1, 2.
Joseph Highmore (1692–1780) attrib.: A seated lady in a landscape. 1977–12–10–12.
Ernst Ludwig Kirchner (1880–1938): Nude standing in a bath. 1982–3–27–5.
R. B. Kitaj (b.1932): Sides, three studies of a male nude. 1980–2–23–35.
François Lemoine (1688–1737): Head of Hebe. 1850–3–9–1.
Edward Luttrell (active 1673–1723): A group of eight pastels. See Croft-Murray pp. 436–8, nos 1–8.
Odilon Redon (1840–1916): Cellule d'or. 1949–4–11–80.
John Singer Sargent (1856–1925): Paul Helleu lying in a field. 1959–1–2–4.

There is also a pastel drawing of Blind Fortune with a Monkey King, by Edward Luttrell, made on a copper plate prepared with a mezzotint ground (1981–11–7–1).

Paste Prints

There are two paste prints in the collection. One is of Christ washing the disciples' feet (Schreiber 2776; 1845–7–24–4) and is described by Dodgson as B33. The other was acquired after the publication of Dodgson's catalogue and shows St Dorothy (Schreiber 2842; 1926–12–14–7). For the latest theory of how they were produced, see Cynthia Bowman, *Print Quarterly*, II 1985, pp. 4–11.

Photographs

The Department has never collected photographs as such, and, unlike many Print Rooms both on the Continent and in the United States, makes no pretence to illustrate the history of photography. Nevertheless, over the course of time very many photographs have entered the collection, almost invariably as reference material. They have, therefore, in general been placed in the various documentary series. Large numbers will be found among the series of portraits under their respective sitters; in the series of topographical prints under places; in books in the Departmental library; and in the master series, both as reproductions of paintings, drawings and sculpture.

In recent years, an unpublished survey of the British Museum's photographic collections has been made by Alan Donnithorne of the Conservation Department. The survey included collections both in this and other departments of the British Museum and numerous rarities were uncovered. On historical and conservation grounds some of the more important items in this Department are now being extracted and mounted in a new series of select photographs.

The following list draws attention to some of the more interesting items or caches of photographs in the Department:

1 D. O. Hill and R. Adamson: a series of calotype portraits *c*.1845, including David Roberts, William Etty, Dr T. Monro, etc. 1857–2–28–2 to 27 (list).

2 Bryan Edward Duppa: two examples of the Duppa process (hand-painted albumen prints mounted on zinc plates) together with a copy of the patent specification, 1854. 167 a.29; 1935–10–28–1 to 3.

3 William Lake Price: the building of the Reading Room of the British Museum in progress, 1855. 1855–5–12–325; 1855–8–11–161.

4 James Robertson: a group of scenes in the Crimean War, salted paper prints 1854. 1958–7–12–271 to 280.

5 Roger Fenton: view of the front of the British Museum 1857. 1857–7–11–77.

6 John Gregory Crace: view of St Paul's from the south side of Blackfriars Bridge, salted paper print 1857. Crace collection VI–289.

7 William Lake Price: Portrait of Richard Ansdell, *c*.1857. 1929–2–9–165.

8 Gustave Le Gray: sea views *c*.1857. 1957–3–14–60 to 62.

9 Édouard-Denis Baldus: View of the Ste-Chapelle Paris, *c*.1860. 1948–2–14–238.

10 Bissons Frères: View of the Rue de la Grosse Horloge, Rouen, *c*.1860. 1948–2–14–240.

11 Charles Clifford: Views in Spain, *c*.1860.1948–2–14–270 to 281 (list).

12 Robert MacPherson: Views in Rome, *c*.1860. 1986 U. 1–11.

13 Julia Margaret Cameron: illustrations to Fruits of the Spirit *c*.1860, published by Colnaghi and Co. 1865–1–14–1294 to 1302 (list).

14 Album of portraits of British Museum officials, statesmen and others, *c*.1850–60, collected by Robert Cowtan. 210* b.11; 1943–11–15–1 (no list).

15 Cundall Downes and Co: album of portraits of members and associates of the Society of Painters in Watercolours, *c*.1865. 210* b.9; 1923–6–12–34 to 69 (list).

16 H. G. Ponting: British Antarctic Expedition 1910–13. 1931–4–11–1 to 42 (list).

There are also several large groups of early reproductions of drawings and other works of art:

17 Benjamin Delessert: salted paper prints after prints by Marcantonio, 1853. 179 c.2, 180 c.1; 1854–5–13–393 to 427.

18 Bissons Frères: salted paper prints after drawings by Rembrandt, 1853–8. 179 c.23; 1854–3–12–425, etc.

19 C. Thurston Thompson: three groups *c*.1856 after drawings in the BM (1856–10–11–124 to 126), at Windsor (1857–5–20–446 to 496), and in the Louvre (1857–7–11–42 to 74) (lists).

20 Roger Fenton: salted paper prints after drawings in the BM, 1857 (1858–10–9–1 to 41); also albumen prints, 1859 (1859–12–10–1082 to 1090) (lists). Other photographs by Fenton are in the Central Archives and the Department of Greek and Roman Antiquities.

21 Fratelli Alinari: after drawings in the Uffizi, *c*.1858. 1858–6–26–409 to 458.

22 Philip Henry Delamotte and

T. Frederick Hardwich: salted paper prints of the Revely collection of drawings in North Wales, 1858. 179 b.1; 1936–4–2–5(1–65). Also some individual impressions, 1860–10–13–169 to 198.

23 Adolphe Braun et Cie: several large groups of carbon photographs, e.g. 1868–8–8–1 to 1273 (list).

For W. H. Fox Talbot's illustrations to W. Stirling-Maxwell's *Annals of the Artists in Spain*, see 165* c.7.

See also s.v. Browning, Gernsheim, London (Potter collection), National Photographic Record, Processes of Engraving, Raphael.

Piranesi, Giovanni Battista
(1720–1778)

The Department possesses some 53 drawings by Piranesi of architectural subjects, many being interior views, purchased in two groups in 1905 and 1908 (1905–11–10–63 to 65, 1908–6–16–1 to 46). The collection of his etched work is very incomplete because many of his series of prints were published with text and have therefore been kept in the British Library. In particular, it does not include the *Prima Parte di Architetture e Prospettive*, the four-volume *Antichità Romane*, the set of fireplace designs *Diverse maniere d'adornare i cammini*, or any of the minor archaeological publications. The series of *Vasi, candelabri e cippi* is incomplete.

The entire collection is marked off against the list in Henri Foçillon, *Piranesi*, 1914. The major items are:

1 *Carceri*. The first edition is mounted, the later reworked edition is in a bound volume (164 c.2).
2 The views of Rome. All loose prints, arranged according to the catalogue in A. M. Hind, *Giovanni Battista Piranesi*, 1922. Including variant states of the same image.
3 The long etchings of Trajan's and the Antonine columns have been mounted and are kept framed: 1926–5–11–35, 36.

See the catalogue of the 1968 exhibition *Giovanni Battista Piranesi, his Predecessors and his Heritage*. The Department library contains a volume with photographs of almost all the exhibits (Ee 5 25). There is also a caricature of Piranesi drawn by Ghezzi in 197 d.4 (1859–8–6–126).

Plates, Blocks and Stones

The Department has only collected a small number of examples of the actual printing matrices from which impressions have been made. Most of these have some particular historic or technical interest. There is a complete manuscript list of such items compiled by A. M. Hind in 1934, to which later acquisitions have been added. It is Departmental policy in general that these blocks and plates should not be reprinted; the only exception to this has been the edition of 150 impressions from the blocks of Blake's illustrations to Thornton's Virgil published in 1977.

Among the most interesting are:

Woodblocks
1 37 woodblocks by Dürer (q.v.).
2 8 vignettes by Thomas Bewick.
3 17 woodblocks by William Blake for Thornton's Virgil. 1939–1–14–2 to 18.
4 7 woodblocks by Edward Calvert. 1904–6–16–3 to 9.
5 William Harvey, The assassination of Dentatus after B. R. Haydon. 1866–7–14–103.
6 Various blocks by illustrators of the 1860s, including Arthur Boyd

Houghton, Fred Walker and
G. J. Pinwell.

Copper plates

7 Cristofano Robetta: The adoration of
the Magi, Allegory of Love. One plate
engraved on both sides.
1888–1–17–13.
8 Hans Burgkmair: Venus and Mercury.
Etched steel plate. 1862–10–11–184.
9 Lambert Hopfer: Three ornamental
panels. 1982 U.4538 to 4540.
10 Valentin Sezenius: Four plates.
1878–12–14–476 to 479.
11 Gerhardt Janssen: Orpheus and the
animals. Steel plate. 1862–10–11–185.
12 22 plates by William Blake illustrating
the Book of Job. 1919–5–28–13 to 34.
Also an electrotype of one of the plates
for the Songs of Innocence and
Experience. 1926–8–16–1.
13 J. M. W. Turner: 49 cancelled plates
from the Liber Studiorum.
1945–12–8–321 to 367. Also two steel
mezzotint plates from the 'Little Liber'.
1942–8–10–2,3.
14 Edward Calvert: Two plates.
1904–6–16–1, 2.
15 Samuel Palmer: The Bellman.
1926–9–3–1.
16 Charles Keene: 21 etched plates.
1903–12–19–1 to 21. Also 3 plates of
the Edwards family. 1930–7–3–1 to 3.
17 J. M. W. Whistler: The Menpes
children. 1904–8–10–3.
18 Sir F. Seymour Haden: The Breaking
up of the Agamemnon. 1911–7–26–1.
Also four others. 1935–12–14–22 to
25.
19 Camille Pissarro: La Vachère,
Baigneuse (D 93, 115).
1924–4–14–1, 3.

Stones and lithographic plates

20 Jean François Millet: Le Semeur.
1957–6–20–2.

21 Camille Pissarro: La Convalescence.
1924–1–12–364.

Miscellaneous

22 Camille Corot: Landscape with rider.
Cliché-verre. 1925–1–20–4.
23 The etching tools of Sir Francis
Seymour Haden. 1910–8–11–1 to 9.
24 The wood-engraving tools of Edward
Whymper. 1911–7–14–49 to 66.

See also s.v. Kelmscott and Vale Press
for other blocks by Burne-Jones and
Ricketts and Shannon.

Playing Cards

A collection of playing cards, built up
piecemeal during the first three quarters of
the xixc., was catalogued in 1876 by
W. H. Willshire: *A Descriptive Catalogue of
Playing and other Cards in the British
Museum.* This includes a small number of
packs that have remained in the British
Library. The collection is arranged
according to the catalogue by country, and
within each country by types. The
numbering is in a single series: Italian
1–14; Spanish 15–36, French 37–102,
Flemish 103–10, Dutch 111–15, German
116–66, English 167–243, Varia 244–9.
The Oriental packs (250–5) were
transferred to the Department of Oriental
Antiquities in 1971.

After 1876 many other cards were
acquired, notably groups from the Meyrick
collection (1878–10–12–1 to 345) and the
collection of Miss E. Estridge
(1904–5–11–23 to 53). These have been
allocated numbers supplementary to
Willshire's, and placed in the Willshire
series. Annotations have been made in the
Department's working copy of Willshire,
but the main record of new items is a card
index.

In 1895 Lady Charlotte Schreiber

bequeathed her collection as a supplement to that already in the Museum (1896–5–1–1 to 1660, list). All duplicates were returned to her executors. This collection is kept separate from the general collection, and is arranged according to the catalogue prepared by Freeman O'Donoghue and published by the Trustees in 1901: *Catalogue of the Collection of Playing Cards bequeathed to the Trustees of the British Museum by Lady Charlotte Schreiber.* This is organised slightly differently from Willshire: packs are catalogued before sheets, and within each section the arrangement is by country and within each country by type. There is a new numbering sequence for each country. The numbers of packs are: Italian 152, Spanish 58, Portuguese 1, French 193, German 379, Swiss 27, Dutch 25, Flemish 15, Russian 4, Polish 1, Swedish 4, Danish 1, English 174, American 9; the Indian, Japanese and Chinese cards were transferred to the Department of Oriental Antiquities in 1971. The sheet cards are numbered separately.

While the collection was still in Lady Charlotte's possession, she published three large volumes with facsimile illustrations under the title *Playing Cards of various ages and countries* in 1892, 3, 5 (168 c.9–11). Lady Charlotte's own manuscript catalogue of her collection is in the Department library.

Reference to packs with particular subject-matter is made in various entries in this Index. One pack frequently requested, the memory cards of William Bowes of c.1605, is placed as Willshire E179.4 (1878–6–8–15 to 73). Francis Barlow's original drawings for 61 playing cards of the Popish Plot and other historical subjects are at 199* a.27 (1954–7–10–4(1–61)); Croft-Murray pp. 135–48.

Polyautography

The earliest lithographs published in Britain came out under the title *Specimens of Polyautography*. Apart from many single-sheet prints placed under the names of their artists, the Department possesses two albums collected by Thomas Fisher and bound together in 1818, which contain nearly 400 early British lithographs. 190* b.1, 2; 1874–7–11–902 to 1283 (list).

Polygraphs

There are only two polygraphs in the collection: a pair of varnished works on canvas after Philip James de Loutherbourg (1740–1812) of Summer and Winter (1982–6–19–1, 2).

Popular Prints

Anonymous popular prints have never been deliberately collected in this country, and as a result those that are in this collection are here by accident more than design. In very recent years a portfolio of popular prints has been started, and items will gradually be transferred to it. But as yet it contains little. British and Foreign popular prints are most likely to be found among the satire and history series, and a few are in the series of portraits. Another group will be found among the anonymous British woodcuts and mezzotints. See Thomas Gretton, *Murders and Moralities, British Catchpenny Prints 1800–1860*, 1980, which includes a number of items from this collection.

Pornography

A few items of pornographic or obscene subject-matter may only be seen by written request to the Keeper of the Department. These include:

1 The drawn 'copies' by Waldeck of the Modi by Marcantonio. 1868–3–28–376 to 396 (no list).
2 An album of XVIIIc. French drawings with the title 'Histoire Universelle'. 1977 U.455(1 to 73a).
3 Etchings by and after Thomas Rowlandson. 1977 U.507(1 to 110). Also eight copper plates. 1977 U.491 (1 to 8).
4 Eric Gill, drawings of sexual organs. 1977 U.504(1 to 132).
5 Illustrations and plates by Charles Mozley for Fanny Hill. 1973–10–27–35 to 86 (list).

There are also single-sheet works by or after Cruikshank, Le Blon, Mauron, Mellan, Monnier, Parmigianino, Rops, Charles Turner and Vivant-Denon as well as a number of early Italian and anonymous English engravings. Furthermore, twenty-one books of prints or reproductions are at present kept in the restricted category; they are all included in the Book Index and are shelved in case 201*.

Portraits

The main series of engraved portraits is described on pp. 41–6. This entry complements the information given there, by drawing attention to groups of portraits kept apart from that series. Unfortunately, only a few of these portraits, mostly of British sitters, have been entered on the blue slip indices.

There are some 600 portrait drawings in the collection. There is an incomplete blue slip index for British sitters only. More useful is the 1974 catalogue *Portrait Drawings XV–XX centuries* compiled by J. A. Gere, which contains full indices both to sitters and to artists for the 450 items of all schools that were included in that exhibition.

Books containing engraved portraits, which are mostly shelved together in cases 206* to 210*, can be traced through the Book Index under the heading Portraits. Works of reference on the subject in the Departmental library, besides H. W. Singer's *Allgemeiner Bildniskatalog* (Leipzig 1930–6) and the *A.L.A. Portrait Index* (Washington 1906), include the manuscript Breun catalogue (see pp. 66–7).

General

See entries for Brocklebank and Hill.

1 Collectanea Biographica, see Grangerised volumes, pp. 57–8.
2 Richard Bentley and Son, illustrated catalogue of portraits, views and other plates, containing 1214 plates in eight volumes, 1884. The volumes contain impressions from plates which the firm held in stock for reprinting. Case 188.
3 Rudolf Lehmann (1819–1905): 102 portrait drawings, chiefly pencil, of eminent person of the late XIXc. 1906–4–19–1 to 102 (list in alphabetical order of sitters). These were prepared for *Men and Women of the Century . . . portraits and sketches by Rudolf Lehmann*, 1896. (210 b.10; containing 80 plates).
4 There is a very large collection of lithographs by Richard James Lane (1800–72), most of which are portraits. See the Book and Artist Index, and the register 1912–10–12–5 to 483, 1924–3–8–1 to 328.

Royalty and statesmen

5 G. B. Cavalieri: set of 154 portraits of Roman emperors, 1583. 208 a.1; 1884–10–11–1 to 154 (list).

6 Portraits and caricatures, mostly drawings and watercolours including some by L. I. Kiel, collected by Count Nesselrode, Chancellor of the Russian Empire, illustrating diplomatic circles, mostly Russian, *c.*1830–50. 197* d.6; 1939–7–11–3(1 to 63).

7 A collection of seventeen scrapbooks of cuttings compiled and presented by Miss E. S. Price. The first ten are of the English Royal Family, mostly from Edward VII to George VI. The next five are of European Royal Houses, including Yugoslavia, Italy, Belgium, Denmark, Spain, Russia, Greece, Albania etc. The last two are of statesmen, including Churchill, Hitler, Lloyd George, Chamberlain, etc. All case 186*; 1973–10–27–18 to 34.

8 A group of about 250 photographic postcards of XXc. members of Royal families. 210* b.12.

American

9 See the oil painting by Gilbert Stuart of Joseph Brandt (1742–1807), Captain of the Six Nations.

British

10 See the entries on the Cheylesmore collection and on Altered Plates (Sligo collection).

11 See the Grangerised volumes of Clarendon and Whitelocke (p. 55) for XVIIc. portraits.

12 See the Grangerised volumes of Pennant (pp. 55, 58–9) for portraits of persons connected with London.

13 See engravings by William Faithorne, arranged in five albums alphabetically by sitter.

14 See Houbraken's 'Heads of Illustrious Persons' arranged in three albums in the order of ver Huell's catalogue.

15 See s.v. Downman for his 'first sketches of portraits of distinguished persons'.

16 A volume of 145 soft-ground etchings, chiefly portraits of artists, by William Daniell after George Dance (1741–1825). These include 73 not published in Dance's *Collection of Portraits*, two vols, 1808–14. Mostly proofs before letters, with ms. list of portraits and notes on the sitters. 209* b.6; 1925–5–11–26(1–146). See also 199 a.13; 1856–10–5–1 to 19 for Daniell's drawings after Dance.

17 George Dance, various pencil portraits. See Binyon II: nos 1–8 were engraved by Daniell for the series described above; 9–27 were not engraved.

18 A group of pencil portraits of artists by Henry Edridge (1769–1821). 1867–4–13–525 to 535.

19 Sir George Hayter (1792–1871): Portraits of men and women. 199* a.11,12; 1895–12–14–3 to 60. Binyon 12, 13.

20 William Home Clift (1803–33): Album of portrait drawings. 199 b.3; 1898–8–3–8 to 48. The album has its own index of sitters.

21 Sir John Mellor (1862–1929): Portraits of members of the Parnell Commission and other legal figures. 200 a.5; 1930–7–12–1 to 74.

22 A collection of twelve volumes of lithographs by Charles Baugniet (1814–86) includes many portraits of British sitters. Case 230*; 1877–4–14–107 to 705, list).

23 A portfolio labelled 'Ipswich Museum Portraits' contains 61 lithographs by T. H. Maguire (1821–95) dated 1849–52 of eminent scientific men of the period (1882–6–10–100 to 160). A

duplicate set of the plates
(1852–4–24–9 to 69) has been
distributed in the main portrait series.

24 An album of anonymous drawings
*c.*1880s of printsellers and characters
who were constant attendants at
Hutchin's Auctions, with text.
210* c.4; 1892–4–11–116(1 to 25).

French

25 There are 48 French portrait drawings
by the Clouets and their school, among
them 32 bequeathed by George Salting
which come from the collection of
Ignatius Hugford (1703–78).
1910–2–12–52 to 84 (list, including
title-page).

26 See engravings by Robert Nanteuil
(1630–78). The collection has been
marked off against Robert-Dumesnil
as well as Petitjean & Wickert.

27 See the extra-illustrated Letters of
Mme de Sévigné (p. 56) for many
French portraits. There are two
volumes of index to sitters
(Ss 7.8, 9).

German

28 A set of nine large genealogical trees
engraved by Matthias Seutter *c.*1760 of
German, Austrian and other ruling
houses. 1919–10–14–36 to 44 (list).

Postage Stamps and Covers

There are no postage stamps in the
collection. The national collection will be
found in the British Library (which houses
the Tapling collection) and the National
Postal Museum. A group of 29 envelopes
parodying the envelope designed by
William Mulready is in 165* a.23* (various
registration numbers). A portrait of Queen
Victoria engraved by F. Joubert is taken
from a plate intended for a postage stamp
(see O'Donoghue 265). A montage by

Donald Evans entitled *Achterdijk* (1974)
consists of six drawings imitating postage
stamps (1975–9–20–5).

Postcards

There is no collection of postcards as such
in the Department. A group of 250
photographic cards of xxc. members of
Royal families is at 210* b.12; various other
cards will be found in the collections listed
in the entry for Religious Imagery. A large
collection, often overlooked, is in the
British Library at the pressmark 1878
a.1–33. The Department does possess a
complete set of the cards of its own
collection published by the Museum
between *c.*1922 and the present (Cc 1, with
a partial index of artists). There is also an
album containing a number of postcards
with drawings by Emil Orlik sent to Robert
and Paula Austerlitz: 200* b.3;
1940–7–22–1 to 28.

Posters

The national collection of posters is in the
Victoria and Albert Museum, and the small
collection of some 600 items in this
Department has not been deliberately
expanded since the early 1930s. It does not
purport to offer a survey of the history of
the medium, but rather contains examples
of the work of many of the more famous
artists who have designed for it. There is a
manuscript handlist arranged by country,
and within each country by artist or
designer. The following countries are
represented: America, Belgium, England,
France, Germany, Holland, Poland,
Russia, Spain and Switzerland.

Notable groups or items within the
collection are:

1 7 posters by Toulouse-Lautrec (Moulin
Rouge-La Goulue, Divan Japonais, Jane

Avril, Caudieux, May Belfort, Au Concert, La Passagère du 54).

2 117 French posters from the First World War. 1920–11–13–2 to 132.

3 Russian Revolutionary posters. 1921–2–10–1 to 13; 1931–5–9–3 to 28.

4 27 posters by Sir Frank Brangwyn. 1943–12–11–579 to 605.

5 Fred Walker, poster for Wilkie Collins *Woman in White*. 1912–6–12–475.

Not included in the handlist, and not strictly posters, is a group of mid-XIXc. advertisements and handbills for theatres, freaks, lectures, performing animals, the eidophusikon, etc. contained in a separate portfolio (1862–10–11–438 to 572, list).

In the British Library will be found a large collection of British and French posters of the First World War (TAB 11748a), and a miscellaneous group including some Russian anti-Capitalist posters (CUP 645 c.12).

Potter, Helen Beatrix
(1866–1943)

In 1946 Captain K. W. G. Duke gave the Department the complete set of watercolour illustrations to *The Tale of the Flopsy Bunnies* of 1909 (1946–11–21–1 to 28). The Tate Gallery was given the watercolours for *The Tailor of Gloucester*. The Victoria and Albert Museum Library possesses a mass of other material: see the catalogue by Anne Stevenson Hobbs and Joyce Irene Whalley, *Beatrix Potter, the Leslie Linder Bequest*, 1985. The copyright in the illustrations remains with the publishers, Frederick Warne and Co.

Processes of Engraving

Under this title is a portfolio which contains specimens of many curious printmaking methods as well as technical elucidations of more usual methods. Among the latter are progressive states of a chromolithograph by Miss C. B. Leighton of before 1859 and progress proofs of a collotype and a colour woodcut. Among the former are examples of acrography, Brulegravures, embossed printing, etching from stone and on celluloid, glyptography, nature printing, Palmer's patented transparent medium, papyrography, photogalvanography, printing from rubber plates and an item inscribed as being 'printed from electricity 1792'. An historic item is a diploma of the Vienna Lithographic Society, which carries the portraits of Senefelder and others, each drawn by the artist himself.

Other collections of actual examples of printmaking techniques are:

1 W. J. Stannard, *Art Exemplar, a guide to distinguishing one species of print from another*, *c*.1860. 1911–10–20–1(1–97) (no list).

2 Norman R. Eppink: *101 Prints*, *c*.1970. Case 289.

Many original treatises on the art of printmaking can be traced through the Book Index under the headings of the names of the various processes; most are shelved in the Lll press.

Railways

The Transport portfolio (q.v.) contains sixteen miscellaneous prints on railways, including:

1 The North Star, Stephenson's patent locomotive engine, lithograph by C. F. Chiffins. 1848–2–8–1.

2 Tring cutting, 1837, aquatint by J. C. Bourne. 1956–7–17–17.

3 South Devon railway, 1852, lithograph by F. Jones. 1956–7–17–21.

There are three bound volumes:

4 London and Birmingham Railway, 1839 (lacking the title-page and plates XIII, XXXVI), lithographs by J. C. Bourne. 172* b.20; 1955–7–9–53 to 80.

5 Six views on the Dublin and Drogheda Railway, n.d., etchings by E. Radclyffe after J. E. Jones. 172 a.36; 1958–10–16–3(1–6).

6 Le Métro, a portfolio with wood-engravings by Serge Glumac. 250 a.12; 1930–1–11–207(1–12).

Items kept in other series include:

7 Brandling Junction Railway, Newcastle-upon-Tyne, c.1842. Etching after T. H. Hair. 1978 U.672.

8 View from the Box Tunnel, and Sonning Cutting; lithographs by J. C. Bourne (from 'The History and Description of the Great Western Railway' 1846). 1938–8–6–1, 2. Bourne's preparatory drawing for the Box Tunnel is in the collection, 1974–10–26–54.

9 Crace collection: see portfolios XXXI 20–7, 38–9 (Euston, King's Cross, Primrose Hill tunnel); XXXIV 113–14 (London Bridge); and XXXVI 154–5 (Nine Elms, Vauxhall).

10 George Scharf (q.v.): Birmingham Railway on the Hampstead Road, drawing. 1862–6–14–409 (mounted imperial).

Raphael (Raffaello Santi) (1483–1520)

There are about 40 drawings by Raphael in the collection which are kept in the order of the catalogue *Raphael and his Circle*, 1962, by Philip Pouncey and J. A. Gere. A more recent publication of the drawings, by J. A. Gere and Nicholas Turner, is the catalogue of the Raphael exhibition held in 1983; this also included almost every drawing by him in British public and private collections.

The most important collection of prints and photographs after Raphael's paintings and drawings was assembled for Prince Albert between 1853–61 by Carl Ruland. This is now on loan to the Department from Her Majesty the Queen. The 5342 items are mounted on large sheets in 50 portfolios in the order of the catalogue written by Ruland. The collection can be most conveniently studied on the microfiche made by the Warburg Institute in 1985, of which a copy is in the Department.

The Department's own collection of prints after Raphael is kept in seven ordinary portfolios and one outsize one. The arrangement is that given in Ruland's catalogue, and the Department's copy has been given a sequential numbering and marked off with the holdings. 418 of these are in the 1837 inventory (V. 4–7) (list).

A few interesting groups are kept apart from the main series:

1 A collection of 68 engravings by different engravers of the Madonna della Seggiola formed and presented by John Dillon, inserted into a large album. 1865–4–8–1 to 68 (list).

2 A mounted series of engravings by Giovanni Ottaviani of the frescoes in the Loggie of the Vatican, hand-coloured by Giovanni Volpato, in three boxes. 1869–4–10–2574 to 2618 (no list).

3 A mounted series of hand-coloured engravings by Sir Nicholas Dorigny of the frescoes of Cupid and Psyche in the Farnesina, Rome. V 7.1–10 (no list).

Other bound sets of prints can be traced through the Book Index.

Reeve, James (1833–1920)

Assistant and then Curator of the Norfolk and Norwich Museum 1847–94, and Curator of its successor, the Norwich Castle Museum, 1894–1910. His entire collection of etchings and drawings by artists of the Norwich school was purchased by the Museum in 1902. There is a complete list in the register (1902–5–14–1 to 1285) as well as a manuscript catalogue in the Department library (167 c.4). There were 481 drawings and watercolours, including unrivalled groups of works by members of the Cotman family, and 702 prints, together with six bound volumes as follows:

1 Catalogues of exhibitions of the Norwich Society of Artists 1805–25. 167 c.5, 6.
2 Biographical sketches, letters, etc. of the Cotman family. 167 c.7.
3 Biographical sketches, etc. of the Crome family. 167 c.8.
4 Biographical sketches, etc. of other Norfolk and Norwich artists who had died before 1898. 167 c.9.
5 Original letters by J. S. Cotman to Mrs Cotman and Mr and Mrs Dawson Turner. 167 c.11.

See also s.v. Cotman.

Religious Images

Two volumes purchased in Rome in about 1837 by W. C. Trevelyan contain a collection mounted around 1800 of prints of the most varied kinds of religious subject-matter. The title is *Raccolta in Rami di alcuni fatti del Vecchio Testamento e di varie Sagre Imagini del N. S. Gesu Cristi, e di Maria Santissima* etc. A few prints have been extracted but the volumes remain substantially intact. 1871–4–29–53 to 384, 385 to 637. A homogeneous series of engravings by Joseph and Johannes Klauber, published in Augsburg in the late XVIIIc., has been mounted into a volume (160 d.6; 1890–12–20–27(1–618)). They are arranged by subject: the life of Christ, the sacraments, saints, feasts, etc.

There are also two later collections of devotional images of the Virgin and saints, both of similar character. The contents are almost entirely late XIXc. and early XXc. chromolithographic cards, photographs and cuttings, arranged in alphabetical order.

1 Two volumes containing 963 items of Christ and saints; and the Virgin Mary. Collected by the Rev. E. H. Dallimore. Transferred from the Library. 250 b.3, 4; 1938–7–28–1 (no list).
2 Three volumes arranged as follows: Male saints A–H; Male saints I–Z; Female saints and groups. Presented by Sister M. E. Gwendolyne Hayes. Z 4 38–40; 1952–6–14–3 (no list).

Finally there are three groups of drawings:

3 Thomas Frank Heaphy (1813–73): Drawings from early likenesses of Christ and other Christian antiquities. 201 c.3; 1881–6–11–358 to 402. Binyon II p. 294.
4 Louisa Twining (1820–1912): The life of Christ, being tracings from manuscripts and some reproductions. 199 b.6; 1897–10–8–1(1–70). Binyon IV p. 213.1.
5 idem: Illustrations, mostly copies and tracings of paintings and manuscripts in the British Museum, of the Apostles' Creed, and for her books *Symbols and Emblems of Christian Art*, 1852, and *Types and Figures of the Bible*, 1855. 199* b.11; 1901–5–29–1 to 3. Binyon 2–4.

For books of prints on religious subjects, see the Book Index under Christian (for the life of Christ), Relics, Reliquaries, Religious Allegory/Orders/Usage, Saints.

Rembrandt van Ryn (1606–1669)

The Department's collection of Rembrandt's drawings is one of the best balanced in existence, and that of his etchings perhaps the best. The drawings have been catalogued by A. M. Hind, *Rembrandt and his School*, 1915, and are kept in Hind's order in 13 boxes. The Departmental desk copy has a concordance with Benesch's Corpus inserted. Hind believed there were 114 drawings by Rembrandt himself (in 9 boxes) and relegated 52 to an appendix of doubtful works and copies (4 boxes). Currently only about 85 are believed to be by Rembrandt. The etchings are in 26 boxes arranged in the order of A. M. Hind, *A Catalogue of Rembrandt's Etchings*, 1923. There is a supplementary box which contains some additional impressions, as well as copies. Later impressions from the original plates will also be found in three bound volumes: H. L. Basan, *Recueil de quatre-vingt-cinq estampes originales par Rembrandt*, *c.*1807/9 (157* b.26), G. J. M. Creery, *A collection of two hundred original etchings*, 1816 (157* b.28), and M. Bernard and Alvin-Beaumont, *Les cuivres de Rembrandt*, 1906 (case 72). Prints and reproductions after Rembrandt's paintings are kept in three portfolios in iconographical order.

The Department library contains an XVIIIc. volume with four items bound together: the unique copy of the printed bill of sale of Rembrandt's collection of drawings and prints in 1658, together with a translation; a manuscript extract and translation from the Amsterdam municipal 'Book of Securities' regarding 6952 guilders due to Titus van Ryn as balance from the sale of 1665; a manuscript catalogue of the Earl of Aylesford's collection of the works of Rembrandt; and an XVIIIc. French translation of the 1656 inventory of Rembrandt's possessions (72 a.5).

See also the catalogues of the exhibitions 1899, 1938 (which contains a summary listing of the entire collection), 1956, 1969 (on the late etchings) and 1984 (Rembrandt and the Passion), and C. White, *The Drawings of Rembrandt*, 1962.

Reynolds, Sir Joshua (1723–1792)

Binyon (III pp. 196–221) describes eleven drawings by Reynolds, to which can be added twelve later acquisitions. Binyon 12 and 13 are two books of sketches and notes made while in Italy in 1752. The first was made at Florence and on the journey from there to Rome (201 a.10; 1859–5–14–305), the second on the journey from Florence to Venice, and in Venice (201 a.9; 1859–5–14–304). The forgeries box contains three examples of drawings signed Reynolds (1939–7–25–1 to 3).

The collection of prints after Reynolds was mounted in twelve albums in 1895, arranged in alphabetical order of sitter, six being of male sitters, four of female, and two of subject paintings. They contain 1056 prints, mostly from Aa 1–13 in the 1837 inventory; supplementary items are in two extra portfolios.

There are two separate bound groups of prints after Reynolds (both case 20*). The first is a set of mezzotints by S. W. Reynolds published in 1820, bound in four volumes (1875–5–8–810 to 1179, list). To this has been added a supplementary volume of unpublished plates given by Mr E. E. Leggatt (1901–10–14–47 to 76, list). The second is a four-volume set of engravings from the works of Reynolds published by Henry Graves in 1865, consisting of mezzotints by a large number of engravers. To these was added a fifth volume (numbered 8) published also by Graves in 1900; the last includes a number of reprints of the S. W. Reynolds plates.

The collection is marked off against the Departmental copy of Edward Hamilton, *Catalogue of the engraved work of Sir Joshua Reynolds*, 1884. The sitters are noted in the blue slip index of portraits, and are listed in the portrait catalogue by O'Donoghue and Hake. See also exhibitions 1978 and Whitley Papers p. 71.

Rome

The series of foreign topography contains two portfolios of views of Rome. Other views are contained in the *Speculum Romanae Magnificentiae* published by Antoine Lafréry (174 c.31; 1947–3–19–26(1–185), list; 84 of these prints are bound in an album, the rest are distributed) and in the set of *Vedute Romane* by Piranesi (q.v.). There is also a similar series by Luigi Rossini (case 253; 1870–7–9–417 to 517, list). This album also contains the bird's-eye view of Rome of 1765 etched by Giuseppe Vasi (1870–7–9–518 to 529). See also the Book Index s.v. Topography, Rome. The collection also contains a large number of watercolours of Rome and its surrounds by Italian and British watercolourists of the XVIII–XIXc. The most notable are:

1 Giovanni Battista Busiri (1698–1757), 67 drawings. 1884–10–11–211; 1919–4–12–4 to 12; 1925–4–6–12 to 68 (lists).
2 Carlo Labruzzi (1748–1817), 64 watercolours. 1955–12–10–10(1–64), no list, formerly an album, now broken up and mounted.
3 Francis Towne (1740–1816), three albums (of 32, 25 and 17 watercolours), now broken up and mounted, made during his visit to Rome in 1780–1, and bequeathed by him to the British Museum. Inventory Nn 1–3 (list); Binyon IV pp. 198–202.
4 John 'Warwick' Smith (1749–1831), 22 watercolours made in 1776–81. 1936–7–4–6 to 51 (list), formerly an album, now broken up and mounted, also containing views of Tenby and Caldy Islands.
5 Thomas Jones (1742–1803), two sketchbooks with views of Rome and surrounds. The first bought 2 December 1776 (198 a.8, 1981–5–16–17(1–94), list), the second bought 17 February 1777 (200 b.10; 1981–5–16–18(1–38), list).

There are various collections of prints of miscellaneous views of Rome, mostly of the XVIIc., in the British Library: see, for example, C. 134 g.11; 559* b.25; 3 Tab 34.

See also exhibitions 1981, and (for XVI–XVIIc. artists) 1984.

Royal Academy of Arts

The Department possesses a complete set of Royal Academy catalogues from 1769 to 1849 extra-illustrated by J. H. Anderdon (see p. 56). The library contains many pamphlets, books and exhibition catalogues connected with it. See also the catalogue of the Department exhibition of 1969, *Royal Academy Draughtsmen 1769–1969*, by Andrew Wilton. This contains 338 entries arranged in groups: history, portraits, presidents, founder members, associates and academicians.

Rubens, Sir Peter Paul (1577–1640)

The collection of drawings is arranged in the order of the catalogue by A. M. Hind, *Rubens, Van Dyck and other Artists of the Flemish School*, 1923. Hind catalogued 118 drawings as by Rubens himself, with another ten in an appendix. More recent scholarship has reattributed many of these. A new catalogue remains to be compiled, but see the exhibition catalogue of 1977 *Rubens Drawings and Sketches* by John Rowlands, which includes every drawing in the collection now thought to be by Rubens, along with numerous loans from British and foreign collections. Hind includes as his number 118 the so-called 'Costume Book', which contains mostly costume studies as well as copies after monuments, paintings and tapestries, German prints, drawings made in the Near East and Persian miniature paintings (197 d.7; 1841–12–11–8(1 to 39). It has been published by K. L. Belkin as volume XXIV of the *Corpus Rubenianum*, 1980. After the publication of Hind, a group of sixteen drawings from the Peel collection was transferred in 1935 on permanent loan from the National Gallery (q.v.).

The collection of prints after Rubens is arranged in seven portfolios according to the order and numbering given by Max Rooses, *P. P. Rubens, Histoire et description de ses tableaux et dessins*, 1886–92. It has also been marked off against Voorhelm Schneevogt, *Catalogue des estampes gravées d'après Rubens*, 1873.

Salting, George (1835–1909)

Son of a Danish merchant who had made a fortune in Australia; educated in England where he settled in 1857. From 1865 till his death he devoted his entire life and fortune of about £30,000 a year to his collection which he bequeathed to the National Gallery, the British Museum and the Victoria and Albert Museum. The Department was permitted to select those of his prints and drawings that it wanted, with the remainder going to the V&A. The total came to 433 (1910–2–12–1 to 433, list). 1–291 were drawings: 1–46 Italian, 47–101 French, 102–110 German, 111–221 Dutch and Flemish, 223–291 British. The most important were 17 Rembrandts, 18 Turners and a group of 33 portrait drawings by the Clouets or their school. 292–433 were prints: the most important were 49 Rembrandts and 21 Marcantonios. See the catalogue of the 1910 exhibition of drawings from the Salting bequest.

Scharf, George (1788–1860)

A Bavarian artist who settled in London in 1816. He made a large number of sketches and watercolours of topographical subjects and everyday life during the Regency and early Victorian periods, which have come to the Department by purchase from his widow in 1862, and by bequest from his son Sir George Scharf, the first Director of the National Portrait Gallery, in 1900. His drawings are full of anecdote and give information on such varied topics as shops, beggars, advertising methods, road-making, inquests and the Lord Mayor's Show. They also show the British Museum at many stages of the building operations between 1828–50.

The collection was summarily catalogued by Binyon (IV pp. 33–7) before the drawings were arranged into their present grouping of six bound volumes and five mounted solander boxes. The mounted drawings were selected on grounds of quality, while the others were arranged into a rough thematic grouping. No attempt was made to follow Binyon's fairly random order, and no concordance exists between the two. Similarly the register gives a complete listing of the drawings (1862–6–14–1 to 1196; 1900–7–25–1 to 181), but since the arrangement in the albums differs, there is no way of finding the location of any particular item from its register number. The following is a synopsis of the contents of the six bound albums:

1 Advertising, beggars, building operations, country types, election scenes, furniture, London types, Lord Mayor's show, uniforms, musical performers, orientals, schools, shipping, liveries.
2 Street cries and musicians, trades, transport, coffee houses, kitchens, hospitals, public houses.
3 British Museum, courts of law, exhibitions, Guildhall, Parliament, inquests, lectures.
4 London topography, shops.
5 London environs.
6 London topography.

There are also three sketchbooks:

7 Sketches made at the British camp in the Bois de Boulogne in 1815 during army service in the Waterloo campaign (Binyon 10). 198 a.23; 1900–7–25–122(1–37).
8 Scenes and figures in London streets 1823–8 (Binyon 11). 198 a.24; 1900–7–25–121(1–29).
9 Scenes in the streets and everyday life in London 1825–40 (Binyon 12). 198 a.25; 1900–7–25–120(1–60).

Schreiber, Lady Charlotte (1812–1895)

A daughter of the Earl of Lindsay; her first husband was Sir Josiah Guest, the Welsh iron magnate, and after his death she managed the business for some years. Her second husband, Charles Schreiber, was her children's tutor. She was a distinguished Welsh scholar, and her great collection of English pottery and porcelain was presented to the Victoria and Albert Museum in 1884. She presented her collection of fans (q.v.) to the Department in 1891, and in 1893 a number of games (q.v.). Various supplementary items were added in the next few years. Her collection of playing cards (q.v.) was bequeathed in 1895. Montague Guest (q.v.) was one of her sons. See Frank Herrmann, *The English as Collectors*, 1972, pp. 329–43.

Sculptors

The series of prints after works in sculpture is described above, p. 40. The Department also possesses drawings by artists who worked primarily or occasionally as sculptors. The following list is not exhaustive, and the drawings referred to may well not, in fact, relate to sculpture:

AMERICAN Shapiro.
BRITISH Armitage, Bacon, Butler, Caro, Chantrey, Dobson, Epstein, Flaxman, Frink, Fullard, Gibbons, Gibson, Gill, Hepworth, Hermes, Kenny, Kirk, Leighton, Martin, Meadows, Moore, Nicholson, Nimptsch, Nollekens, Paolozzi, Pierce, Rysbrack, Sandle, Stevens, Tucker, Watts, Westmacott, Derwent Wood.
FRENCH Barye, Bouchardon, Degas, Dubuffet, Gaudier-Brzeska, Gauguin, Maillol, Matisse, Puget, Renoir, Rodin.
GERMAN Klinger, Kollwitz.

ITALIC Algardi, Bandinelli, Bernini, Canova, Cellini, Foggini, Guidi, Michelangelo, Pierino da Vinci, Raffaello da Montelupo, attrib. to Rossellino, Francesco da San Gallo, Verrocchio. SCANDINAVIAN Sergel, Thorwaldsen. SPANISH Picasso.

Shakespeare, William (1564–1616)

The main groups of illustrations to Shakespeare's plays are:

1 One portfolio from the bequest of H. S. Ashbee (see Illustrations to Authors). It contains illustrations to all the plays, with a separate wrapper for each play. The entire series is registered in alphabetical order of play as 1900–12–31–2005 to 2298.

2 Thirty-six illustrated editions of the plays in the Departmental library (see the index), plus various recent catalogues and pamphlets on the subject.

3 Three volumes containing 899 proofs of wood-engravings to all the plays cut by the Dalziels (q.v.) from designs by Sir J. Gilbert 1858–60 (248 b.1–3).

4 A broken-up copy of the Boydell (q.v.) Shakespeare of 1803–5 (inventory Dd 6.6, no list). The plates have been distributed in the master series, while the text is at Oo 7.6.

5 An extra-illustrated copy of the Second Folio edition of Shakespeare's plays, containing six watercolours by William Blake and illustrations by other artists (200 b.12; see above p. 59).

About 200 portraits of Shakespeare are kept in a separate portfolio, and portraits of many actors in Shakespearean parts will be found in the main portrait series. A particularly fine group of portraits of Garrick is in the Burney (q.v.) collection. There are also numerous prints and drawings on Shakespearean subjects scattered through the master and engraver series. See, for example, lithographs by Delacroix, and drawings by Alexander Runciman and Henry Fuseli. See also s.v. Toy Theatre.

Sheepshanks, John (1787–1863)

A Leeds cloth manufacturer. His first collection was of Dutch and Flemish prints and drawings, which he sold en bloc to the dealer William Smith, who passed it on to the British Museum in 1835 for £5000. He then began to collect contemporary British paintings which he presented to the nation in 1857 (now in the Victoria and Albert Museum). The drawings were registered as 1836–8–11–1 to 812, and there is a separate inventory of them drawn up by Carpenter. The prints are in a separate inventory volume with a unique numbering sequence from 1 to 7694. They were combined with the Dutch and Flemish prints already in the collection and most were mounted in a series of 41 albums (plus a few unnumbered ones); a few were placed in the parallel sequence of unmounted etchings. These albums are often referred to (not strictly accurately) as the Sheepshanks series.

An ornate cabinet in the Keeper's study came with the collection, and is now known as the Sheepshanks cabinet (case 205). It has a plaster composition in the pediment designed by Erasmus Quellinus, painted to simulate bronze. The rest of the woodwork is an early XIXc. confection. On the cabinet's provenance from Bernardus de Bosch (1742–1816), see B. Haak 'Het portret van een Amsterdamse verzamlaars-familie uit de 18e eeuw', *Antiek* I. It now houses the pornographic material and part of the collection of blocks and plates.

Shipping

There is a portfolio of prints of shipping. The British section contains 42 prints and drawings of a miscellaneous group of ships by various arists. It includes the *Great Eastern* 1856, the *Great Britain* 1843, the *Archimedes* 1839, and types such as convict ships, East and West Indiamen and others. The drawings are by Richard Cook (1784–1857) of Roman galleys (1882-3-11–996 to 999) and by C. H. Muller in 1834 of xv–xvic. vessels. Other prints in this portfolio are mentioned in the entry on Naval History.

The section of foreign shipping contains prints from the following countries: America 3, China 3, Holland 44, France 63 (including a series of etchings by J. P. Guéroult du Pas, *Les Différens Bâtimens de la Mer Océanne*, 1709; 1924-6-19–1 to 61), Germany 2, Italy 12, Spain 1.

In addition, there are many single prints of shipping and shipwrecks kept in the master and engraver series. Some of these have been noted on the subject cards on the duty desk. Interesting groups will be found among the engravings by R. Pollard (British, Dutch, Spanish and French frigates of 1788) and the prints after Thomas Baston (HMS *Blenheim*, the *Royal George*, the *Royal Sovereign*, the *Britannia*, the *Royal Ann*, of 1710–30). See also s.v. Yachting.

Among the drawings, two by William and John Cantiloe Joy of 1858 should be noted: Men-of-War at Spithead, and Ships in a Storm (1883-12-8–2, 3; Binyon 1, 2).

Shrimpton and Giles Bequest

By the will of William Giles (d.1939), the sum of £3000 was bequeathed as capital to establish a fund, to be known as the 'A. M. Shrimpton and William Giles Bequest', whose object was to encourage the art of colour printing. The Keepers of the Departments of Prints and Drawings in the British Museum and the Victoria and Albert Museum were appointed Trustees. A schedule suggested ways in which this object could be achieved, and specified that prints must be in colour, and preferably from relief metal plates or wood blocks; aquatint and lithograph were allowed if necessary, but one-plate colour etchings or drypoints were excluded. Between 1943–9 the income was applied to purchases for both departments, as well as the Circulation Department of the V&A. From 1950–60 a biennial competition was held, organised by the V&A, with the winners being awarded purchase prizes. In 1960 the capital was increased by another £3600 given by Mrs M. T. Leggatt, trustee for the remainder of the Giles estate. In the early 1960s the income reverted to being spent on individual acquisitions. From 1968 to the present it has been used to fund a prize at the Bradford International Print Biennale.

Silhouettes

There is no collection of silhouettes as such, and a far better collection will be found at the National Portrait Gallery. A number of silhouette portraits are placed in the main portrait collection, and can only be found by searching through the O'Donoghue and Hake catalogue. An example is the portrait of Nevil Maskelyne of 1792 from the Banks collection. The only significant group of cut silhouettes is in an album by Jane E. Cook (case 35; 1939-3-6–13(1–35)).

See also s.v. Cut Paper, the Book Index s.v. Silhouettes, and prints after Moritz von Schwind and Skating Scraps (188* b.2).

Silk, Works on

Examples of engravings printed on silk include:

1 Cornelis Cort after Giulio Clovio, Christ on the Cross, hand-coloured (see the 1986 catalogue of Florentine XVIc. Drawings under no. 97). 1895–9–15–1407.
2 John Spilsbury (engraver), A new and most accurate map of the roads of England and Wales 1921–8–18–1.
3 The Ceremonies to be observed at the Royal Coronation of Queen Victoria. 1902–10–11–8776 (placed with English History 1838).

A portrait of Edward Ellice MP (1787–1863) is woven out of silk thread. 1921–4–11–112. An impression of *England at one view. The statistical pocket handkerchief*, a mid-Victorian wood-engraving by M. U. Sears, is printed on linen (1952–8–1–1). Other items printed on silk are some admission tickets in the Banks collection: C 2. 183 to 199, and 1661 to 1673.

Skating

There are two collections of skating prints and drawings in the Department:

Fowler collection

Given by Dr G. H. Fowler in 1924, with a supplementary gift in 1938 (1924–7–12–1 to 183; 1938–1–3–1 to 13). The collection is mounted in a large album of 97 pp. in the following order: Netherlands (XV–XIXc.), England (XVIII–XIXc.), France (XVIII–XIXc.), Germany and Austria (XVIIIc.). Several minor unregistered items are in a separate portfolio. The collection contains reproductions of paintings and prints as well as original prints, and was put together by J. van Buttingha-Wichers.

Cannan collection

Presented by Miss F. L. Cannan in 1931 (1931–11–14–57 to 668). The collection includes reproductions and photographs, as well as original works, to illustrate skating and events on ice, including topography, caricature, historical and other scenes, from the XVI–XXc., some being in colour. It is registered in the following order: drawings (57–160), prints (161–619), books (620–646), glass prints (647–668). The single items are mounted on 147 mounts in six solander boxes. The mounts are arranged as follows: English (1–77), Netherlandish (78–124), others (125–147). A few of the best drawings have been extracted and mounted with the main collection. The most interesting of the books are two albums labelled 'Skating Scraps' (188* b.1,2) which contain a miscellany of reproductions.

There is a finding list which serves as a catalogue to both the Fowler and Cannan collections. See also Frost Fairs, Sporting Prints and Drawings.

Sketching Club

The Club was founded in 1799, and members spent evenings together drawing a chosen subject from literature or the imagination. The Department possesses a group portrait of members of the Sketching Club of 1836 by John Partridge (1887–11–16–2). Examples of works produced at the evening sessions include John Sell Cotman's Weird Scene of 1803 (1902–5–14–39), and illustrations to *A Difficult Passage* by John James Chalon (1956–12–19–1) and Clarkson Stanfield (1956–12–19–2).

Slade, Felix (1790–1868)

A wealthy amateur, and founder of the
Slade professorships at Oxford,
Cambridge and London Universities. The
greatest of his bequests to the British
Museum was his collection of glass, but he
also bequeathed his very choice collection
of prints. He was renowned for his extreme
fussiness for perfection of impression.
They were registered as 1868–8–22–12 to
8853 (list). The main sections are as
follows: single-sheet prints 12–2163,
portraits 2164–2497, and illustrations
taken from periodicals and books
2871–7102. Eleven books occupy the
numbers 7903–8853. There were only 23
drawings, all connected with book
illustration (7588–7611). See the
exhibition guide of 1869 to the prints from
the bequest exhibited in the King's
Library, and the pamphlet for the 1968
exhibition in the same location: *Felix Slade,
Collector and Benefactor.*

Sloane, Sir Hans (1660–1753)

The foundation collection of Sir Hans
Sloane purchased by Parliament in 1753
included both printed books and
manuscripts. Among them were large
numbers of prints and drawings mounted
into albums, whose arrangement seems to
have been largely but not entirely by
subject-matter rather than artist. The
albums of prints seem to have passed via
the Department of Printed Books to the
new Department of Prints and Drawings,
and there is no record of their arrangement
before the inventory of 1837 by which time
they had been reorganised and
incorporated with the prints from the
Fawkener and Cracherode collections.
The albums of drawings, on the other
hand, came via the Department of
Manuscripts, and can be reconstructed
almost in their entirety, since most of them
were described in a manuscript catalogue
made by Carpenter in 1845 (cf pp. 8–9)
before they were broken up. There were
seven main albums which contained the
collection of drawings of primarily artistic
interest; these were nos 5214, 5223, 5224,
5226, 5227, 5236 and 5237 of the
following list, which were numbered by
Carpenter from 1 to 7. In addition to these
(and certainly of a different format) were
the Bolten and Dürer albums (5217, 5218)
and the two van Huysum albums (5284,
5285).

The Sloane manuscripts were allocated
the numbers 1–4100; the series of
additional manuscripts then begins at
4101. But for some reason the albums of
Sloane drawings were omitted, and only
subsequently given the numbers 5018–27
and 5214–5308. Most of these albums
have remained in the Department of
Manuscripts. The following are the ones
which are now in this Department,
ignoring those which have been transferred
back to Manuscripts. See also Popham's
article on Sloane material in the Print
Room in the *British Museum Quarterly*,
XVIII 1953, pp. 10–14.

3981 'Officium Beatae Mariae Virginis'.
Manuscript containing 12 engravings by
Israhel van Meckenem. Transferred in
1897. 158 b.1*; 1897–1–3–1 to 12.
5214 301 miscellaneous drawings, mostly
Dutch and Flemish of the XVIIc. including
Hollar's Tangier panoramas and shipping
drawings by the van de Veldes. Inventory
T 10; now broken up.
5217 'Bolten van Swol Teekeninge 1637'
on cover. Inventory Ii 6; the album
containing 424 drawings survives in c.152.
See Popham (Catalogue of Dutch and
Flemish Drawings) V, pp. 96–136.

5218 'AD Teeckening 1637', being Sloane's Dürer album. Almost all the 229 drawings have now been extracted, but the album survives in c.152. Inventory C 7.

5219 'Vischen, Vogelen, Dieren, Vruchten 1637'. Containing a miscellany of items, mostly Dutch XVIC., still in the album c.152. Inventory C 6; transferred in 1845 to Manuscripts, returned to Prints and Drawings 1886. See Popham V pp. 208–20.

5220 Still in Dept Manuscripts. Folios 12, 18, 19, 29 containing various monstrous animals extracted and transferred in 1928 (1928–3–10–96 to 99).

5221 Drawings by Frans Post dated 1645 of scenes from the expedition to Brazil of Maurice of Nassau in 1637–44. Being the original drawings for the book *G. Barlaei rerum per octennium in Brasilia historia*, Amsterdam 1647. Transferred in 1928. 197* a.2; 1928–3–10–90(1 to 32).

5223 65 Italian drawings. Inventory A 20; now broken up.

5224 88 Italian drawings. Inventory A 17; now broken up.

5226 193 drawings, mostly Italian and German. Inventory A 7; now broken up.

5227 113 drawings, mostly of heads, and mostly Italian. Inventory A 6; now broken up.

5234 Still in Dept Manuscripts. Folio 89 (Jan Scorel, View of the ruins of Bethlehem) extracted and transferred 1928 (1928–3–10–100).

5236 186 Dutch, Italian, French drawings. Inventory A 21; now broken up.

5237 166 Dutch, Italian, French drawings. Inventory A 22; now broken up.

5239 Watercolours of church vessels and ecclesiastical ornaments by Adolphus Gaab, Joseph Grisoni, P. S. Bartoli and John Talman. Transferred in 1928. 197* d.3; 1928–3–10–91(1 to 48).

5249 Anonymous designs for ornament

and flowers. Transferred in 1928. 197 b.17; 1928–3–10–92(1 to 52).

5251 Landscapes attributed to J. van der Vaart (1647–1721). Transferred in 1928. 197 a.7; 1928–3–10–93(1 to 12).

5259 Still in Dept Manuscripts. Folios 13 and 227 (mezzotint by J. C. Le Blon of male genitals and an anonymous English woodcut of 1552 of a monstrous child) extracted and transferred 1928 (1928–3–10–101,2).

5261 166 drawings of quadrupeds, including Dürer's Elk and Walrus and 32 drawings by George Edwards (1694–1773) (now taken out). Not in 1837 inventory; album survives in c.203.

5264 Still in Dept Manuscripts. Folios 23 (Jacopo de' Barbari, Dead partridge) extracted and transferred 1928 (1928–3–10–103).

5270 Early copies of John White's drawings of Virginia, etc. Transferred in 1893, but not registered. 199 a.3. Cf s.v. White.

5275–6 Two albums of flower drawings by Maria Sybilla Merian. Inventory N 1,2. 198* b.5,6.

5277 79 drawings by Nicolas Robert of plants, birds, shells etc. Inventory A 16; transferred in 1845 to Manuscripts, returned to Prints and Drawings 1886. Now c.203.

5278 65 drawings by Nicolas Robert of plants, birds, shells, etc. Inventory A 16; provenance as for 5277. Now c 203.

5279 40 drawings of animals, birds, plants, etc. by various artists. Inventory C 5; provenance as for 5277. Now 199* b.3.

5281 Heinrich Füllmaurer and Albrecht Meyer, drawings of plants for the woodcut illustrations in L. Fuchs *De Historia stirpium commentarii insignes*, Basle 1542. The album also contains drawings of surgical operations, and allegorical and other compositions. Transferred in 1928.

197* d.2; 1928–3–10–94(1 to 205).

5283 305 drawings of plants by various artists, including Dr Massey, Mr Catesby and Jan van Huysum (1682–1749). The Huysum drawings have been taken out and mounted. Inventory N 5; c.203.

5284–5 265 drawings of plants by Jacob van Huysum (*c*.1687–1740). See Binyon IV pp. 285–8. Inventory N 3,4 c.203.

5289 Still in Dept Manuscripts. Folios 245–7 (mezzotints of plants by E. Kirkall) extracted and transferred in 1928 (1928–3–10–104 to 106).

5308 Jewellery designs by Hans Holbein II. Transferred in 1860, but not registered. Album broken up. See Croft-Murray pp. 558–70, nos. 4–184.

Two other volumes in the Department seem never to have had Manuscript numbers, and perhaps came via Printed Books:

Min 269 Jacques Le Moyne: *La Clef des Champs*, London 1586. 162 a.25; 1952–5–22–1(1 to 48).

Min 273 Attributed to Ellen Power: 38 drawings of flowers, plants, birds. 198 a.18; 1975 U.1589(1 to 38); Croft-Murray I p. 3.

See also exhibitions 1960.

Smith, William (1808–1876)

The outstanding print dealer of his age, and benefactor of the Department. He and his brother George took over their father's business in Lisle Street in 1835, and both retired in 1848. During his professional career he was the intermediary in the purchase of the Sheepshanks collection, of large sections of the Coningham collection (1843–5–13–1 to 504, 1845–8–9–1 to 1757, 1845–8–25–1 to 829), of items purchased at the Beckford sale (1848–11–25–1 to 562, 1849–5–12–1 to 200) and of many other single prints and groups of prints. After his retirement he presented a large collection of satires and sketches by Gillray and other artists (1851–9–1–1 to 1398) and in 1850 a collection of rare auction catalogues of the XVIII–XIXc.

Sporting Prints and Drawings

There is a separate series of mounted sporting prints. It is arranged in five royal solanders, eight imperial, three atlas, and one antiquarian plus one portfolio. The organisation is partly by engraver and partly by designer, but there is a card index which enables all the prints in this series to be traced, as well as the many other sporting prints kept in other series under the names of the artist or engraver. The collection is also marked off against the standard catalogue by Frank Siltzer, *The Story of British Sporting Prints*, 1929. There are a number of drawings of sporting subjects. The largest single group is by James Pollard (1933–10–14–105 to 256, presented by Arthur du Cave): 16 are mounted, the rest are in an album and a sketchbook (198 a.16**). There is also a group of five race horses by James Seymour (1940–10–12–3 to 7).

The catalogue of the exhibition held in 1983, *Sporting Life, an Anthology of British Sporting Prints*, by Paul Goldman, is arranged by categories and covers a very wide range of sports: archery, athletics, animal baiting, ballooning, bowls and croquet, boxing and wrestling, coaching and trotting, cricket, fencing, fishing, football, golf, horse-racing, hunting, rowing and yachting, shooting and hawking, skating, tennis and rackets, and a miscellany. An appendix gives a checklist of the prints in the collection that are described by Siltzer. An earlier exhibition of sporting prints was held in 1933 with the aim of encouraging gifts (see BMQ VIII, pp. 69–70); it was only moderately successful, and the collection remains very weak in the area of classic British sporting prints. By far the best collection is that of Paul Mellon in the British Art Center in Yale, of which a catalogue by Dudley Snelgrove has been published: *British Sporting and Animal Prints 1658–1874*, 1981.

See also s.v. Balloons, Skating, Transport, Yachting.

Stothard, Thomas (1755–1834)

There is a large collection of drawings, mostly illustrations for books and other decorative purposes. Part is mounted (royal, imperial and antiquarian sizes), while the remainder is kept in four bound volumes and four portfolios. Many of the drawings came from the Vaughan (q.v.) bequest (1900–8–24–220 to 489) and that of Miss Julia Sharpe (1946–4–13–1 to 180). For the mounted series, see Binyon IV pp. 138–62. The volumes and portfolios are:

1 Illustrations to Shakespeare, Rogers, Scott, Boccaccio, etc. 201 b.7; 1867–4–13–396 to 524. Binyon p. 162.
2 Views and buildings in Britain and France. 199* b.14; 1919–11–15–8 to 97.
3 Pen outlines after Stothard. 199* b.14*; 1935–7–11–5 to 12.
4 Portraits and other sketches. 102A number 55; 1961–2–11–4 to 29.

The following four portfolios, each of which has a list at the front, contain the drawings from the Sharpe bequest:

5 Figure studies, studies from sculpture and for monuments and paintings. 200* a.2; 1946–4–13–various.

6 Illustrations to Rogers. 200* c.1; 1946–4–13–26 to 77, 79, 105 to 107.
7 Illustrations to Langhorne's *Fables of Flora*, Townsend's *Poems*, Gessner's *Death of Abel*, etc. 200* c.2; 1946–4–13–various.
8 Chinese figures, English and foreign topography, etc. 200* c.3; 1946–4–13–various.

The main group of prints after Stothard is the Robert Balmanno collection, mounted into four albums (1849–7–21–1 to 2186, list). These contain many touched proofs, variant states and a very few preparatory drawings. Ten etchings by Stothard from the same collection are kept separately (2187–96). Other prints are kept loose in two boxes. Most of these come from the collections of William Beckford (1849–5–12–344 to 513, list), Sir Charles Price (1859–8–6–644 to 914, list) and Felix Slade (1868–8–22–6816 to 6928, list).

Sutherland, Graham (1903–1980)

In 1980 Mrs Kathleen Sutherland presented a large group of her late husband's work to the Department (1980–10–11–129 to 223). It comprised 28 drawings, 8 sketchbooks and 59 etchings and lithographs. In addition she gave from his collection a drawing by Samuel Palmer titled 'The valley farm' and two of his etchings, plus a sheet of drawings by Henry Moore of ideas for sculpture (1980–10–11–224 to 227).

The Department independently possesses a large group of his early etchings, and a complete portfolio of 'A Bestiary', 1968, which was presented by Dr and Mrs Bernhard Baer (1980–10–11–214(1–26)). The prints have been marked off in Felix Man, *Graham Sutherland, Das graphische Werk*, 1970.

Swain, Joseph (1820–1909)

A group of 665 proofs of wood-engravings cut by Swain was purchased from J. Swain and Son in 1908 (1908–4–14–413 to 1063). They have been distributed: 14 portraits have been placed in the portrait series (399–412), and the rest placed under the names of the designers (A. Ansdell, R. Doyle, F. Eltze, H. Furniss, A. B. Houghton, J. Lawson, J. Leech, Lord Leighton, W. M. Thackeray, J. C. Millais, J. N. Paton, F. W. Walker, A. F. A. Sandys, J. Tenniel, and others).

A later acquisition was an album of proofs of illustrations to *Punch's Pocket-Book* of 1865–81 cut by Swain (248 b.5*; 1914–10–12–32 to 140).

Talman, John (1677–1719)

There are two albums from the collection of the architect John Talman. The first is described in the entry on Sloane (Sloane 5239). The other contains watercolours partly by Talman himself and partly assembled by him. The subjects include the Doge's corno, the tiara made for Julius II, and the morse designed by Cellini for Clement V. Two watercolours by Bernard Lens (1682–1740) of the crown worn by George I at his coronation and of William III in garter robes, which had been removed from the album, were added in 1912 (197* c.2); 1893–4–11–10(1–18), 1912–4–16–44,45. Binyon IV p. 170).

Tate Gallery

A group of 28 XIXc. French drawings was deposited by the Tate Gallery on long loan in the Department in 1963. They were formally transferred in 1975, and assigned the register numbers 1975–3–1–29 to 56. The drawings are by Boudin, Daumier, David, Delacroix, Flandrin, Guys, Harpignies, Ingres, Eugène Isabey, Menzel and Puvis de Chavannes. Since 1975 certain duplicate impressions of prints (notably a group of etchings by Stubbs) have been transferred from this Department to the Tate Gallery.

See also s.v. Turner.

Theatrical Material

The Departmental library contains 58 books of prints which can be traced in the index under the heading Theatre. Portraits of British actors and actresses can be traced through O'Donoghue and Hake, but to their lists must be added the prints in the bequest of theatrical portraits by Richard Henry Bath (1933–10–14–280 to 646, list). Most of these have been placed in the main portrait series, but a number of duplicate impressions have been mounted into an album in alphabetical order of actor/actress. At the end are some fine impressions of double portraits (mostly mezzotints) in scenes from dramas. A few drawn portraits are listed in the catalogue of the 1974 exhibition of Portrait drawings, nos 260–78. A quantity of material relating to the French stage will be found in the extra-illustrated *Lettres* of Mme de Sevigné (see p. 56). See also s.v. Burney, Commedia dell'Arte, Toy Theatres. London theatres will be found in the main collection of topography of London (q.v.); the best sources for provincial theatres are the coloured aquatints in J. Winston, *The Theatre Tourist*, 1805 (173 a.12).

An unpublished handlist was produced by E. Croft-Murray in 1954 listing 103 items of theatrical material in this Department, with a few additions from the Library departments. It includes drawings, watercolours, prints and illustrated books, and covers actors, stage and costume designs, and theatres. The most notable drawings are the following:

1 Stefano della Bella, 58 costume designs. 1887–5–2–3 to 60.
2 Baccio del Bianco, 31 costume designs after della Bella. 1887–5–2–61 to 91.
3 Giuseppe Galli Bibiena, various stage settings.
4 Samuel de Wilde, portraits of actors and actresses. M 32.1–19.
5 Carl Friedrich Schinkel, design for a scene in König Yngurd. 1895–10–15–1.
6 Mary Hamilton, Mrs Siddons' dresses and attitudes in various characters. 1876–5–10–816 to 896.
7 Attrib. to Henry Hodgins, designs for stage sets. 1857–6–13–1183 to 1191.
8 Charles Ricketts, costume and stage designs. 1933–6–10–1 to 8.

To Croft-Murray's list may be added the following:

9   23 subjects from the opera Il Pomo d'Oro 1668, etchings after L. Burnacini. 1891–4–14–111 to 133.
10 John Devoto, Album of 93 drawings, many of which are designs for stage scenery. 201 b.3; 1891–6–27–1(1–91). Also another similar design, dated 1724. 1962–12–8–7.
11 Michael Angelo Rooker, A scene painter in his studio, watercolour. 1968–2–10–32 (see S. Rosenfeld, BMQ XXXIV 1969, pp. 33–6).
12 Three scenes from P. A. Wolff's Preciosa, anonymous German etchings. 1967–7–22–9 to 11.
13 André Dunoyer de Segonzac, drawings of Isadora Duncan, Nijinsky and Ida Rubinstein. 1951–7–14–1 to 15.
14 Oskar Kokoschka, 7 stage settings for Weber's Oberon 1956. 1967–10–14–3 to 9.

15 Richard Winnington, album of humorous drawings of characters from films. 197* d.13; 1956–11–22–1 to 17.

Tinsel Prints

There is one example of a XVc. tinsel print in the collection: St Dorothy, 1895–1–22–18 (Schreiber 1398; Dodgson A80). Ten specimens of XIXc. prints with foil additions are at the end of volume 9 of the Toy Theatre (q.v.; 168* c.2). See 1886–11–27–12 to 15, and 1958–7–2–264 to 269.

Title-pages

There is a separate portfolio of title-pages taken out of books, arranged by country of publication: Denmark, France, Germany, Great Britain, Italy, Netherlands, Switzerland. There is also a section of printers' marks. The contents all come from a gift from Sir Augustus Wollaston Franks: 1895–10–31–1 to 1152 (list). Other printed title-pages are kept in the series of cuts from XVc. books and Italian woodcuts, or under the names of the designer or engraver: see for example Hans Holbein, Urs Graf, Jost Amman and Claude Mellan. A few drawings by Rubens for title-pages are described as numbers 204ff. of the 1977 Rubens exhibition catalogue. The British Library has two collections: those of Joseph Ames (Ames 1–9) and of John Bagford. For the latter, see Melvin H. Wolf, *Catalogue and Indexes to the Title-pages of English Printed Books Preserved in the British Library's Bagford Collection*, 1974.

Topography

The separate series of topographical prints is described above, pp. 47–9, where references are also given to the published catalogues of the collections of topographical prints and drawings from the library of George III and elsewhere kept in the British Library. It cannot be overstressed that the topographical collections in the BL are in general much more extensive and much finer in quality than those in this Department. The present entry supplements the information given in pp. 47–9, by describing the other topographical prints and drawings kept in other series in the Department, and the means of tracing them.

Illustrated books containing topographical prints

Many of these can be traced by subject through the Book Index, not under the heading 'topography', but under the name of the continent, country or town depicted. The individual plates in some 203 books of British topography have also been indexed and can be found in the blue slip index to British topographical prints. Other plates can sometimes be traced through the indices to the bibliographies of the library of J. R. Abbey and other standard reference works.

Single-sheet topographical prints kept in the master or engraver series

There is no way of tracing these, apart from a few which have been included in the blue slip index to British topographical prints.

Topographical drawings and watercolours

There are topographical indices in Croft-Murray and Hulton's catalogue of British drawings, and in the five volumes of the catalogue of Dutch and Flemish drawings. There is an incomplete blue slip index of topographical subjects of drawings (both mounted and in sketchbooks) of the British school, and an incomplete blue slip index of topographical subjects for drawings of foreign schools.

The following list, arranged alphabetically by country, gives a small selection of some of the more useful groups of mounted drawings, albums of drawings, sketchbooks (and a few bound collections of prints) of topographical interest in the Department.

GENERAL

1 A portfolio of miscellaneous topographical drawings is at 200* a.1. The artists included are F. Franks, Vianelli, G. Witting, J. Faure.
2 George Keate (1729–97): Views in France, Italy, Savoy, Switzerland taken during a tour 1754–6. 201 c.4; 1878–2–9–106 to 338. Binyon 1.
3 Robert James Elliot (1790–1849): Views in South America, the Pacific, Australia 1820–2. 197* c.3; 1907–11–18–37 to 116.
4 Sir Charles John Holmes (1868–1936): 75 sketchbooks drawn in Spain, New York, Venice, Switzerland. 102A; 1937–3–13–198 to 272.
5 Ambrose Poynter (1796–1886): Views in France and Italy. 200 b.20; 1965–12–11–44(1–83).

AFRICA

6 Lieut. Andrew Motz Skene (d.1849): Drawings of St Helena. 198 a.26; 1884–11–8–12.
7 Laetitia Jervis Terry (1808–56): Drawings and lithographs of Sierra Leone. 1950–9–5–1 to 11.
8 Charles Wellington Furse (1868–1904): Sketches at sea and in South Africa. 102*; 1907–10–18–19.

AMERICAS

9 Frans Post (*c.*1612–80): Scenes connected with the expedition of Prince Maurice of Nassau to Brasil 1637–44. 197* a.2 (Sloane 5221); 1928–3–10–90(1–32).

10 Capt. Frederick Franks (d.1844): Views in North America 1824, watercolours. 198* a.2; 1880–9–1–1654 to 1730.

11 Lady Maria Callcott (1785–1842): Views in South America. 199* b.9; 1845–4–15–14(1–261). Binyon 2.

12 See separate entries for John White and Captain Cook.

AUSTRALIA

13 Charles Rodius (1802–60): Drawings of Aborigines. 197 d.8; 1840–11–14–64 to 81.

14 S. T. Gill (1818–80): Lithographs of gold-mining. 1969–6–14–16 to 39.

CHINA

15 William Alexander (1767–1816): Watercolours of Chinese subjects. 198 c.1; 1865–5–20–193 to 274 (list). Binyon I pp. 17–22.

EGYPT

16 See separate entry.

FRANCE

17 Gabriel Perelle (*c.*1603–77) and Israel Silvestre (1621–91): Album containing etchings of French views. 191* b.16*; 1975 U.729–1064.

18 Silvestre, Le Pautre and others: Album of engravings of Versailles. 250 a.1; 1889–12–18–33 to 169 (list).

19 See also s.v. Dawson Turner.

GREAT BRITAIN

20 Anonymous: Views in Great Britain, mostly in East Anglia, 1830s. 199 a.14; 1957–11–29–1 to 40.

21 John Laporte (1761–1839): Views in Britain and Ireland. 200 a.3*,3**; 1899–8–5–8 to 128 (list). Binyon 3,4.

22 William Daniell (1769–1837): Unpublished drawings made during his voyages round Great Britain 1814–24. 201 b.1,2; 1867–6–12–265 to 373. Binyon 25,26.

23 Francis Nicholson (1753–1844): 25 watercolours of Stourhead. 1944–10–14–124 to 148. Also 47 pencil sketches for the above: 1956–11–14–1 to 47.

24 Attributed to S. H. Grimm (1734–94): Sketches of Althorp and on the Thames at Barnes and Mortlake. 198 a.15*; 1919–7–12–1 to 97.

25 William Gawin Herdman (1805–82) and sons: two portfolios of watercolours of Liverpool made in the 1850s and later. 1981–11–7–38 to 222 (list).

26 Thomas Hornor (active 1800–40): Album of watercolours of the Vale of Neath, Glamorganshire 1817. 198 b.6*; 1937–10–8–165(1–28).

27 Joseph Farington (1747–1821): 56 drawings of the Clyde. 201 c.1**; 1936–4–9–1 to 55, 1936–6–13–4. Also Views of the Forth from its source to the sea. 201 c.1*; 1922–2–11–1 to 78.

28 J. C. Nattes (1765–1822): Views in Scotland 1799. 201 b.14; 1948–7–9–1 to 43 (list).

29 George Fennel Robson (1788–1833): 41 sketches of the Grampian mountains 1812. 198 b.6**; 1937–11–20–3(1–40) (no list).

30 See separate entries for London, Kaye (for Grimm collection), Buckler, Davy.

GREECE

31 Pauline, Lady Trevelyan (1816–66): Sketches in Greece 1842. 200 c.8; 1880–9–11–1384 to 1479 (list).

INDIA

32 J. Ridge (dates unknown): Views in India, *c.*1824–8. 200 b.14; 1970–12–2–25(1–57) (list).

33 R. Havell after J. B. Fraser: Views in the Himalaya mountains, aquatints. 243*; 1866–12–8–64 to 84.

34 Egron Sellif Lundgren (1815–75): Drawings of life in India 1857–8. 1915–3–13–56 to 71 (list).

35 William Simpson (1823–99): 4 Views in India, with others in Greece and elsewhere. 1900–4–11–33 to 41; Binyon 1–9 mounted.

36 Lady Maria Callcott (1785–1842): Views in India and Italy. 199* b.8; 1845–4–15–13(1–167). Binyon 1.

ITALY

37 Luca Carlevaris (1665–1731): The preparatory drawings for his set of etchings of Venetian views. 197 d.2; 1886–10–12–596(1–86).

38 Antonio Visentini (1688–1782): The preparatory drawings for the engravings *Prospectus Celebriores Venetiis* after Canaletto. 197* d.7.

39 Major J. P. Cockburn (*c.*1799–1847): Views in Italy 1817. 200 c.13; 1949–12–13–1 to 17.

40 Samuel James Ainslie (1806–74): 9 Italian sketchbooks. 102*; 1874–7–11–2309 to 2802. Also mounted watercolours of Etruscan antiquities. See Binyon 1–112.

41 See also s.v. Rome.

JAPAN

42 Georges Ferdinand Bigot (dates unknown): Three albums of prints of Japanese scenes *c.*1882. 191* a.14 (1919–11–16–1(1–26)); 192* a.27 (1983 U.2372(1–42)); 192* b.14 (1922–7–12–20(1–29) and 1937–1–29–2(1–31)).

MALTA

43 V. Feneck and others: Costume and topography of Malta. 197 c.17; 1933–11–28–2(1–53) (no list).

NETHERLANDS

44 Theodosius Forrest (1728–84): A tour through Flanders and many parts of Holland in the year 1769. Manuscript with drawings and watercolours. 198 a.44; 1981–7–25–7(1–17) (list).

45 See also the Beudeker atlas in the Map Room of the British Library. To Joan Blaeu's *Toonneel der Steden van de Vereenighde Nederlanden* and part of the *Atlas Major*, the collector Christoffel Beudeker added hundreds of maps and views of the Netherlands to form a collection of outstanding importance in 24 volumes. BL C 9d,e.

RUSSIA

46 Jean-Baptiste Le Prince (1734–81): Etchings and aquatints of Russian daily life and scenes. 1853–12–10–663 to 797 (list).

47 Evdokime Egoroff (1832–91): 68 prints of Russian subjects. 191* a.10; 1905–7–12–1 to 68.

SCANDINAVIA

48 Patrick Gibson (1782–1829): Views in the Faroe Islands. 201 c.2; 1880–9–11–1356 to 1383 (list).

49 Capt. Frederick Franks (d.1844): Views of the Faroe Islands 1818, watercolours. 198* a.1; 1880–9–11–1731 to 1754.

SWITZERLAND

50 John Robert Cozens (1752–97): 24 watercolours of Swiss scenery. 1900–4–11–9 to 32.

51 W. L. Leitch (1804–83): Views of Switzerland and the Rhine. 199 b.5; 1887–6–13–1 to 37. Binyon 3.

52 See separate entry for the R. W. Lloyd collection.

TURKEY
53 Luigi Mayer (active 1776–92):
Portfolio of 10 large watercolours of
Constantinople, 1788. 1947–3–19–16
to 25 (list). Also a volume of views in
the Ottoman Empire, including some
of Samos and Sicily. Case 195;
1960–2–12–1(1–52) (no list).
54 Capt. J. B. Estcourt (dates unknown):
Sketchbook with watercolours made
during the survey of the rivers Tigris
and Euphrates, 1855–7. Case 204;
1962–7–9–1(1–98) (no list).

Toy Theatre

In 1886 the Department purchased the
collection formed by Mr Ralph Thomas. It
is arranged in nine volumes by publisher or
type, and includes some original drawings
as well as coloured and uncoloured
versions of the same print. Many were both
published and designed by West 1811–54;
others were designed by well-known artists
like George Cruikshank and William
Heath. The subjects are very varied,
including pantomimes, tragedies (e.g.
Shakespeare), popular dramas, naval and
military battles, and portraits. The entire
collection is listed in the register at
1886–5–13–17 to 1961, but unfortunately,
when the collection was later mounted into
the albums, a different order was often
adopted and the register numbers
obscured. For this reason references have
to be given to the numbering sequence
within each volume. One set of portraits
described in alphabetical order at 761–967
can be found in volume two, numbers 63ff.

1 William West, Theatrical characters.
168* a.1.
2 William West, New theatrical
characters, combats and portraits.
168* a.2.

3 William West, Theatrical scenes.
168* a.3.
4 William West, Theatrical characters,
combats, pantomimes, tricks, scenes,
etc. 168* c.1.
5 Hodgson and Co, Theatrical characters,
portraits, tricks, scenes. 168* a.4.
6 Hodgson and Co, Theatrical groups,
scenes, etc. 168* b.1.
7 J. H. Jameson, Theatrical characters,
portraits, scenes. 168* a.5.
8 Bailey, Cole, Creed, Dyer, Edwards,
Green, Hebberd, Marks, Perkins, Skelt,
Smart, Stokes etc. Theatrical characters,
portraits, scenes. 168* a.6.
9 Supplementary and miscellaneous items.
This includes a few items not from the
Thomas collection added in later years;
the most interesting are figures with
applied metal foil. 168* c.2.

Trade Cards and Shop Bills

There are two series of trade cards in the
Department which are kept separately: the
Banks and Heal collections. Most of the
cards are British and most date between
c.1740–1800. The great majority come
from London, although the Banks
collection also has a significant number of
provincial cards. The Banks series was
mounted in the 1950s by Mrs Bernard
Croft-Murray. In 1976 Andrew Parkinson
completed the operation by rearranging the
Banks cards in the same way as the Heal
collection, with new sections added or
omitted as appropriate. He also compiled
manuscript lists of all the cards in both
collections; these lists have been bound in
five volumes.

In both series the various trades are
divided into 131 groups alphabetically
(from agricultural implement
manufacturers to woollen drapers), within
which the cards are arranged alphabetically
by merchant. Cards of unspecified

tradesmen are in group 132, while foreign cards are in a single sequence as group 133. Each group has its own number, and each individual card a sub-number. A proper reference, therefore, will be of the form Heal 54.6 (Mr Dechemant the dentist). In the case of the Heal collection there is no other register number; the Banks cards come from inventory D2, but since there is no concordance between the inventory and location numbers, the latter are used instead of the former.

All the cards are mounted on boards in cabinets which are housed outside the Department. They are therefore best consulted on the microfilm which has been made of the entire series. Parkinson's manuscript lists of both collections follow the sequence of their arrangement. There is an index of trades, which gives cross-references from other trades to the 131 recognised classifications. There is an index of engravers and publishers for the Banks, but not the Heal, series bound into the beginning of the Parkinson list. There is also an old blue slip index by name of tradesman for the Banks (but not Heal) collection, but this only gives references to inventory numbers and does not give the present location of the card.

Banks collection

Under this name and in this series is kept every trade card in the Department that does not come from the Heal collection. The great majority of these does indeed come from the collection of Sarah Banks (q.v.), but others came from Sir A. W. Franks (q.v.), the Fielden collection and other sources. There are about 6000 items in all, mainly of the period 1770–1810. There is a separate sequence for inns, filed by town with a cross-reference by proprietor. Since the Banks collection is rich in provincial cards, an index has been provided of towns in Britain and abroad represented in the collection. Some other cards are mounted into an album (242 a.34).

Heal collection

Formed by Sir Ambrose Heal (1872–1959), of the famous firm of furnishing specialists. Heal was a great authority on the history of London shops and trades, on which he published many articles and books, and formed his collection as part of his research materials, all of which he bequeathed to the British Museum. His collection of about 9000 items covers the same area as the Banks collection, but with some earlier cards and later additions. The main series of cards has included within it many related items such as newspaper cuttings, letters, shop bills, headed paper and reproductions, often taken from the Banks collection and the Bagford Bills in the British Library. There is an additional section of manuscript shop bills (mostly duplicates) kept at the end. There is also a separate sequence for inns, filed by county and town (with an index of proprietors where they are known). The mounts of the cards bear copious annotations in Heal's hand.

Besides the series of trade cards described above, Heal's research material included 10 boxes containing original prints and reproductions related to other aspects of London shops. They are arranged as follows: views of Old London Bridge (2), of New London Bridge, maps, views of shop facades and interiors, views of streets with shop facades, and 4 boxes of portraits of shopkeepers and tradesmen. The other research materials are Heal's own lecture and research notes, containing detailed lists of London goldsmiths, cabinet makers and upholsterers, and 24 folders listing locations of shop signs in XVIIIc. London.

The Department does not possess any examples of the later type of card, also known as trade cards, which were offered by firms from the later XIXc. to the present day as inducements to purchase their goods: the most familiar examples are cigarette cards. The British Museum has, however, been offered as a bequest the collection of E. C. Wharton-Tigar, which is a virtually definitive series of about a million examples of such cards. This will be kept as part of the Museum's central archaeological store, and does not come under the curatorial control of this Department.

Trades

This entry describes scenes of men practising a professional skill; for street vendors see s.v. Cries. See also s.v. Trade Cards (of which a few carry illustrations of their trades) and Industrial Scenes.

1 Jost Amman: Panoplia omnium . . . artium, woodcuts 1568. 159 d.11; 1904–2–6–103(1–131).

2 Jacquinet: Plusieurs modèles . . . en l'art d'arquebuzerie. Plates 2–4 show interiors of gunsmiths. 161 c.23(17); 1937–9–15–447(233–5).

3 Engravings after Jan Stradanus (van der Straeten): Nova reperta. 157* a.38; 1948–4–10–4(191 to 209).

4 Engravings after Francesco Maggiotto by Giovanni Volpato showing various trades. 1890–4–15–247 to 254; 1917–12–8–818 to 821.

5 Thomas Rowlandson, 5 of a set of 12 plates of Country characters, 1799. George 9482–7.

6 George Cruikshank, 13 from a set of 15 etchings of London characters, 1827–9. Reid 1391–1405.

7 W. H. Pyne: Microcosm . . . of the arts, agriculture and manufactures of Great Britain, 1806. In 92 sections with an alphabetical list of contents. 166 b.21; 1863–7–25–78 to 198.

8 A. S. Hartrick: drawings of peasant types in the Cotswold country, 1898–1900, with descriptive notes on their occupations. Mounted royal; various inventory numbers. See also etchings by Stanley Anderson.

Transparencies

A copy of Edward Orme, *An Essay on Transparent Prints, and on Transparencies in General*, 1807 is in the Department (167* c.51; 1922–10–17–20). It contains various specimens of transparencies. The series of English History for 1814 contains three other examples published to celebrate the peace on 1 August. There is also one watercolour transparency, a view of Netley Abbey by moonlight, dated 1820, by John Linnell (1956–12–24–1).

Transport

There is a portfolio of unmounted transport prints which contains a miscellany of prints and reproductions on such subjects as coaches, mails, steam carriages, caravans, trams, cycles, etc. All the best examples of the type have been mounted. There is an imperial solander solely devoted to transport prints: the contents are almost entirely coaching prints, with a few steam carriages. Fourteen further examples which have been mounted in other sizes have been included in the series of select sporting prints (royal, atlas and antiquarian size). A complete listing of the Department's holdings of prints recorded by Siltzer is published in the catalogue *Sporting Life* (see s.v. Sporting Prints). Siltzer, however, did not include steam carriages or vessels in his catalogue, and for this reason the five prints of these curiosities in the imperial transport solander are worth recording:

1 Steam Carriages (the Autopsy, Era and Infant) built by Mr Walter Hancock. 1871–8–12–5333.
2 Patent steam carriage by W. H. James. 1871–8–12–5334.
3 The Enterprise steam omnibus built by Mr Walter Hancock. 1871–8–12–5335.
4 The New Steam Carriage invented by Mr Goldsworthy Gurney. 1938–11–4–3.
5 View of British steam vessels, 1947–3–19–53.

A view of Leicester Square in 1753 with the Prince of Wales going to Court in a sedan chair, engraved by Parr, will be found in the Crace collection (XVIII.17).

The collection also contains an album of original drawings by an unidentified designer, together with some hand-coloured engravings, of carriages from the early xixc.: 198 c.16, 1856–10–11–31 to 97.

Turner, Dawson (1775–1859)

A Yarmouth banker and collector, and patron of Crome and Cotman (q.v.). A small part of his collection, a total of 146 items, was purchased from his sale in 1859; this included 32 British drawings (1859–5–28–115 to 146). He married Mary, daughter of Francis Palgrave, and her work together with that of five of their six daughters is represented in the Department: these are Maria Hooker b.1797, Elizabeth Palgrave b.1799, Mary Anne Turner b.1803, Harriett Gunn b.1806, Hannah Sarah Brightwen b.1808.

The part of the collection of drawings, prints and books which descended down the Palgrave side of the family was presented to the Department by the Rev. Francis Palgrave and Miss Annora Palgrave in 1941 (1941–12–13–1 to 695). It included three interesting albums:

1 Mostly drawings by Mrs Dawson Turner and her daughters Elizabeth and Mary Anne, as well as 5 drawings by J. S. Cotman (ff. 16, 20, 49, 54, 66 verso), 2 by C. R. Cockerell for his reconstructions of ancient Athens and Rome (ff. 61, 68), and portrait drawings of members of the family (ff. 81–5) and of John Crome (f. 80). 186 a.22; 1941–12–13–1 to 155 (no list).
2 One hundred original sketches of French, chiefly Norman, antiquities, drawn in 1819, mostly by Mrs Dawson Turner and Elizabeth Turner. 198* a.13; 1941–12–13–156 to 238a (no list).
3 Drawings mostly by Elizabeth Turner chiefly illustrating her continental tours of 1836 and 1837. 186 b.11; 1941–12–13–239 to 495 (no list).

The volumes of F. Blomefield's *History of Norfolk* collected and annotated by Dawson Turner and extra-illustrated by his family are now in the British Library (Add. Mss. 23013–62, 23064, 23065).

Turner, James Mallord William (1775–1851)

The Department possesses 116 drawings and watercolours by Turner and one sketchbook; a complete list of all these works is available for consultation. Most of the drawings and watercolours come from four bequests: 13 from the John Henderson (q.v.) bequest (1878–12–28–38 to 50); 18 from the Salting (q.v.) bequest (1910–2–12–272 to 289); 6 from the Sale bequests (1915–3–13–48 to 50, 82 to 84); and 61 from the Lloyd (q.v.) bequest

(1958–7–12–387 to 447). The sketchbook is of *c.*1845 and contains 70 leaves, 10 of which contain sketches (1981–12–12–15, presented by Mrs Edward Croft-Murray; included in the gift was an account book of the engraver W. B. Cooke concerning his dealings with Turner during the years 1817–24). The collection also includes three drawings of Turner: one by J. T. Smith of Turner in the Print Room (1885–5–9–1648; Binyon 1), the others by Sir Edwin Landseer of back and side views, in the second Redleaf album (199 b.16; 1981–5–16–20(45,46)).

The works on paper from the Turner Bequest were housed in this Department from October 1931 until their return in 1986 to the Tate Gallery, where they are housed in the newly built Clore Gallery. A microfilm of the entire Bequest is available for consultation in the Print Room. The Department library contains a photocopy of his will with its four codicils, together with a cancelled codicil. The British Library contains a group of autograph letters from 1809–51 (Add. Mss. 50118–9) and the notes for his lectures as Professor of Perspective in the Royal Academy (Add.Mss. 46151).

The collection of prints by and after Turner is arranged as follows:

1 The Liber Studiorum. There were 71 published plates, and 20 other ones begun but left unpublished. They are mounted and arranged in 13 boxes in the order of A. J. Finberg, *The History of Turner's Liber Studiorum*, 1924; the Department copy is marked. Most of the impressions were presented (1861–10–12–2223 to 2237) or bequeathed (1900–8–24–1 to 104) by Henry Vaughan, or given by W. G. Rawlinson (1913–7–12–12 to 19). There is also a complete set in the original wrappers (165 a.20; 1923–7–14–31 to 101). Annexed to the series is a box of the 47 plates of the later continuation of the Liber Studiorum by Sir Frank Short.

2 The so-called Little Liber mezzotints are contained in royal portfolio number 64 of the main collection of mezzotints. The collection is complete with the exception of R 802.

3 The main series of engravings after Turner's work is unmounted and arranged in 11 portfolios in the order of W. G. Rawlinson, *The Engraved Work of J. M. W. Turner*, 1913; Rawlinson 812–832 are in an outsize antiquarian portfolio. The England and Wales series (Rawlinson 209–312) used to be housed in the 5th portfolio of this series; it has now been arranged separately in 6 other portfolios. The collection includes many proofs touched by Turner himself.

See s.v. Plates for the 49 cancelled plates from the Liber Studiorum, and 2 from the Little Liber. See also exhibitions 1959, 1966, 1969, 1975 and 1981.

Twopeny, William (1797–1873)

A very large collection of drawings by this antiquarian draughtsman was bequeathed in 1874. They are all listed in the register as 1874–2–14–104 to 1937, and catalogued by Binyon IV pp. 214–43. There is also a manuscript catalogue compiled by Twopeny himself (Cc 4.15) and a volume of index (Cc 4.7). The arrangement of the drawings is:

1 13 large albums containing finished drawings made in England with the title *Drawings of ancient architecture*, arranged by sections: domestic buildings XII–XVIIc. (8 albums), churches XI–XVIIc. (2), wall paintings, stained

glass and tiles (1), ancient furniture and metal work (1), miscellaneous (1). 290 b.1–13; Binyon 1–13, with full list.

2   8 small albums labelled *Sketches* which contain pencil sketches of cathedrals, houses, churches and castles, including interior views, windows and furniture. 290 d.9–16; Binyon 14–21, with partial description.

3   17 small volumes labelled *Nugae* with dates on the spines from 1820–65, containing slight studies, chiefly details of buildings and architecture, with notes and measurements. 290 d.17–33; Binyon 22–38, with no description.

Vale Press

224 blocks for woodcuts employed in the publications of the Vale Press were bequeathed in 1937 in the joint names of Charles Ricketts and Charles Shannon. There is a full listing in the register, with notes of the various publications to which the blocks belonged (1937–6–12–323 to 546). In 1946 Mrs Constant Rea presented an album of drawings by Ricketts and Shannon, which included studies for illustrations in the Dial, Daphnis and Chloe and the Vale Press books (200 a.12; 1946–2–9–35 to 124). The register gives a full description and correlation with the woodblocks already in the collection. The Department does not possess any of the Vale Press publications 1898–1904; these will be found in the British Library.

Vanity Fair

The Department possesses an incomplete series of the cartoons published between 1869–1908 by Vanity Fair (1943–11–13–298 to 572, and other numbers). It is kept separately in a box, which also contains a list of the prints published in the first 34 volumes. A complete listing with identifications of the sitters will be found in Roy T. Matthews and Peter Mellini, *In 'Vanity Fair'*, 1982.

Vaughan, Henry (1809–1899)

A wealthy collector, who bequeathed items to most of the national museums. He had already presented five Michelangelo drawings to the British Museum in 1887 (Wilde 4, 6, 10, 29 and 53; 1887–5–2–115 to 120, including a copy, W91). In his bequest he added 555 further items (1900–8–24–1 to 555):

1–98 Proofs of Turner's Liber Studiorum, selected to supplement the existing series (the remainder going to University College, London).
99–104 Various prints.
105–161 Old Master drawings.
166–489 Drawings by Flaxman, Lawrence and Stothard.
490–555 Other British drawings and watercolours.

Victoria, Queen (1819–1901)

The Department possesses a virtually complete set of the etchings and lithographs made by Queen Victoria and Prince Albert (1926–1–9–1 to 91, list). 359 portraits of her, both individually and in groups, will be found listed in the catalogue by O'Donoghue and Hake. The Cheylesmore collection (q.v.) contains as well as many portraits (all included in O'Donoghue and Hake), a large number of historical prints covering her life. See the register 1900–10–11–8475 to 9919, 9934 to 10084.

Walker, Fred (1840–1875)

In 1915 Mr E. E. Leggatt presented his collection forming a complete record of the oeuvre of the artist and illustrator Fred Walker. The collection includes original drawings and watercolours, as well as impressions of wood-engravings and photographs, tracings and original letters. 630 such items are mounted on 127 sheets housed in two solander boxes (1915–7–10–1 to 127). There is an index of envelopes kept separately arranged alphabetically by title of the work. Each envelope takes the form of an entry providing basic catalogue information on each work, and sometimes contains extra information as an enclosure inside. There is also a manuscript index book with titles in alphabetical order giving item and sheet numbers.

Wallpaper

There is no collection of wallpaper in the Department. The national collection is in the Victoria and Albert Museum and is described in Charles C. Oman and Jean Hamilton, *Wallpapers: a history and illustrated catalogue of the collection of the Victoria and Albert Museum*, 1982. One German renaissance woodcut that may well be for wallpaper shows a vine pattern with a satyr family. An impression is in the Department (E 2.402; Dodgson I 482.155 as Sebald Beham: it has also been attributed to Dürer).

War Artists

The collection includes a certain number of works made by official and unofficial war artists. The main national collection is, however, that in the Imperial War Museum, and others will be found in many other national and provincial collections. The chief items in the Department are:

1 *The Great War, Britain's Efforts and Ideals* a series of 66 lithographs by 18 artists including Muirhead Bone and Eric Kennington, published by the Ministry of Information. 246 a.1–9; 1918–7–13–80 to 145.
2 Muirhead Bone (1876–1953): drawings made as official war artist on the Western Front and in Great Britain 1916–18. 1919–2–8–1 to 125 (list); some mounted and some in an album 200* c.14.
3 Joseph Pennell (1858–1926): 95 drawings in two volumes, 1916, mostly of munition works but also of balloons and airships over London and aeroplanes at Farnborough. 1917–4–14–2 to 51, 53 to 108.
4 Eric Kennington (1888–1960): two drawings *c*.1917, a Northumbrian with his arm in a sling, and a Belgian landscape by night. 1981–6–20–13,14.
5 Henry Moore (1898–1986): The Shelter Sketchbook, made in the Underground during the Blitz in autumn 1940. Bequeathed by Lady Clark; 1977–4–2–13(1–67), now mounted.
6 Ralph Lillford (b.1932): Three drawings made in Northern Ireland in 1971. 1973–9–15–2 to 4.

Ward, James (1769–1859)

In 1817 Ward presented to the Department a complete collection of all the states of the mezzotints that he had engraved. They were placed loose between the leaves of six large albums, which were described as Ii 8 to 13 in the 1837 inventory. The inventory volume lists each of the 401 prints; the last figure of the inventory number has been written in pencil on the verso of every impression. The titles have been entered in the Catalogue of Select Mezzotints (see pp. 35–6); the Departmental copy of Julia Frankau, *William Ward, James Ward, their lives and works*, 1904, has not been marked off with the holdings.

Watch-Papers

These are small circular engravings intended to be used as liners between the inner and outer cases of a watch. A portfolio contains three groups of watch-papers: a set representing the chief events of the war with France 1758–62 (1870–6–11–1 to 55, no list); a small collection purchased from Mrs H. S. Vinter (1902–10–18–54 to 75, list); and ten items presented by G. D. Sherborne (1927–2–15–21 to 30). A much larger collection will be found in the Clock Room in the Department of Medieval and Later Antiquities.

Watteau, Antoine (1684–1721)

The 59 drawings by Watteau in the collection are arranged in four boxes in the order of the catalogue by Karl Parker published in *Old Master Drawings*, V 1930, pp. 1–28. A more recent catalogue of the whole collection is in Paul Hulton, *Watteau Drawings in the British Museum*, published as the catalogue of an exhibition in 1980.

The main series of prints after his paintings is contained in the two volumes of the Recueil Jullienne, 1736. The Department's copy comes from the collection of John Barnard (1838–5–26–1,2). It also possesses the two volumes of prints after Watteau's drawings, *Figures de différens charactères*, 1726,8 (161* b.4,5; 1859–7–9–2004 to 2137, 2138 to 2354). Other prints after Watteau are kept loose in a portfolio.

Whistler, James Abbott McNeill (1834–1903)

There are only five royal drawings and watercolours by Whistler in the collection. There is, however, also an album containing 18 sketches and 16 letters and other documents relating to Whistler and the Alexander family; it was presented by the Misses Alexander through the NACF in 1958 (200 c.10; 1958–2–8–3 to 36).

The etchings by Whistler are mounted in 7 solanders in the order of the catalogue by E. G. Kennedy, published in 1910. The Department copy is marked with the holdings. There are 5 accompanying volumes of photographs of every state (165* c.16–20). The collection possesses complete sequences of the French set 1858, the Thames set 1871, the set of cancelled plates of 1879 (190* a.24; 1887–12–16–34(1–57)), and the second Venice set 1886 (presented by Dowdeswells and Thibaudeau, 1887–10–10–63 to 88). There are only 5 prints from the first Venice set 1880. A complete handlist is available.

The lithographs are mounted in 6 solanders in the order of the catalogue by T. R. Way of 1905. Of the 160 numbers, all but 32 are in the collection. An album of reproductions was published in 1914 to accompany Way's catalogue (165* c.21).

White, John (active 1585–1593)

English artist, and author of some of the earliest drawings of America. His career is poorly documented, but he made a number of voyages of exploration: possibly with Martin Frobisher to north-west America in 1577, with the first expedition to colonise Virginia organised by Raleigh in 1585 as draughtsman-surveyor, with its successor in 1587, and with the relief expedition in

1590. Three of his drawings are in a manuscript of Thomas Moffett, *Insectorum . . . Theatrum* (Dept. Manuscripts, Sloane 4014, ff. 69r,96r,109r), but all the remainder of his surviving drawings are in this Department, together with a number of copies and related works. Four volumes contained most of the relevant material:

1 An album, formerly in the library of Lord Charlemont, purchased in 1866 and transferred from the Library to this Department in 1906 (199 a.1; 1906–5–9–1, with sub-numbers 1–76). For reasons mentioned below, the album had to be dismantled, and the pages mounted on to the leaves of a new blank volume. This then contained a manuscript title-page and 75 drawings, all by White. In 1933 the drawings were taken out and mounted individually; the album survives empty.

2 In 1865 the Charlemont album was saturated with water, and the drawings offset on to the facing pages. In the rebinding carried out in 1866 before they came to the British Museum, the pages carrying the offsets were mounted into a second album (199 a.2; 1906–5–9–2). Since the first three drawings had been double-spread, there were only 72 offsets.

3 A volume from the Sloane collection (q.v.), Sloane Ms. 5270. This was transferred in 1893 but never registered (199 a.3). It is therefore referred to by its Sloane number and foliation. It is still kept as an album, and contains 113 folios which carry 130 drawings by a number of different hands. None is by John White, but several are copies of his drawings in (1) above or from what may confidently be regarded as lost drawings by him. The remainder are Indians of Brazil close to the work of Jean de Lery,

flora after Dutch originals, and miscellaneous costume studies.

4 A printed book published in Frankfort in four different language editions by Theodor de Bry in 1590 as part 1 of his *America.* It contained a reprint of Thomas Harriot, *A briefe and true report of the new found land of Virginia,* first published in 1588, but added 28 engravings by de Bry himself after drawings by White. Versions of many of these drawings are contained in (1) above, a few are only known in copies in (3) above, and five others are entirely lost. No copy of de Bry is in this Department (though there is a facsimile published in 1972 with an introduction by Paul Hulton); copies of the original Latin, German, French and English editions are in the British Library (Grenville 6834–7 respectively).

Three official catalogues have been published of the above works:

1 In 1907 in volume IV of Binyon, pp. 326–37. He allocated the numbers 1–3 to the three albums, the contents of which he listed in the order that he found them. The first was given sub-numbers (1–75); since he did not give a number to the title-page, his numbers are always one behind the sub-numbers of the inventory. The second was merely mentioned. The third was listed in a summary fashion, with sub-numbers (1–130) allotted to each drawing in it.

2 In Croft-Murray and Hulton in 1960, pp. 26–86. They catalogue the title-page and each drawing of album (1) separately, from 1–76, not in the original (Binyon's) order, but in the putative order in which they were made or by class: 1–31 drawings connected with the

West Indies, 32–60 with Roanoke, 61–2 copies from Le Moyne (q.v.), 63–4 Eskimos, 65–6 birds, 67–71 ancient Britons, 72–6 Orientals. The drawings are kept in five royal solanders in this order, with the three larger ones in the imperial size. 77 is the album of offsets (2) above. 78 is the Sloane volume (3) above, and a complete description is given of the foliation and the drawings on each page.

3 By Paul Hulton in ed. Paul Hulton and D. B. Quinn, *The American drawings of John White 1577–1590, with drawings of European and Oriental subjects*, 1964. The drawings are catalogued in the same thematic order as in the 1960 catalogue, but the lost drawings known only in copies in the Sloane album or in the engravings by de Bry are included in a single numbering sequence, which therefore differs from that of 1960. There is a total of 139 numbers, under each one of which all the known versions are listed.

Another book by Paul Hulton, *America 1585, the complete drawings of John White*, 1984, reproduces all the drawings, including those only known in copies, but supplies no catalogue beyond notes on the plates.

Williams, Iolo (1890–1962)

Museums correspondent of *The Times*, and author of *Early English Watercolours*, 1952. To mark his 70th birthday, he gave 24 drawings by artists previously unrepresented (1960–7–16–1 to 24), and later bequeathed a further selection of 65 drawings designed to fill other gaps in the collection (1962–7–14–4 to 67). See exhibitions 1962.

Wright, Harold J. L. (1885–1961)

A distinguished print dealer, and director of Messrs Colnaghi. He bequeathed to the Department six drawings by Sir Lionel Lindsay (1962–10–13–10 to 15), as well as three manuscripts: a catalogue of prints by Elizabeth Fyfe (240 b.4), notes for a catalogue of prints by Walter Sickert (240 a.1), and the typescript for his published catalogue of prints by Charles Meryon (240 b.3). The rest of his papers are now in the Glasgow University Library (see *Print Quarterly* II 1985 p. 230). His widow, Mrs Isobel Wright (d.1965), arranged for an endowment of £10,000 of her husband's money, plus proceeds of the sale of his pictures, and £10,000 of her own money to provide two scholarships to be administered by the University of Melbourne for students from New Zealand and Australia to study in the Print Room of the British Museum. These are called the Harold Wright and Sarah & William Holmes scholarships (after Mrs Wright's parents). Since 1983 the two scholarships have been combined to provide one scholarship.

Yachting

There is an atlas solander containing 37 mounted watercolours and prints of yachting subjects all of the XIXc., bequeathed by Mr C. P. Johnson (1948–4–10–168 to 204, detailed list). It includes 7 watercolours by T. G. Dutton. Earlier Mr Johnson had presented 6 anonymous drawings of 1862–72, of yachts at Plymouth, Torquay, Harwich, and Cowes (1933–7–8–10 to 15, list). See also s.v. Shipping, Sporting Prints and Drawings.

INDEX

Note This index is highly selective. It only includes headings under which the user is likely to look, and ignores references which are likely to be of little use. It does not repeat cross-references contained in the main text. Entries in **bold** signify that an entry on the subject will be found in the Topic Index.

Aberystwyth 4
Admission tickets 83, 118, 121
Africa 171
Ainslie, S. J. 173
Albert, Prince 77
Alexander, Misses 181
Alexander, W. 1, 24, 112
Almanacs 91
Alphabets 130
Altered plates 76
Amand-Durand 113
Amateurs 76
America 28, 34, 41, 49, 95, 129, 137, 145, 153, 172, 181
Anastatic drawings 77
Anatomy 77
Anderdon, J. H. 56, 57
Animals 77
Anonymous works 77
Antiquities 78
Archer, J. W. 78
Architecture 79
Archives 71–2
Ark Royal 143
Armada 143
Armour 52
Arts and sciences 79
Ashbee, H. S. 108, 126, 162
Australia 172

Authorities for artists 52
Aviation 80

Baer, B. 139, 168
Bagford, J. 80
Ballads 80
Ballooning 80
Balmanno, R. 168
Bandinelli, B. 77
Bank notes 81
Banks, Sir J. 81
Banks, S. S. 82, 101
Barnard, O. 139
Bartolozzi, F. 84
Bartsch, A. 7, 13
Bath, R. H. 169
Baugniet, C. 153
Baxter, G. 84
Beckford, W. 167, 168
Bell, C. F. 69
Bellini, J. 84
Beudeker atlas 173
Bewick family 81, 84
Biblia Pauperum 86
Bill books 72
Binyon, L. 3, 25
    Catalogue of British Drawings 28
Birds 141
Birthday cards 92
Blake, W. 85

Blocks 149
Blockbooks 86
Bolten van Zwolle 165
Bone, M. 180
Books 53–61
Bookplates 86
Botany 141
Bouchardon, E. 105
Boydell, J. 88
Brass-rubbings 88
Bray, D. 135
Breun, H. A. J. 66
Brighton album 86
British Architectural Library 6
British Library 5, 48, and passim
British Museum 88
British Museum Society 89
Broadsheets 90
Brocklebank, P. 90
Browning, R. 90
Buckler collection 90
Buckley, F. 67, 69
Bull, R. 76
Burne-Jones, E. 94, 128
Burney, C. 91
Busiri, G. B. 159
Butterflies 141
Byron, Lord 58

Calendars 91
Calligraphy 91
Callot figures 92
Cannan, F. L. 164
Cards 92
Caricature 93
Carpenter, W. H. 8, 25
Cartoons 94
Cartouches 126
Castiglione, G. B. 96
Catalogues 65
Catlin, G. 95
Cats 131
Cavendish, Lord 95
Cecil, J. 135
Ceremonies 95
Cheylesmore, Lord 95
Chiaroscuro woodcuts 98
China 96, 172
Chinoiserie 96
Christmas cards 92
Cigarette cards 176
Circus 97
Clarendon, Lord 55
Clark, Lady 138
Claude Lorrain 97
Clichés-verre 97
Clouet, F. 154
Coaching 167
Coffee houses 97
Collectanea Biographica 57
Colour printing 98
Colvin, S. 3, 10
Commedia dell'Arte 98
Conservation 98
Constable, J. 132
Contemporary Art Society 99
Cook, R. 102
Cook, Captain J. 99
Copley, J. S. 77
Copyright 100
Corbould, H. 112
Coronations 95, 100
Coryton, P. D. O. 69
Costume 52, 101
Cotman, J. S. 102
Cowtan, R. 88

Crace, F. 103, 119
Cracherode, C. M. 104
Cries 104
Croft-Murray, E. Catalogue of British Drawings 29
Crookshank, C. de W. 105
Crowle, T. 55
Cruikshank, G. 51, 105, 108
Crystal Palace 120
Curiosities 80
Curtis, J. 142
Cust, L. 12
Cut paper 106
Cuttings 67
Cuvillies, F. 79
Czechoslovakia 90

Dallimore, E. H. 157
Dal Pozzo, C. 106
Dalziel Brothers 106
Dance, G. 153
Dasent, W. 143
Davy collection 107
Delany, M. 107
Denon, D. V. 112
Deposit books 72
Designs 144, 177
Dexter, J. F. 108
Dickens, C. 108
Dickes, W. 98
Dighton, R. 108
Dillon, J. 156
Diplomas 118
Docker, A. 98
Dodgson, C. 108
    Catalogue of German Woodcuts 38
Don Quixote 108
Dotted prints 109
Downman, J. 109
Doyle, R. 94
Drawing books 109
Drawings 11, 27–32
Ducerceau, J. A. 109
Duke, K. W. G. 155
Duplicates 110
Dürer, A. 111
Dyck, A. van 111

Eastern Europe 30
Edward VII Galleries 3, 16
Edwards, E. 57
Edwards Anecdotes 57
Egypt 112
Ehret, G. D. 142
Elgin Marbles 112
Ellis, E. 56
Embassies 95
Ephemera 82, 117, 121, 161
Evans, W. 58
Evelyn, J. 77
Exhibitions 14–24
Ex-libris 86
Extra-Illustrated books 54–9
Eyre, J. 116

Facsimiles 113
Fagan, L. vii
Fairholt, F. W. 101, 113
Fans 113
Farington, J. 68
Fashion. See Costume
Fawkener, W. 114
Fenwick, T. F. 115
Festivals 95
Fielden collection 175
Finberg, A. J. 115
Finiguerra, M. 115
Fireworks 95
Fisher, T. 151
Fishes 141
Flaxman, J. 112
Flock prints 116
Florence, H. L. 116
Florentine Picture Chronicle 115
Flowers 141
Forgeries 116
Fowler, G. H. 164
Fowler, W. 116
Fragonard, J. H. 108
Framed works 116
France 30, 44, 49, 52, 102, 122, 154, 172
Franks, Sir A. W. 10, 86, 117
Fraser, Sir W. A. 101

Freedman, B. 93
Freemasonry 118
Frontispieces 126
Frost Fairs 119
Funerals 95
Funeral tickets 83, 118
Furniture 52
Fuseli, H. 58
Fyfe, E. 183

Gainsborough, T. 71
Games 119
Ganymed 139
Garle, Mrs. 123
Garrick, D. 91
Gavarni 119
Geisberg, M. 113
Genealogy 90
George, M. D. 26
  Catalogue of Satires 50
Gere, J. A. viii
  Italian Drawings 32
Germany 31, 37, 44, 49, 53
Gernsheim 40, 119
Ghezzi, P. L. 93
Gilbert, J. 106
Giles, W. 163
Gillray, J. 51, 82, 93, 167
Giorgio, F. di 122
Glass painting 119
Glass prints 120
Gloucester, William Duke
  of 55
Goff, R. C. 120
Gold, S. M. 68
Gould, Sir F. C. 94
Goya, F. 120
Grangerized books 54–9
Graves, A. 69
Gray, M. E. 142
Great Exhibition 120
Greece 172
Greeting cards 92
Greenwood, J. 81
Gribelin, S. 121
Griffin, W. H. 90
Grimaldi, G. F. 104
Grimm, S. H. 127
Guest, M. 121

Hall, C. 121
Harleian manuscripts 121
Harris, T. 120
Hauke, C. M. de 122
Hawkins, E. 49, 122
Haydon, B. R. 112
Hayes, Sister M. E. G. 157
Hayman, F. 108
Hayter, Sir G. 153
Heal, Sir A. 10, 175
Heaphy, T. F. 157
Heathcote, J. 68
Heitz, P. 113
Henderson, J. 122
Heraldry 122
Herdman, W. G. 172
Hill, Sir G. F. 123
Hills, R. 123
Hind, A. M. *Dutch
  Drawings* 30
  Italian Engravings 38
Hipkins, A. J. 70
History 46–7, 123
Hodges, W. 99, 100
Hogarth, W. 124
Holbein, H. 124
Holland, J. 122
Hollar, W. 125, 132, 143
Horne, H. P. 85
Huth, A. H. 125
Huysum, J. van 167

**Illuminated
  manuscripts** 125
Illustrated books 126
**Illustrations to
  authors** 126
India 126, 173
Indices 10
Industrial imagery 127
Insects 141
**Institute of Contemporary
  Arts** 127
Invitations 83, 118, 121, 127
Ipswich Museum 153
Ireland 51
Irving, Sir H. 127
Italy 31, 38, 45, 49, 51, 53,
  173

Japan 173
Jewellery 118, 144, 169
Johnson, C. P. 183
Jones, I. 127
Jones, O. 145
Jones, T. 159
Jones, W. 84, 98
Josi, H. 2, 8, 25

Kaye, Rev Sir R. 127
Kelmscott Press 128
Kennington, E. 180
King's Library 3, 14
Kirkall, E. 128
Knight, R. P. 128
Knowles, J. 58

Labruzzi, C. 159
Lance, G. 69
Landells, E. 128
Landseer, E. 69
Lane, R. J. 152
Laroon, M. 98, 104
Lawrence, Sir T. 128
Layard, G. S. 76
Lear, E. 94
Leggatt, E. E. 70, 180
Lehmann, R. 152
Le Moyne, J. 129
Leonardo da Vinci 129
Le Prince, J. B. 102, 105
Letter books 72
Letters and alphabets 130
Lewis, R. E. 119
Library, Departmental 10
Lilliputian figures 92
Linocuts 98
Lippmann, F. 113
Lloyd, R. W. 130
Loans 72, 131
London 48, 131
Loutherbourg, P. J. de 99,
  137, 143, 151
Lucas, Baroness 132
Lucas, D. 132
Lucas, R. C. 133
Lugt, F. *Catalogues de
  Ventes* 65
  Marques de Collections 76

Mackintosh, C. R. 79
Malcolm, J. 133
Malta 173
Manière criblée 109
Manuscripts 66–71, 125
Maps 133
Marryat, Captain 106
Martin, H. W. 56, 134
Mary, Queen of Scots 93, 135
Marx, H. 58
Master series 39
Medical illustrations 135
Medici family 58, 90, 123
Menus 118
Merchants's marks 135
Merian, M. S. 166
Meryon, C. 183
Mezzotints 35
Michelangelo 136
Microfilms and microfiches 73–4
Military 136
Millar, E. G. 137
Miniatures 137
Mitchell, W. 137
Mitelli, G. M. 105
Modern Graphic Art Fund 138
Moll, Baron 138
Monotypes 138
Monro, Dr. 69
Moore, H. 138
Morghen, R. 139
Morin, J. 139
Morland, G. 69
Morris, W. 94, 128
Mosaics 116
Mosmann, N. 139
Mount sizes 6
Museum of London 6
Music 139
Music titles 140

National Art-Collections Fund 140
National Gallery 140
National Photographic Record 141

National Portrait Gallery 14, 41
Natural History 141
Naval History 142
Netherlands 29, 36, 42, 49, 53, 173
New Year Cards 92
Nielli 143
Nollekens, J. 144
Norwich school 157
Nuremberg Chronicle 144

O'Donoghue, F. Engraved British Portraits 43
Oleographs 144
Oriental sub-Department 3, 9, 18, 25
Orlowski, A. 102
Ornament 51, 144
Orpen, Sir W. 94
Ottley, W. Y. 25, 113

Painter-Stainers Company 68
Paintings 14, 145
Palgrave gift 177
Palmer, W. J. 85
Panoramas 145
Panoramic scenes 145
Papillon, J. M. 126, 130
Paris 49
Parkinson, S. 81, 100
Pastels 147
Paste prints 147
Paton, F. 93
Pennant, T. 55, 58
Pennell, J. 180
Percy, J. 69
Periodicals 61–4
Phillipps, Sir T. 115
Photographs 147
Pillement, J. 96
Piranesi, G. B. 149
Plants 141
Plates, blocks, stones 149
Playing cards 92, 150
Polidoro da Caravaggio 94
Pollard, J. 167

Polyautography 151
Polygraphs 151
Popes 45, 123
Popham, A. E. Dutch Drawings 30
Handbook vii, 27
Italian Drawings 32
Popular prints 151
Pornography 152
Portraits 41–6, 78, 152–4
Post, F. 166
Postage stamps 154
Postcards 154
Posters 154
Potter, H. B. 155
Potter, G. 132
Pouncey, P. Italian Drawings 32
Pressmarks 7, 60
Preziosi, A. 102
Price, E. S. 153
Private presses 128, 179
Processes of engraving 155
Processions 95
Pugin, A. W. 79
Puzzle pictures 80, 83

Queen's costume books 101
Quixote, Don 108

Railways 155
Raphael 156
Receptions 95
Redleaf albums 178
Redouté, P. J. 142
Reeve, J. 157
Registers 6, 9
Reid, G. W. 25, 72
Religious images 157
Rembrandt 158
Reproductions 39–40, 113
Resta, S. 70
Reynolds, Sir J. 158
Ricketts, C. 179
Ripa, M. 96
Robert, N. 166
Roberts, J. 91
Rome 159

Rosenheim, M. 87
Rossetti, D. G. 70, 94
Rowlandson, T. 51, 104, 152
Roxburghe ballads 80
Royal Academy 159
Royal Library, Windsor 73, 74
Royal Society 83
Royalty 77, 90
Rozière, E. de 86
Rubens, P. P. 160
Rupert, Prince 77
Russia 102, 155, 173
Rysbrack, J. M. 94

Saints 157
Sale bequest 177
Sale catalogues 65–6
Salting, G. 160
Samplers 80
Satires 49–51, 93
Scandinavia 32, 173
Scharf, G. 160
Schreiber, Lady C. 161
Science 79
Sculptors 161
Sévigné, Mme de 56
Sforza 123
Shakespeare 162
Sharpe, J. 168
Sharpe, S. 70
Sheepshanks, J. 10, 162
Shells 141
Shipping 163
Shop bills 118, 175
Shrimpton and Giles Bequest 163
Sickert, W. R. 183
Silhouettes 163
Silk 164
Simes, J. T. 58
Skating 164
Sketchbooks 11, 27–8
Sketching Club 164
Slade, F. 165
Sligo, Marquess of 76
Sloane, Sir H. 128, 165

Smirke, Sir R. 88
Smith, J. T. 2, 25, 104
Smith, J. 'Warwick' 159
Smith, W. 167
Society of Artists 56
Solander boxes 6
Spain 32, 46
Sporting art 167
Staff 24
Stannard, W. J. 155
Steer, P. W. 70
Stephens, F. G. *Catalogue of Satires* 49
Stone, Sir B. 141
Stones 149
Stothard, T. 168
Street Cries 104
Sulphurs 143
Sutherland, G. 168
Swain, J. 169
Switzerland 32, 102, 173

Tailpieces 126
Talman, J. 169
Tartt, W. M. 58
Tate Gallery 6, 169, 178
Teyler, J. 98
Theatrical material 169
Thomas, B. 70
Thomas, Rev. J. 59
Thomas, R. 174
Tickets 82
Tinsel prints 170
Title-pages 170
Tonks, H. 94
Topography 47–9, 171–4
Towne, F. 159
Toy theatre 174
Trade cards 174
Trades 79, 176
Transparencies 176
Transport 176
Trustees 71
Turkey 46, 53, 102, 174
Turner, D. 177
Turner, J. M. W. 177
Twining, L. 157
Twopeny, W. 178

Valentines 92
Vale Press 179
Vanderbank, J. 108
Vanity Fair 179
Vasari Society 113
Vaughan, H. 179
Velde, W. van de 143, 165
Venne, A. van de 137
Vernet, C. 105
Victoria, Queen 77, 179
Victoria and Albert Museum 5, 65, 74, 119, 144, 154, 160, 163
Vignettes 126
Viner, G. H. 87
Visiting Cards 83
Visitor books 72
Visscher, C. J. 132

Walker, F. 70, 180
Wallpaper 180
Walton, I. 56
War artists 180
Ward, J. 180
Watch-papers 181
Watteau, A. 181
Webber, J. 81, 99, 100
Wharton-Tigar, E. C. 176
Wheatley, F. 104
Whistler, J. A. M. 181
White, J. 181
White, W. 3, 16
Whitelocke, B. 55
Whitley, W. T. 70
Whitman, A. 26
Wiener, H. 140
Williams, I. 183
Wilton, J. A. R. viii
Windsor. See Royal Library
Wirgman, C. 94
Wood-engravings 36, 37, 54
Wren, Sir C. 77, 79
Wright, H. J. L. 183
Wyattville, Sir J. 79

Yachting 183

Zompini, G. 105

NOTES

Notes